McDonnell Douglas MD-11

A Long Beach Swansong

Arthur A C Steffen

McDonnell Douglas MD-11
A Long Beach Swansong
© 2001 Arthur A C Steffen
ISBN 1 85780 117 2

Published by Midland Publishing
4 Watling Drive, Hinckley
LE10 3EY, England
Tel: 01455 254 490   Fax: 01455 254 495
E-mail: midlandbooks@compuserve.com

Midland Publishing is an imprint of
Ian Allan Publishing Ltd

Worldwide distribution (except North America):
Midland Counties Publications
4 Watling Drive, Hinckley
LE10 3EY, England
Telephone: 01455 233 747   Fax: 01455 233 737
E-mail: midlandbooks@compuserve.com

North American trade distribution:
Specialty Press Publishers & Wholesalers Inc.
11605 Kost Dam Road, North Branch, MN 55056
Tel: 651 583 3239   Fax: 651 583 2023
Toll free telephone: 800 895 4585

Design concept and layout
© 2001 Midland Publishing and
Stephen Thompson Associates

Printed in England by
Ian Allan Printing Ltd
Riverdene Business Park, Molesey Road,
Hersham, Surrey, KT12 4RG

Contents

Photograph on the previous page:
**Lufthansa Cargo was the last customer for the
MD-11. Check Captain Siegmund 'Archie'
Doelker is at the controls of the carrier's fourth
freighter, D-ALCD, on the delivery flight from
Long Beach to Frankfurt on 17th September
1998.** George Hall/Clay Lacy – Lufthansa Cargo

Photograph on this page:
**The first MD-11, N111MD, is parked next to a
DC-3, N26MA, on the compass rose. The old lady
was originally delivered to Pennsylvania-Central
Airlines in November 1939 and was brought up
to Long Beach for the tri-jet's first flight
ceremony in January 1990.** McDonnell Douglas

Photograph on the opposite page:
**The frontal view of this World Airways MD-11
shows the superbly aerodynamic cockpit, the
advanced wing and winglets design, and the
clean tail assembly.** McDonnell Douglas

Introduction

Dream no small dream; it lacks magic.
Dream large; then make the dream real –
Donald Wills Douglas

This thought of the founder of the Douglas Aircraft Company (DAC) put a stamp on the design and development of the propeller and jet aircraft built by what once was the world's second largest aircraft manufacturer.

For DAC the jet age in commercial aviation started with the introduction of the famous DC-8 in 1958. When production stopped in 1972 a total of 556 aircraft of the different series had been built.

Although Boeing sold nearly twice as many examples of its competing 707, today's figures speak for the reliability and ruggedness of the Douglas product. Currently 233 DC-8s are still in service compared to 102 commercial 707s.

With the wide-body DC-10, which was placed into service in 1971, McDonnell Douglas (MDC) once more proved the company's importance and influence in the airliner marketplace. Not only did the DC-10 outlast its rival, the Lockheed L-1011 TriStar, the aircraft

also established an enviable reputation for reliability and profitability. The DC-10 has shown itself to be both enduring and adaptable. The ongoing FedEx MD-10 programme is a further prove of the tri-jet's qualities. Today 404 of the total 446 aircraft built are still in service around the world.

When the last DC-10s were nearing completion on the assembly line of the Douglas Aircraft Company in Long Beach, California, in 1988, a new wide-body airliner was taking shape: the MD-11. The DC-10 was to be the last aircraft with the 'DC' prefix. In 1983, a name change, which would incorporate the company's full name, was decided upon by the Douglas management. All commercial would carry the designation MD, for McDonnell Douglas. The name was introduced on the successful Super 80 family, the Super 81 and 82 series being renamed the MD-81 and MD-82.

The first aircraft to carry the new name from the start of development was the MD-83, later followed by the MD-87, the MD-88 and the MD-90. The successor to the DC-10 was appropriately named MD-11.

MDC was well ahead of the competition with the new state-of-the-art tri-jet. Airbus launched its A340 half a year later than the MD-11, while Boeing did not launch its 777 twin-jet until late 1990. At the time MDC saw a market for over 300 aircraft of the new tri-jet. The majority of the launch customers were operators who selected the aircraft to replace their DC-10 fleet like American Airlines, Alitalia, Finnair, Japan Airlines , KLM, Korean Air, Swissair and Thai International. FedEx, launch customer of the freighter version, selected the aircraft to expand its large Douglas wide-body fleet.

Production problems, a major managerial reorganisation and layoffs severely hampered the MD-11 programme and as a result the first flight, originally scheduled for March 1989, was delayed until January 1990. The advantage of an early introduction and early deliveries, specifically ahead of Airbus Industrie's A340, dwindled.

Once in service, a serious shortfall in range performance was reported by several airlines. Notably, American Airlines president Robert 'Bob' Crandall's airing of his unhappiness with the aircraft's initial performance did not contribute to the aircraft's sales success. The downturn for the MD-11 programme came on 2nd August 1991, when Singapore Airlines cancelled its order for 20 aircraft, citing the confusion over of the aircraft's range performance. Although MDC addressed the performance problems with a series of Performance Improvement Packages (See Chapter One for more details) the MD-11's image was damaged beyond repair.

At the Farnborough Air Show in the UK in September 1996, Lufthansa Cargo announced a first order for five MD-11Fs with an option for seven additional aircraft. Selection of the MD-11F by Lufthansa was viewed as a major milestone due to the airline's reputation as a world leader in the air cargo business. However, the German cargo giant would prove to be the last customer to take delivery of the wide-body workhorse.

After the McDonnell Douglas-Boeing merger in August 1997, Boeing announced the project strategy regarding the company's jetliners produced by its Douglas Products Division in November of that year. For the twin-jet programmes it meant the phase-out of the MD-80 and MD-90. In the case of the MD-11 the decision was taken to continue to offer the aircraft in both passenger and freighter versions. However, with a decrease in orders for passenger aircraft, marketing efforts would focus on the freighter market. Within the Boeing production range the aircraft was well-placed between the 767 and 747 freighters.

The moment of truth for the MD-11 however came in June 1998, when Boeing Commercial Airplane Group (BCAG) President Ron Woodward announced the phase-out of the MD-11 programme: 'Since our last MD-11 market forecast in November, demand for new MD-11 passenger and freighter aircraft has declined. Despite our best marketing efforts, it became clear to us that there simply was not enough customer interest in either the passenger or freighter versions of this airplane to justify keeping the production line open'. When the last aircraft for Lufthansa Cargo left Building 84 in June 2000, the MD-11 production line was closed for ever. Building 84 was the assembly site of all McDonnell Douglas tri-jets.

A tribute was paid to a great aircraft when the last example, fuselage number (f/n) 646, was towed across Lakewood Boulevard to the flight line, with a 'The perfect end to a perfect era' sticker on the forward fuselage.

As of 1st March 2001, 195 of the total of 200 aircraft were in service with 23 operators around the world. Since their introduction in 1990, airline MD-11s have carried 133,007,670 passengers. Passenger and freighter aircraft together have flown 2,631,208,212 statute miles and accumulated 5,294,701 revenue hours.

With American Airlines, Swissair and other airlines parting from their MD-11 passenger aircraft within the next few years, the MD-11's future role will mainly be in cargo operations. Not only FedEx and Lufthansa Cargo, but also Gemini Air Cargo and UPS Airlines have added the rugged workhorse to their freighter fleet.

It cannot be disputed that the production delays and performance shortfalls did indeed jeopardise the MD-11 programme to a great extent. After all problems had been sorted out, the aircraft proved to be the workhorse it was designed to be. However by that time, Airbus and Boeing had penetrated the market with new wide-body aircraft and were successfully selling the A340 and 777, even to the most loyal McDonnell Douglas customers.

After the merger the MD-11 legally became a Boeing product and today is generally referred to as the Boeing MD-11. Since the majority of the MD-11s built carry the McDonnell Douglas name, this nomenclature is used throughout the book; see Chapter Four for more details. As the last of the 'MD' line, the mighty MD-11 is a living tribute to a pioneering aircraft manufacturer.

In Chapter Five, the daring double-deck MD-12 design and other projects are described which would have taken McDonnell Douglas into the 21st century.

A separate chapter has been devoted to the MD-10. Federal Express Corporation's decision to convert the many American Airlines and United Airlines DC-10-10 aircraft acquired, as well as part of the company's own Series -10 and -30 fleet, gave rise to the MD-10 programme. The refined workhorse carries on the enviable reputation for reliability and profitability of the famous McDonnell Douglas DC-10.

Arthur A C Steffen
Dreieich, Germany   May 2001

Bibliography

McDonnell Douglas MD-11 Aircraft,
Program and Product Reviews
Flight Times
McDonnell Douglas, Douglas Aircraft
Company, Long Beach, California, USA.
Aero magazine, Boeing Commercial Airplane
Group, The Boeing Company, Seattle,
Washington, USA.
Boeing News, The Boeing Company, Seattle,
Washington, USA.

ACAR International – Airways
John Wegg, Sandpoint, Idaho, USA.

Aviation-Letter
Lundkvist Aviation Research, Pahoa, Hawaii,
USA.

Jet Airliner Production List
J R Roach & A B Eastwood,
The Aviation Hobby Shop, West Drayton,
Middlesex, England.

JP airline-fleets international
Ulrich Klee, Bucher & Co., Publikationen,
Zürich-Airport, Switzerland.

Luftfahrt Journal
Hamburg, Germany.

Acknowledgements

Following my McDonnell Douglas DC-10 and KC-10 Extender publication in the Aerofax series it seems appropriate to pay tribute to the company's last tri-jet workhorse: the MD-11.

First of all, my thanks to the people at Midland Publishing for their support of the project.

I would like to record my appreciation to the following persons particularly: Don Hanson, retired Media Specialist, Douglas Products Division; John A Thom, Boeing Media Relations; Patricia M McGinnis, Boeing Historical Archives; Leslie Nichols, Editor-in-chief Aero Magazine, the Boeing Company; the late Harry Gann, former Douglas Aircraft Company Historian; Dietrich Seidl, Lufthansa Cargo Media Relations; Christoph Titze, Lufthansa Fleet Planning; Marlyse Bartis, Swissair Photo Archives; Detlev Anders, World Airways; A J Altevogt, Mike Badrocke, Frank E Bucher – Bucher & Co; Mark Busseniers – Exavia; Dario Cocco, Jeffrey S DeVore, Ken Ellis, Eddy Gual – Aviation Photography of Miami; Reiner Geerdts – Luftfahrt Journal; P J Gralla, Ricky-Dene Halliday, World Airline Fleets; George W Hamlin, Theo Handstede, Heiko Hauptreif, Harald M Helbig, Derek Hellmann, Bill Hough, M Kaspczak, Jan C D G Keesen, Achim Leich-

ner, Fred Lerch, Michael F McLaughlin, Malcolm Nason, Pierre-Alain Petit, Frank Poetsch, H Quander, Nico G J Roozen, J Ross, Nicky Scherrer – VIP Photoservice; A J Smith, Arnold Verwiel, Rolf Wallner and John Wegg – Airways.

Although most of the air-to-air and factory scene photographs were obtained before the McDonnell Douglas and Boeing merger, I wish to thank the Boeing Historical Archives for their permission to publish this material.

I would also like to express my thanks to the following companies, institutions and organisations for supplying documentation and photographic material: Air International Magazine, Alitalia, AlliedSignal, American Airlines, Delta Air Lines, Euro Aviation Slides, Federal Express, Finnair, General Electric Aircraft Engines, Honeywell, Japan Airlines, KLM, LTU, Lufthansa Cargo, Martinair Holland, NASA, Rolls-Royce plc, Sabena, Swissair, The Aviation Data Centre, United Technologies – Pratt & Whitney, VARIG, VASP and World Airways.

Some photos shown were bought at slide conventions. If the photographer is unknown, 'Author's collection' is used in the caption. I would like to apologise for using these slides without stating the photographer's name.

Chapter One

Evolution of a Wide-Body

Final assembly work on the first aircraft is conducted on the East Ramp of the Long Beach site. McDonnell Douglas

As early as 1979, production of larger models of the efficient DC-10 was under consideration at McDonnell Douglas in Long Beach. Using the same nomenclature as for the DC-8, Douglas had three different variants under study. The DC-10 Series 61 would be a domestic-range model, while the Series 62 and 63 would have intercontinental ranges. Both the Series 61 and 63 tri-jets would be 40ft (12.1m) longer than the 182ft (55.4m) length of the existing DC-10s, and the Series 62 would be 26.7ft (8.1m) longer. Maximum capacity of these variants would be over 500 passengers, compared to the maximum of 380 for the DC-10s currently in service. Plans of the extended fuselage DC-10s called for a 5ft (1.5m) tip extension on the wings and powerplants in the 52,000 to 55,000 lb (231 to 244kN) thrust range.

Although these planned series did not make it into production, it was a clear indication of what Douglas had in mind as a DC-10 successor. In 1982, further studies of an advanced and stretched DC-10 evolved. Named the MD-100, in line with the nomenclature used for the narrow-body MD airliners, the long-range aircraft would be offered in two versions. The MD-100 Series 10 was a 6ft 6in (1.95m) shorter version of the DC-10 with a capacity of 270 passengers in a typical three-class cabin layout. The Series 20 was 20ft. 6in (6.2m) longer than the DC-10 and offered seating for 333 passengers in the same cabin configuration.

Advanced development work on the new tri-jet, which was now named MD-XXX, started in 1984. At the time Douglas proposed two versions of the aircraft, named the MD-11X-10 and the MD-11X-20. Whereas the MD-11X-10 had the same fuselage as the DC-10, the MD-11X-20 would feature a fuselage stretch of 22ft 3in (6.7m). The aircraft would be powered by GE CF6-80C2 or P&W PW4460 engines. The envisaged range for the -10 was to be 6,500nm

(12,038km) and 6,000nm (11,112km) for the -20. Both aircraft would have an advanced three-crew flightdeck.

When McDonnell Douglas gave approval for the MD-11 to be offered to the airlines in July 1985, the aircraft featured an advanced two-crew cockpit and the fuselage length of the MD-11X-20. The final refined MD-11 design was an 18ft 6in (5.66m) stretched DC-10-30 derivative. The stretch included the insertion of an 8ft 4in (2.54m) plug forward of the wing and another 10ft 2in (3.12m) plug aft of the wing. The projected range was 6,700nm (12,000km) with a passenger load of 276 in a three-class configuration, up to 405 in an all-economy layout. The aircraft featured an all-new two-crew advanced glass cockpit, redesigned wings with winglets, and new turbofans.

The official production go-ahead for the widebody aircraft was announced on 30th December 1986, almost one year behind schedule. At the time McDonnell Douglas had received orders and commitments for 92 aircraft from 12 airlines and leasing companies.

inboard ailerons and spoilers, in conjunction with low speed outboard ailerons, are installed. In the wing-redesign DAC made extensive use of aluminium and composite materials. While the inboard ailerons and flaps have a composite material skin over a metal structure, the outboard ailerons and flaps are made completely from carbon/epoxy. The spoilers consist of an aluminium honeycomb and skin construction. The tail section features a vertical stabiliser with a two-segment rudder for directional control. The straight inlet duct of the tail engine installation is an aerodynamic design feature which assures an optimal performance and freedom from inlet distortion and the associated operational losses. A further advantage of this configuration is the ease of assembly and the optimum utilisation of the rear fuselage. The most notable change in the tail section is the 30% reduction in size of the MD-11 horizontal tail in comparison to the DC-10-30. While the horizontal tail area on the DC-10 measures 1.338ft² (120.4m²), the area on the MD-11 was reduced to 920ft² (82.8m²). This reduction along with use of composite materials for the elevators and horizontal stabiliser trailing edges resulted in a substantial weight reduction of 1.900 lb (855kg). A new, aerodynamic and tapered tailcone was designed for the MD-11. The forward part of the tailcone is made of aluminium and the aft part is made of carbon/epoxy. The combined aerodynamic features contributed to higher fuel efficiency, reduced drag and added range. Another novelty for the MD-11 was the installation of a 2.000 gallon (7,570 litre) fuel tank in the horizontal stabiliser for added fuel capacity and centre of gravity control.

As had been the case with the DC-10, McDonnell Douglas built a MD-11 development fixture (DF) which was a full-scale representation of the aircraft. Though it was not required to fly, the DF was built to tolerances which simulated those of an airworthy airliner. Thus the fixture provided a precision base for the development of wiring, cables, and systems installations throughout the aircraft. It was used by engineers and planners to determine proper equipment installation, routing, clearance, and similar specifications requiring three-dimensional investigation.

The DF included many simulated parts fabricated from a variety of materials, as well as production components and structural sections from the DC-10 development program. For the MD-11, its kinship with the DC-10 enabled development of a highly advanced new generation of wide-body aircraft in a relatively short time yet with optimum confidence in systems reliability.

MDC launched four models from the start. Three models, a passenger, a combi and a freighter version were derived from the standard MD-11 fuselage length; the fourth model, an extended range version had the same fuselage length as the DC-10. The extended range aircraft was designed to carry 277 first and economy class passengers up to 8,870 statute miles (14,274km) non-stop. However, plans to produce this variant were dropped in 1988.

The design of the MD-11 was the evolutionary result of joint efforts by the manufacturer and many airlines. The aerodynamic configuration of the aircraft had been established and verified by development testing in high and low speed wind tunnels as well as full scale flight testing on the DC-10. Using a former Continental Airlines DC-10-10, N68048, extensive test flights were conducted to test the application of the new aluminium and carbon fibre winglets. DAC, in a co-operative effort with NASA (National Aeronautics and Space Administration), actually was the first aircraft manufacturer to flight-test winglets on a transport aircraft. The

flight tests, which started in August 1981, were conducted from the McDonnell Douglas Flight Test facility in Yuma, Arizona, and Edwards Air Force Base, California. The impressive winglets on the test aircraft extended 10ft 6in (3.18m) above the wing and 2ft 6in (0.61m) below. A further variant was flight-tested which extended 7ft (2.1m) and 2ft 6in (0.61m) downwards. After evaluations had shown these winglets offered the same drag reduction and at the same time a weight reduction because of its smaller size, these were fitted to the MD-11.

The MD-11 wing combines advanced airfoil designs and a 35° of sweep to provide a maximum operating efficiency for long range operations at a maximum cruise speed of Mach 0.87. The aircraft has a wingspan of 169.5ft (51.7m) and a wing area of 3.648ft² (339m²) including the winglets. The winglets each have a 40ft² (3.7m²) area. The MD-11 wing features full-span leading edge slats. Coupled with the powerful large-chord double-slotted trailing edge flaps, an extremely effective high-lift system is formed. For lateral control, all-speed

Parts for the MD-11 came from a worldwide network of subcontractors and suppliers as shown in the diagram on page 12. Subassembly responsibilities were also dispersed from Long Beach throughout the McDonnell Douglas Corporation. For instance, the production of the MD-11 nose subassembly was transferred to the MDC plant in St. Louis, Missouri, while control surface assembly was moved to Tulsa, Oklahoma, and the massive banjo rings were fabricated at the MDC facility in Torrance, California.

Because of their sheer size of deployment, two sequences of the operations were eye-catching. The wings of the MD-11 were manufactured by McDonnell Douglas Canada at its Malton, Ontario plant, adjacent to Toronto's Lester B Pearson International Airport. Upon completion they were shipped by boxcars to the plant in Long Beach. General Dynamics' Convair Division in San Diego was the subcontractor for the manufacturing of the main fuselage sections. The sections were transported by barges to Long Beach Harbor and then transported by truck to the Long Beach assembly plant.

When Convair decided to focus on its core business and to end production of the MD-11 fuselage sections as of December 1995, a state and local 'red team' was formed in December 1994 in an effort to keep this manufacturing in California and to avert job losses in the state. The team consisted of officials from McDonnell Douglas, United Aerospace Workers/Labor Employment Training Corporation, the California Trade and Commerce Agency, Southern California Edison and the California Employment Training Panel. The team's efforts led to a $5.5 million California Employment Training Panel (ETP) award to McDonnell Douglas. As a result more than 100 jobs were saved and nearly 400 jobs were created at the plant in Long Beach. The first MD-11 fuselage built by workers trained with funds from the ETP contract was completed on 18th July 1996.

With DC-10 production coming to an end, assembly of the first MD-11 started on 9th March 1988, and the first flight of the new wide-body was planned for March 1989. The assembly of the final DC-10, f/n 446, destined for Nigeria Airways, was completed in October 1988, the same month the marriage of the wing and fuselage of the new wide-body took place.

In 1989, a massive restructuring plan was announced by John F McDonnell, the Chairman and CEO of McDonnell Douglas, in an effort to produce aircraft on time and on budget.

Dark clouds hang over Long Beach with suppliers not adhering to their delivery schedules and production problems increasing due to labour unrest and strikes. As a result, the first flight was delayed until April 1989. Also, the production of the highly successful MD-80 and development work on the upcoming MD-90 interfered with the MD-11 programme which badly needed skilled personnel. Furthermore, the complexity of the MD-11 programme caused problems which Boeing had also experienced during the early days of their 747-400. With three basic versions and, initially, three engine/airframe combinations being offered, production planning became increasingly difficult. The lack of skilled workforce and mounting supplier problems caused the programme to slip further behind schedule and it was not until September 1989 that the first aircraft was quietly rolled out of the final assembly building.

It is of interest to note that there actually never was a prototype. The complete test and certification program was carried out with five MD-11s which were ultimately delivered to customer airlines. The control system was proof-tested and the system operation was demonstrated on the first production aircraft before its maiden flight from Long Beach Municipal Airport on 10th January 1990. Piloted by chief project pilot John Miller, a former Royal Air Force Vulcan test pilot, and co-pilot Tom Melody, chief pilot advanced technology and special projects, MD-11 N111MD flew for 2hr 56min on its first test flight from its home base to the McDonnell Douglas Flight Test facility in Yuma, Arizona. Also aboard the flight were Fred Schreiner, flight test co-ordinator, and Jack Bowman, specialist flight engineer. Since the programme had slipped eight months behind schedule, the aircraft did not receive the MDC livery and was flown in bare metal with a gold-accentuated burgundy 'McDonnell Douglas' title on the upper fuselage and 'MD-11' titles on the tail section and winglets. The logos

Built to the exact dimensions of the actual aircraft the development fixture permitted early development of wiring, cockpit, avionics and other installations before the start of production. McDonnell Douglas

McDonnell Douglas leased a Continental DC-10-10, N68048, to flight test the winglets for the MD-11. McDonnell Douglas

The massive aluminium and carbon fibre winglet extends 7ft (2.1m) above and 2ft 6in (0.61m) below the wing surface. Martinair Holland

tests of the advanced avionics systems. The aircraft also performed a first long range flight of 8hr 30m. The full MDC 'house' colours livery, consisting of different shades of burgundy painted cheatlines and one gold lining, was applied to the aircraft.

N311MD (f/n 449), the third MD-11, took off from Long Beach on its maiden flight on 26th April 1990 and was the only Pratt & Whitney PW 4460 powered test aircraft. On Ship No. 3 the 'house' colours were applied only to the tail section while the fuselage was kept in white, displaying a burgundy 'McDonnell Douglas' title.

The fourth aircraft, N411MD (f/n 450), took to the sky on 5th of June 1990. Ship No. 4 underwent navigation checks during flights over the North Pole the following month. The aircraft took off from Anchorage, Alaska, on 31st July on a 16hr 35m flight, the longest recorded flight of a commercial tri-jet. Besides testing the navigational systems in the arctic region, special attention was paid to the workload on the two-men cockpit crew on a long range flight.

The fifth and last test aircraft to join the test sisterships was MD-11 N514MD (f/n 453). The aircraft was used for Function & Reliability (F&R) tests.

Towards the end of the test programme McDonnell Douglas flew this aircraft on a round the world tour for the final long range F&R tests. The aircraft was operated with simulated up to 'full house' payloads on the three long distance route proving flights with FAA officials aboard. After a short flight from Yuma to Dallas/Fort Worth on 22nd October 1990, the aircraft took off for Seoul, South Korea that same day. The 6,316nm (11,697km) distance was flown in a record 14hr 50min. On 24th October the aircraft departed Seoul for London Gatwick and covered the 6,083nm (11,266km) distance in 13hr 20min. Flight DACO 514 came to an end on 25th October after a 13hr 05min flight from London Gatwick to Yuma. The 6,078nm (11,256km) segment included an overhead visit to the North Pole to check navigation accuracy.

During the stops in Dallas/Fort Worth, Seoul and at London Gatwick, officials and staff from three MD-11 customers (respectively American Airlines, Korean Air and Air Europe) were invited to take a look at the new wide-body airliner.

Upon return, pilots, engineering and FAA staff had gathered valuable information about long range cruise performance, fuel consumption and the safe and reliable operations of the different systems.

Originally ordered by Air Europe, the aircraft was leased to Delta Air Lines by Mitsui & Company, having already carried the livery of the Atlanta-based carrier during the flight tests.

of 27 airlines and leasing companies which had ordered the aircraft were displayed on both sides of the forward fuselage. The test and certification programme was based out of the Yuma facility and involved over 400 people between Yuma and Long Beach.

After its first flight to Yuma N111MD (f/n 447) conducted evaluation tests on performance and handling and was used for certification trials of the GE CF-6-80C2D1F engines. Anticipating an impending FAA requirement, the Douglas team voluntarily performed the '100 Percent Rejected Take Off (RTO) test with worn brakes. Traditionally, the RTO is performed with new brakes and tires. But for the MD-11 certification, Ship No. 1's carbon brakes were machined down to within 95 percent of the maximum allowable wear limit. Then, the flight team made five landings on those brakes and tires before performing the RTO. Very often, an RTO ends with brakes in flames and the aircraft towed off the runway. But the test, performed at Edwards Air Force Base because of its long runway, went off without a hitch.

The second aircraft in the test programme, N211MD (f/n 448), was flown from Long Beach to Yuma on 1st March 1991. Ship No. 2, which was also powered by GE engines, conducted

The rigorous, almost 2,000hr test and certification programme was completed within ten months following the first flight. An important part of the certification programme's efficiency can be attributed to the cooperation of Douglas Flight Test team and FAA staff. FAA members flew on development testing flights, a first for the Douglas Aircraft Flight Test team. Also, the test information was electronically transmitted to the FAA as soon as it was collected, another first. This new system speeded the process and improved communications between the two groups. In a ceremony at Washington's Dulles International Airport on 8th November 1990, the type and production certificate for the GE powered MD-11 was presented by Admiral James B Busey, Federal Aviation Administration (FAA) administrator, to Douglas Aircraft Company president Robert H Hood Jr. The certification brought to a close the most carefully planned and intense flight test program in Douglas history.

Certification of the P&W powered MD-11 followed on 18th December 1990. Certifications for Category IIIb fail-operational automatic landings were obtained for the PW and GE powered aircraft on 23rd April and 17th May 1991 respectively. The MD-11 was the first US-built commercial airliner to be designed to meet the requirements of the newly founded European Joint Airworthiness Authorities (JAA), later renamed Joint Aviation Authorities. The JAA issued the certificate of airworthiness, under the JAR-25 (Joint Airworthiness Regulation), for the MD-11 on 17th October 1991. During a ceremony at Long Beach on 29th November 1990 the first MD-11 was handed over to launch customer Finnair. The new widebody was parked beside a Douglas DC-2, which was delivered to Pan American in 1935 and now belongs to the Boeing Museum of Flight in Seattle. The picture truly portrayed the evolution of Douglas Aircraft Company's commercial airliners. Finnair officially took delivery of the aircraft on 7th December and placed the new tri-jet into service on 20th December 1990.

After the first aircraft had been delivered to Finnair, other airlines like American Airlines, Korean Air and Delta Air Lines soon received their first MD-11s. It was American Airlines which first made the world aware that there was something amiss with the MD-11; the aircraft had a performance problem which had already become evident during the flight test programme. Although performance guarantees were made by General Electric and Pratt & Whitney, both the GE and P&W engines

burned too much fuel which resulted in a shortfall of either range or payload. The specific fuel consumption (sfc) of the PW4460 was 6.7% above the guaranteed specifications while the CF6-80C2D1F was 4.5-5.3% above. To make things worse, the airframe proved to be more drag-prone and heavier than expected.

American Airlines and Asian carriers particularly had selected the aircraft for non-stop transpacific flights and the shortfall in range and payload had a serious impact on their operations.

Meanwhile Airbus was promoting its new long range A340 and Boeing had launched its new twin-jet, the 777, in October 1990. Both aircraft were serious competitors to the MD-11 and the aggressive marketing efforts of both Airbus and Boeing forced McDonnell Douglas to take immediate steps to rectify the performance problems of their aircraft.

In 1991, DAC came up with a drag reduction programme to be implemented in three phases. Phase I of the A1 PIP (Performance Improvement Program) included the addition of outboard wing trailing edge splitters which reduced drag by 0.7%. In January 1992, Phase II was introduced as A-1 Package 1. Drooping

the outer ailerons by four degrees during the cruise and the installation of seals at the outboard slats brought a benefit of 1.5%. The result was an increase in range of 100nm (185km). With A-1 Package 2, which included structural modifications to the wings, the wingbox and undercarriage, the maximum takeoff weight (MTOW) was increased from 618,000lb (280,572kg) to 625,000lb (283,750kg) in November 1992. The modifications allowed the carriage of more fuel which resulted in a range increase of 250nm (463km) or an additional 7,000lb (3,178kg) in payload. The A-1 Package 3 included a further modification to the ailerons, enabling them to droop during take-off. With the ailerons deflected the take-off field length was decreased by 500-900ft (150-270m), which permitted a higher MTOW.

The Phase IIIA package was introduced in late 1993 and resulted in a total drag reduction of 1%. The package included changes to the pylon fillet, the installation of aileron seal plates and the positioning of the windshield wipers from a horizontal to vertical position.

In 1994, DAC introduced Phase IIIB which made possible a further 1.5% drag improvement by the installation of a new, larger intake

Until mid-1996 the fuselage sections, manufactured by General Dynamics' Convair Division, were transported by barges from San Diego to Long Beach Harbor and trucked to the plant. McDonnell Douglas

The assembly of the first MD-11 started on 9th March, 1988. The nose sections of the first MD-11 (f/n 447) and the last DC-10 (f/n 446) are depicted. McDonnell Douglas

on the aft engine which was 400 lb (180kg) lighter. The larger intake was one of the few changes in the PIP which could not be retrofitted. The first aircraft on the production line which had the new intake installed was f/n 575, delivered to KLM in November 1994. The final part of the PIP, Phase IV, came in early 1995. A further 1.2% drag reduction was accomplished by a wing and undercarriage seal package and a redesigned flap hinge fairing.

In the meantime the engine manufacturers had also accomplished improvements and modifications. A -1.5% fuel burn was realised by General Electric with improvements in the high pressure compressor, high pressure turbine and tail pipe. Pratt & Whitney achieved a 2.7% reduction in fuel burn by improving the booster, high-pressure turbine, low-pressure turbine and fan toggle, and a modification in the inlet cowl. With all modifications performed the aircraft met its original design goal, transporting 298 passengers over a 6,840nm (12,655km) distance.

On 29th August 1995, an MD-11 landed at NASA's (National Aeronautics and Space Administration) Dryden Flight Research Center, Edwards, California. This would not normally be regarded as a spectacular event, but it was in fact the first landing ever of a commercial transport aircraft under engine power only. In partnership with McDonnell Douglas Aerospace (MDA), Pratt & Whitney and Honeywell, helping to design the software, NASA developed a propulsion-controlled aircraft (PCA) system following a series of incidents in which hydraulic failures resulted in the loss of flight controls. For the MD-11, the PCA system used standard autopilot controls already present in the cockpit, together with new programming in the aircraft's flight control computers. The aircraft demonstrated software used in the flight control computer that essentially landed the MD-11 PCA without a need for the pilot to manipulate the flight controls and without the use of conventional, hydraulic controls.

The milestone flight was flown by NASA research pilot and former astronaut Gordon Fullerton, together with John Miller, DAC MD-11 chief pilot, Tim Dingen, DAC MD-11 pilot and Wayne Anselmo, MD-11 flight test engineer.

Although not installed in customer aircraft as yet, aircraft manufacturers have decided that a PCA system will be valuable for use in the design of future aircraft.

An MD-11 successfully demonstrated its exceptional performance during a series of simulated engine-out operations en route to and at the high-altitude airport in Lhasa, Tibet, on 12th September 1996. MDC conducted the flight for China Southwest Airlines to demonstrate simulated engine-out manoeuvres under the constraints of operations in the altitudes and environment encountered at airports in the Himalayan mountains. Lhasa's Gonggar Airport is 11,600ft (3,538m) above sea level. The flight demonstrated several critical safety capabilities that would be important in selecting the best aircraft for use to airports located at high altitude. The aircraft's performance under these previously undemonstrated engine-out conditions exceeded all requirements. The test demonstrated that the MD-11's performance also at high elevation fields is not only safe, but absolutely superior.

The wing panels were manufactured by McDonnell Douglas in Canada and shipped by boxcars to the Long Beach plant. Here the wing panels are joined to the centre wing box. McDonnell Douglas

After fuel tank installations were completed, the centre fuselage section was joined to the wings and wing box. McDonnell Douglas

A view through the forward fuselage stretch barrel shows two nearly completed nose sections. McDonnell Douglas

At this station in the production line noses were attached to the forward fuselage sections. The section in the foreground awaits mating with a nose section while rearmost fuselage section is in the process of being mated. McDonnell Douglas

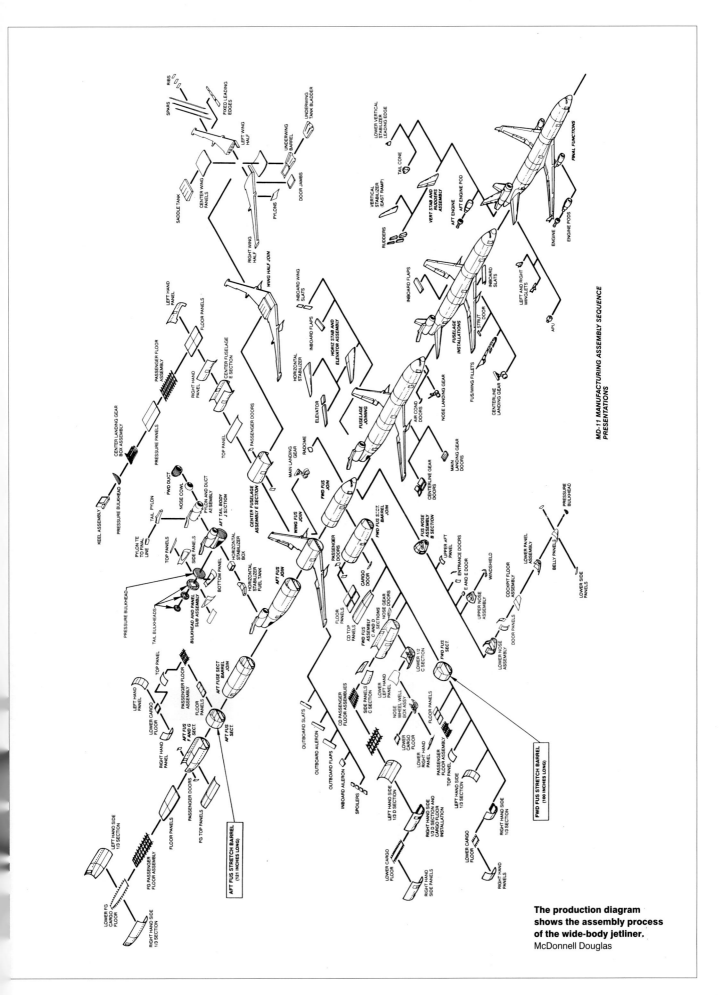

**The production diagram
shows the assembly process
of the wide-body jetliner.**
McDonnell Douglas

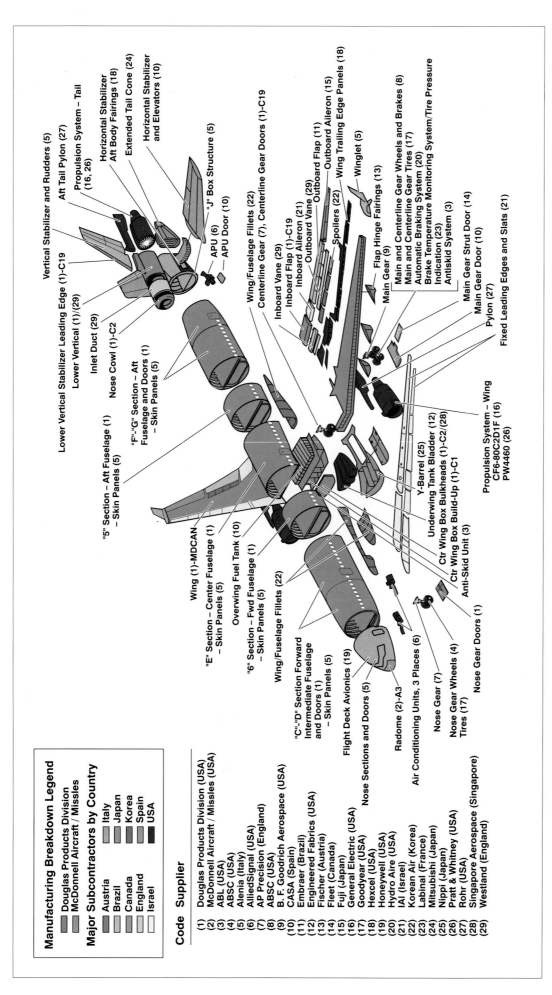

The component manufacturers diagram provides an overview of the components produced by DAC, McDonnell Douglas Aerospace and major subcontractors from around the world. McDonnell Douglas

Above: **The giant forged rings in the aft engine air duct serve as the main vertical spars for the stabiliser.** The Boeing Company

Below: **The first MD-11 is shown in an advanced stage of assembly.** McDonnell Douglas

Bottom: **The new aerodynamic tailcone is moved on a rollered cradle to mate with the rear fuselage section.** McDonnell Douglas

Top: **The tail mounted engine support structure has been mated with the rear fuselage section. The German flags were placed on the tooling fixture because it was the first fuselage built for Lufthansa Cargo.** The Boeing Company

Centre: **A look down the assembly line. Notice the cockpit section of the next aircraft through the aft air intake.** McDonnell Douglas

Above: **The final assembly line. The aircraft's bare aluminium skins are still covered in the anodised finish.** McDonnell Douglas

Left: **Assembly continues outside on the East Ramp with the installation of the engines, winglets and the pre-assembled tail fin.** McDonnell Douglas

Below: **Delta Air Lines' MD-11** *The Centennial Spirit* **obtained its beautiful livery in the Long Beach paint shop.** McDonnell Douglas

Bottom left and right: **The first MD-11 being towed across Lakewood Boulevard to the West Ramp in 1989. Only eleven years later the last aircraft, with a 'The perfect end to a perfect era' and 'MD-11 Final Assembly' sticker, is towed to the flight line.** McDonnell Douglas/ Boeing Company

Right: **Before the first flight, the aircraft's magnetic navigation instruments are checked. A Saudi Arabian MD-11F is parked on the compass rose at the Long Beach plant.**
The Boeing Company

Centre right: **A historic day. The first MD-11 takes off from Long Beach Municipal Airport for its maiden flight on 10th January 1990.** McDonnell Douglas

Below right: **The first aircraft displayed the logos of prospective customers on the forward port- and starboard fuselage. 1st line: FedEx, Korean Air, Swissair, Alitalia, Finnair, Mitsui and Thai Airways International. 2nd line: Guinness Peat Aviation, Nigeria Airways, China Airlines, Minerve, LTU, Delta Air Lines and China Eastern. 3rd line: Air Europe, JAT, ILFC, Garuda Indonesia, VARIG, VIASA and Zambia Airways. 4th line: ZAS, American Airlines, Air Zaire, Aero Lloyd, AOM and Evergreen.** McDonnell Douglas

Above: **The first flight is cause for celebration as flight crew members prepare to board the new tri-jet. From left are Tom Melody, co-pilot; Fred Schreiner, flight test coordinator; John Miller, chief project pilot; and Jack Bowman, MD-11 technical specialist.** McDonnell Douglas

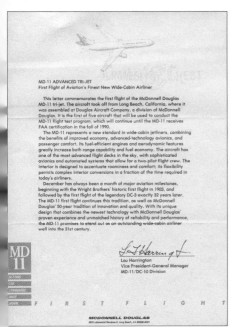

Letter of Lou Harrington, Vice-President Douglas Aircraft Company, and first day cover commemorating the first flight of the MD-11. McDonnell Douglas

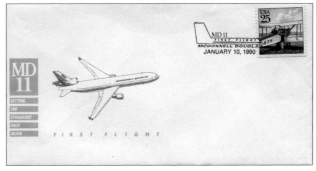

A spectacular top view of the first MD-11 during a test flight. McDonnell Douglas

The second test aircraft, N211MD, painted in the full McDonnell Douglas 'house colours', flies over the city of Long Beach, California. McDonnell Douglas

Opposite page:

Top: **The third test aircraft, N311MD, was the first aircraft powered by Pratt & Whitney engines and obtained only a part 'house colours' paint scheme.** McDonnell Douglas

Centre: **MD-11 N90178 (f/n 560) on final approach to Edwards Air Force Base, California, home of NASA's Dryden Flight Research Center.** J Ross – NASA

Bottom: **The first MD-11 was handed over to Finnair during a ceremony at Long Beach on 29th November 1990. The DC-2 parked beside the MD-11 was originally delivered to Pan American in 1935 and is now owned by the Boeing Museum of Flight in Seattle, Washington.** McDonnell Douglas

Chapter Two

The MD-11 Family

For the MD-11, MDC followed the DC-10 concept and offered three different versions of the new jetliner from the start of production. The all-passenger version (MD-11P), the 'Combi' (MD-11C) for mixed passenger and cargo transport and the all-freighter model (MD-11F) were available to meet the different customer requirements. A further version, the Convertible Freighter (MD-11CF) was introduced in August 1991.The fifth and final version, the so-called ER – Extended Range – was launched at the Singapore Air Show in February 1994. Unlike the DC-10 family of aircraft which included medium range versions, all MD-11 variants were conceived as long range airliners.

The all-passenger MD-11 proved to be the most successful aircraft in the family. A total of 131 examples left the Long Beach plant for delivery mainly to international operators. The range of this version is 7,865 statute miles (12,655km), carrying 298 passengers in a typical three-class layout.

The development of the combi aircraft was initiated by Alitalia. Only five aircraft of the type were built. With 183 passengers and six main deck pallets the MD-11C has a range 7,730 statute miles (12,435km).

In December 1994, the first MD-11CF was delivered to Martinair Holland. The Dutch carrier was the first airline to order the Convertible

The mighty MD-11, a state-of-the-art and impressive airliner. McDonnell Douglas

Freighter aircraft. The Dutch carrier looked back at years of profitable DC-10-30CF operations and selected the MD-11CF as its new workhorse. The second airline to order the aircraft was World Airways. DAC built six MD-11CFs between 1994 and 1995. With an arrangement for all passenger or all cargo layout, the aircraft was ideal for the two carriers which operate in both fields. In the passenger layout the range of the aircraft is the same as the base passenger aircraft. In the freight mode, the aircraft will carry a payload of 196,928 lb (89,325kg) over a 4,540 statute miles (7,310km) distance.

The first MD-11F was delivered to FedEx in May 1991. A total of 53 aircraft of the successful all-freight version were built. With a payload of 200,151 lb (90,787kg) the aircraft can fly a distance of 4,540 statute miles (7,310km).

As the last member in the MD-11 family, the extended range version was ordered by World Airways and Garuda Indonesia. Equipped with a 3,000 gallon (11,355 litre) supplemental fuel tank, this long range version provides a maximum range of 8,300 statute miles (13,355km) at a maximum take-off weight of 630,500 lb (285,990kg). If McDonnell Douglas had not already solved the range problems with the base MD-11, the MD-11ER proved even more to be a true long range airliner . Although the ER-option was available for all MD-11 variants it was only delivered on passenger aircraft, hence the designation MD-11ERP. As was the case with the combi aircraft, only five extended range aircraft were built, both representing the lowest production runs of all MD-11 variants. When the MD-11 production line closed in June 2000 a total of 200 aircraft had been produced:

Version	Built
MD-11P	131
MD-11C	5
MD-11CF	6
MD-11F	53
MD-11ERP	5

A total of 446 DC-10s were built between 1971 and 1988, bearing the fuselage numbers 1 through 446. DAC continued with fuselage number 447 for the first MD-11 built, the 200th and last aircraft being fuselage number 646. Thus altogether the company built 646 wide-body tri-jets. The MD-11 is one of the world's most advanced, versatile, reliable, fuel-efficient and environmentally friendly jetliners in service. With its three engines, the aircraft is not subject to the ETOPS (Extended Range Twin Operations) regulations imposed on Boeing and Airbus long range twin-jets. However, after the cessation of production, the MD-11 will most probably prove to be the world's last commercial wide-body tri-jet to be built.

Engines

Each of the world's three major engine manufacturers, General Electric, Pratt & Whitney and Rolls-Royce, developed engine variants to power the new tri-jet. From the start of the programme McDonnell Douglas was able to offer a multiple engine choice for the different MD-11 models and address the different needs and requirements of the airlines interested to purchase the aircraft.

Although the DC-10 had been studied with R-R turbofans, the aircraft was in fact only built with General Electric and Pratt & Whitney power plants. Not since the days of the DC-8 had there been a McDonnell Douglas product with Rolls-Royce engines.

The General Electric CF6 engine was developed for the DC-10 and was GE's first successful commercial engine. GE took the technology which had been developed for the TF39, powering the military Lockheed C-5 Galaxy and adapted it for civilian use.

The CF6-80C2, which has a 93-inch (2.36m) diameter fan, is a direct derivative of the reliable CF-6-50 used on the DC-10-30 and was developed to meet airline needs of the late 1980s and the 1990s. The engine was first tested in May 1982 and was certified in mid-1985. International co-operation was the hallmark of the CF6-80C2 programme. Work on the engine was also being performed by SNECMA of France, MTU of Germany, Volvo Flygmotor of Sweden and Fiat Aviazione of Italy. The thrust ratings of the different versions range from 52,500 to 61,500 lb (233 to 273kN).

The CF6-80C2 version for the MD-11 is the highest rated 61,500 lb thrust CF6-80C2D1F engine which has a length of 160.9in (4m) and a total weight of 9,135 lb. (4,144kg).

The Pratt & Whitney PW4460 and PW4462 engines are members of the PW4000 high-thrust, commercial engine family, developed for the biggest, wide-body aircraft. P&W designed the PW4000 with a large engine core that allows thrust growth by increasing the fan diameter and changing the low-pressure spool. With a 94-inch (2.38m) diameter fan, the first series of PW4000 engines covered a thrust range from 50,000 (222kN) to 62,000 lb (275kN). Launched in 1982, the engine was certified in 1986. Besides the MD-11, these engines power Airbus A300 and A310 aircraft, the Boeing 747 and 767. While the PW4460 engine is rated at 60.000 lb (266 kN) take-off thrust, the higher-rated PW4462 delivers 62,000 lb (275 kN) thrust. Both engines measure 132,7in (3.37m) in length and have a complete weight of 9,400 lb (4,264kg).

The GE and P&W engines are 'high bypass ratio' turbofan engines. The bypass ratio is the proportion of airflow through the fan at the front of the engine and airflow through the engine core. A high bypass engine not only develops more power, it also is more fuel efficient and quieter. Both the GE and P&W engines are equipped with a FADEC (Full Authority Digital Engine Control) system which interfaces with the aircraft's electronic auto-throttle and flight management systems and contributes to the fuel economy and reliability.

Because of the larger fan diameter of the P&W engines one can notice a difference in size and shape between the cowlings of the GE & P&W wing-mounted engines. Whereas there was a remarkable difference between the straight cowling profile of the GE aft engine and the P&W 'coke bottle' look aft engine on the DC-10, there is no difference in the aft engine air intake cowlings of the GE and P&W powered MD-11s.

The third engine type to be offered for the MD-11 was the Rolls-Royce RB211-524L 95-inch (2.41m) turbofan engine, which was later

renamed Trent 665. A derivative of the -524 Series, the -524L version was planned with a take-off thrust of 65,000 lb (289kN), with a potential growth to 80,000 lb (355kN). The higher thrust was achieved through the utilisation of a larger diameter wide-chord fan and improved core components. The engine had an overall length of 150in (3.8m) and a total weight of 13,589 lb (6,177kg). UK charter operator Air Europe was to be the launch customer for the Rolls-Royce powered MD-11 but the bankruptcy of parent organisation International Leisure Group forced the airline to cease operations in 1991. Subsequently the outstanding orders and options were cancelled. Although Rolls-Royce continued with the development of the engine for a short period, no other airline was interested in acquiring this engine/airframe combination and ultimately the Rolls-Royce engine option for the MD-11 was dropped.

Engine	Take-off thrust
GE CF6-80C2D1F	61,500 lb (273kN)
P&W PW4460	60,000 lb (266kN)
P&W PW4462	62,000 lb (275kN)
R-R RB211-524L (Trent 665)	65,000 lb (289kN)

	Fan Diameter	Engine length
GE CF6-80C2D1F	93in (2.36m)	160.9in (4m)
P&W PW4460/PW4462	94in (2.38m)	132,7in (3.37m)
R-R RB211-524L (Trent 665)	95in (2.41m)	150in (3.8m)

Although General Electric supplied the majority of the engines for the MD-11, Pratt & Whitney's share grew tremendously compared to the DC-10 programme, when the engine manufacturer had only managed to capture orders to equip a total of 42 out of 446 aircraft built (respectively 22 for Northwest Orient and 20 for Japan Airlines).

Of the 200 MD-11s delivered, 119 aircraft were equipped with General Electric engines. GE CF6-80C2D1F-powered aircraft were ordered by Alitalia, American Airlines, City Bird, FedEx, EVA Air, Finnair, Garuda Indonesia, KLM, Lufthansa Cargo, Saudi Arabian Airlines, Thai Airways International, VARIG and VASP.

Of the remaining 81 aircraft, 67 were delivered with Pratt & Whitney PW4460 engines and 14 aircraft with the higher thrust PW4462 variant. The airlines which ordered PW4460-powered MD-11s are China Airlines, China Eastern Airlines, City Bird, Delta Air Lines, Japan Airlines, Korean Air, LTU International Airways, Swissair and World Airways.

Martinair Holland was the only carrier to order the PW4462 engine for its entire MD-11 fleet. FedEx selected the engine for the last three ordered aircraft while three of the original Swissair aircraft were equipped with the power plant. Saudi Arabian VIP Aircraft selected the PW4462 for the two VIP MD-11s.

The wing engines (number one and three) hang from pylons which extend below and forward of the wing. An important installation design element was that the standard pylon can either carry a GE or P&W engine without modification. The aft engine hangs from a pylon-beam at the bottom of the vertical stabiliser. The position of the engine-to-pylon rear mount is movable for the different engine installations.

Ease of maintenance was an important factor in the design of the engine system installations. The large pylon-hinged nacelle doors expose the entire engine and the cowl door and split thrust reverser allow easy access. For simplicity and reduced spare engine costs, these remain on the aircraft during an engine change. A self-contained built-in platform for maintenance and inspection is located at the aft engine. With the proper ground support equipment available, a wing-mounted engine change takes eight hours. The tail engine change takes 12 hours.

The so-called 'fourth pod' option, which enabled the DC-10 to transport a spare engine, was not considered for the MD-11. First, the basic engine can be transported by highway truck without a special permission. Second, DC-10 and MD-11 freighter aircraft can transport a spare engine on the main deck around the world in due time, thus eliminating the labour- and time-consuming installation of the extra pylon and spare engine.

Cockpit

Being not merely an extended DC-10 able to carry more passengers, the MD-11 incorporates the state-of-the-art technologies of the 1990s. The two pilot flightdeck features the latest advances in electronic control technology. The flightdeck and avionics systems were designed by Honeywell Sperry Commercial Flight Systems in conjunction with airline flight operations and engineering personnel through the medium of the MD-11 Cockpit Advisory Committee.

Since computerised system controllers perform automated normal, abnormal and emergency checklist duties for the MD-11's major systems, the flight crew requirement was reduced from three to two persons. The so-called Aircraft Systems Controllers (ASC) consist of five separate dual channel computers which monitor the proper operation of the aircraft systems, taking over the functions formerly carried out by a flight engineer. During normal operations, when the cockpit is configured for flight, all annunciators on the overhead panel will be extinguished. The 'dark cockpit' confirms to the crew that no abnormalities are present. A light will only come on to alert the crew if an abnormality occurs.

The Electronic Instrument System (EIS) consists of six identical colour cathode ray tube displays (CRTs) which display flight instrument and aircraft systems information. The 8in x 8in (20.3cm x 20.3cm) CRT Display Units (DU) are arranged in two horizontal groups of three on each side of the landing gear handle. The outer two DUs are Primary Flight Displays (PFDs). Inboard of the PFDs are the Navigation Displays (NDs) with five pages selectable from the captain's and first officer's EIS control panels.

Inboard of the left ND is the Engine Alert Display (EAD). Inboard of the right ND is the Systems Display (SD) with ten selectable pages. The SD pages are selectable from the Systems Control Panel (SCP) located immediately aft of the throttle quadrant on the pedestal.

As mentioned, each pilot has his/her PFD which combines the functions of the Flight Mode Annunciator (FMA), IAS/MACH indicator, Attitude Director Indicator (ADI), baro altimeter, radio altimeter and vertical speed indicator. Additional items include taxi speed, V speeds (V_1, V_2, V_R), flap/slat position, flight director, bank angle limits, flight-path angle and windshear information, amongst others. Approach and landing information is also displayed on the PFD.

The ND shows aircraft position, waypoints, navigation aids, airport locations, weather information, ground speed, true air speed, wind speed and direction, distance and time to the next waypoint, weather radar and heading. The GE CF6-80C2D1F EAD shows each of the parameters N_1 (low pressure rotor, % rpm), N_2 (high pressure rotor, % rpm), EGT (exhaust gas temperature) and FF (fuel flow). P&W-powered aircraft have an additional EPR (engine pressure ratio) read-out.

The SD includes the secondary engine display which shows engine oil pressure, temperature and quantities, gross weight, centre of gravity, stabiliser trim, total fuel, cabin altitude, cabin rate and APU parameters. Other pages selectable on the SD provide information about the aircraft systems.

The dual Flight Management System (FMS) automates the lateral and vertical navigation to reduce pilot workload and to enhance precision control of the aircraft. To provide simple and positive aircraft control, dual Flight Control Computers (FCC) are installed.

In October 2000 the penultimate MD-11 (f/n 645) started flight tests of a new flight management system for Lufthansa Cargo's fleet. Upon certification of the new Honeywell Pegasus 920 FMS, which is Future Air Navigation System (FANS) capable, it will be installed in all of the cargo carrier's MD-11 freighters.

The pedestal houses the captain's and first officer's FMS multifunction control displays, throttles, engine start and fuel switches, systems control panel, audio control panels and data printer. The ASC, air, electrical and fuel system control panels as well as fire shut-off handles are located in the overhead panel.

The MD-11 can be equipped with advanced systems like the Traffic Alert and Collision Avoidance System (TCAS), Satellite Communication (SATCOM), Global Positioning System (GPS) and Ground Proximity Warning System (GPWS).

Excellent pilot vision was inherited from the DC-10 cockpit. The flat windshield panels and slightly curved clearview panels give unimpeded vision. The advantages of the flat windshields are a minimum amount of reflection and distortion, not achievable on curved wind-

shields as used on the 747, maximum strength and optimal wiper efficiency. The large side windows provide an excellent aft view, enabling each pilot to see the winglets during taxying and close quarter manoeuvring. Since the forward cut-off is less than 57.4ft (17.5m) excellent forward-and-down vision is vision is obtained during taxying. Upward forward vision is 39°.

A significant feature are the openable clearview windows, permitting a rapid egress in case of emergency. Adequate vision is assured in case of bird or hail strike damage since the clearview windows may be opened at speeds up to 286mph (460km/h). The openable windows also allow the cleaning of cockpit windows without the need for ground support equipment.

On the comfort side, a heat-soaked cockpit can be cooled down through cross ventilation before the air conditioning is in operation. Crew comfort is further enhanced by the cool air 'eyeball' diffusers located at each crew station. In order to eliminate wide temperature variations in the windshield and clearview window area, an additional 'air curtain' is supplied by the air conditioning system ducting.

Flight crew seat comfort was a high priority for the MD-11. Pilots from a umber of major airlines were invited to help in the selection process. The crew seats can be operated electrically in both the vertical and horizontal direction and have a manual override system. A high degree of comfort was achieved in seat design. The entire back support moves up and down, and forward and aft to match the contour of a crew member's back. Furthermore, the seat bottom pan and cushion are designed to follow the body contour while not allowing the cushion to bottom out. An outstanding feature of the captain's and first officer's seat is its capability to track 11 inches (28 cm) in the fore and aft direction, allowing crew members to place a food tray on their laps or stretch to a relaxed position in conjunction with the reclining seat backs.

The right observer's seat may be positioned between and slightly aft of the engine control pedestal and at the same eye reference height as the two pilots. This provides the observer with excellent visibility of the instrument panel and outside the aircraft. An optional second observer's seat could be installed aft of the captain's position while a foldable third observer's jump seat against the port side cockpit wall was also available as an option.

Ample stowage space is provided within reach of the seated pilots for all required manuals and documents. The cockpit is furnished with a crew coatroom which is located in the rear left area of the compartment. Finally, space is also provided for crew luggage.

As is common today on nearly all wide-body aircraft operating extra-long range flights, separate rest areas for cockpit and cabin crew can be installed. The optional cockpit rest area is located at the forward port side entry door and is equipped with two telescoping bunks. The

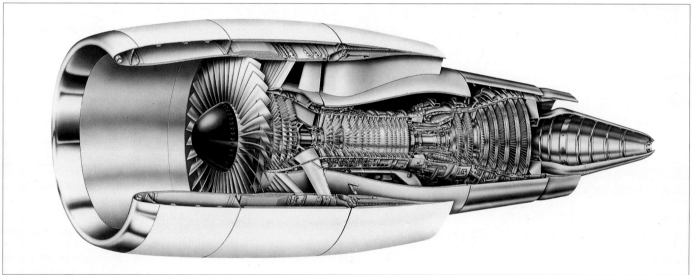

Top left: **The CF6-80C2 93-inch high bypass turbofan for the MD-11 is a direct derivative of the successful CF6-50 used on the DC-10-30.** GE Aircraft Engines Photographic Services

Top right: **Pratt & Whitney offered two versions of its PW4000 high-thrust engine for the MD-11.** United Technologies-Pratt & Whitney

Centre: **Cutaway of the CF6-80C2 propulsion system (includes engine, nacelle and nozzle).** GE Aircraft Engines Photographic Services

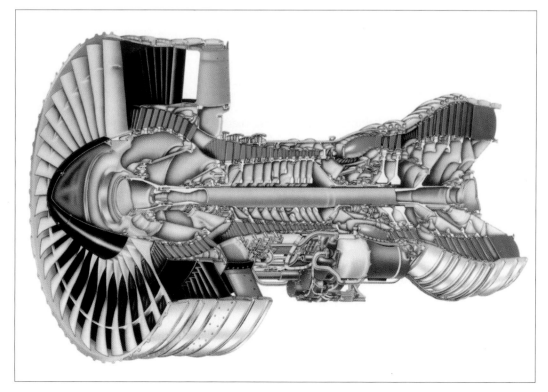

Right: **Cutaway of a PW4000 Series turbofan engine.** United Technologies-Pratt & Whitney

area is sound isolated and is directly accessible from the cockpit without entering the passenger compartment.

The spacious MD-11 cockpit is one of the largest cockpits in today's jet transports and provides uncrowded working conditions for the flight crew. Furthermore, the aerodynamic design of the nose of the fuselage and the V-shape windshield guarantee a minimum of airflow disturbance, resulting in extremely low cockpit noise levels. Through this cockpit design, Douglas achieved the envisaged efficient and comfortable workspace for the MD-11 flight crews.

Convertible Cabin

If McDonnell Douglas had already written the word 'flexibility' in capital letters for the DC-10 interior configuration, this would even more be applicable in case of the MD-11. A comfortable and modern interior was designed with maximum airline flexibility in mind. This was achieved with the co-operative efforts of engineering and passenger service personnel from many of the world's premier airlines. A full-scale interior mock-up was built in two phases. During

Rolls-Royce was a contestant in the engine selection with the RB211-524L 95-inch turbofan engine until the demise of Air Europe.
Rolls-Royce plc

Phase 1, Douglas completed design of architectural concepts; installation of lighting, ceiling and side-wall panels, overhead stowage bins, passenger seats; and fabrication and installation of these items. Phase 2 included the completion of final design details and installation of the public address system, flight attendants panels, and passenger entertainment system.

To simplify MD-11 interiors installations, Douglas teamed up with Flightline Industries. All interior components were delivered directly to Flightline Industries' facility where they were inspected, checked for fit on jigs representing MD-11 cross sections, and assembled into kits. Then, when assembly crews on the aircraft were ready, the kits were delivered in order of installation by scissorlift trucks right onto the aircraft. The result was a reduction in assembly hours and damaged components. The goal of reaching an installation rate of five days for an

entire interior was reached by the just-in-time deliveries.

McDonnell Douglas designed a cabin which would give airlines maximum flexibility in cabin configuration. Galleys, lavatories and coatrooms can be moved in 1-inch (2.54cm) increments on the seat tracks. The water and waste piping runs along either side of the fuselage and connection points have been installed every 40in (102cm). Galleys and toilets can be hooked up to the connection points with flexible plumbing. Potable water is supplied from four 63 gallon (238 litre) tanks located in the forward cargo side-wall tunnel areas. Two 135 gallon (511 litre) stainless steel waste tanks are located in the aft bulk cargo compartment.

The modular flexibility allows MD-11 operators to react to market needs within a short period of time. The majority of reconfigurations, like a three-class to a one-class cabin seating, can be accomplished in 12 to 18 hours.

Passenger seat configurations are numerous. From a typical 22 first, 56 business and 226 economy, they range up to a 409 all-economy seating arrangement. With the flexibility of the total of passenger seats in mind, varied seating arrangements were offered. With increasing demand for more comfort, first class and business class are equipped with sleeperettes. First class normally features a six abreast seating. The ultimate in first class passenger comfort was introduced by Swissair in 1999. With seating reduced to four abreast, ensuring absolute privacy, the airline offers a seat that transforms into a bed 79in (201cm) long and 24in (60cm) wide. At each seat location a large table is installed that enables the passenger to hold a conference, or a dinner, for two. For business class a seven or eight abreast configuration can be incorporated. By virtue of the inherent flexibility of the cabin, eight, nine or even ten abreast seating is available for economy class. In whatever configuration chosen, the wide cabin with its twin aisles provides a feeling of spaciousness in all classes.

The MD-11 has eight cabin doors of which the two port side forward doors are normally used for embarkation and disembarkation of passengers. Except for the overwing door, swift catering is assured through the remaining three starboard doors. The track-mounted doors open inward and then upward, being hidden in the ceiling. Besides ease of operation by the cabin crew, this system provides protection from damage from ground servicing equipment, jetways and wind gusts. All doors have built-in emergency slides securing the evacuation of all passengers within 90 seconds, which is an aviation authority safety requirement. In case of a ditching the slides are used as rafts. With a normal capacity of 30 (maximum 37) passengers for the rafts of the most forward and overwing doors and 70 (maximum 87) passengers for the rafts of the remaining four doors, safe accommodation of all passengers and crew is guaranteed.

Below left: **Because of the length of the GE engine the engine support beam is 4.7in (12cm) longer than that on the P&W equipped MD-11.**
McDonnell Douglas

Below right: **The P&W engine is 24.8in (63cm) shorter than the GE engine. The shape of the P&W engine provides an uncluttered profile of the tail section.** McDonnell Douglas

Bottom left: **Instrument layout was designed in conjunction with airline flight operations through the MD-11 Cockpit Advisory Committee.** McDonnell Douglas

Bottom right: **The MD-11 cockpit is one of the largest and roomiest in today's airliners and a comfortable workplace for the two-man crew.** Swissair

The modern cabin is equipped with overhead stowage compartments along the sidewalls and standard centreline compartments. The modular overhead stowage bins accommodate lavatory flexibility. Additional space for coats and garment bags can be obtained by the installation of a further coatroom in the overwing centre section of the cabin.

Brightness in the cabin is provided by the 11.69in x 17.19in (29.7cm x 43.6cm) passenger windows which are 75% bigger than the Airbus A340 windows. Fluorescent lamps in the overhead, lower and upper side wall light the passenger cabin. Whereas the overhead lights give direct light, the side wall lights give indirect illumination. The lights can be regulated sepa-

rately in each cabin section and contribute to the pleasant environment at any time of day.

The high standard of passenger comfort is also met by the advanced audio-visual entertainment systems supplied by different manufacturers. At the start of the MD-11 programme McDonnell Douglas selected Matsushita Avionics Systems to supply its Advanced Passenger Entertainment and Service System, called APES, for the MD-11. The state-of-the-art digital multiplex system incorporates many advanced functions and features. The entertainment portion of APESS provides passengers with audio quality that matches the quality found in home stereos. Through headphones, listeners are given access to a variety of stereo

Above left: **Four abreast seating in the forward cabin provides ultimate comfort and absolute privacy for first class passengers.** Swissair

Above right: **In a spacious seven abreast business class configuration no passenger is more than one seat from an aisle.** Swissair

Left: **By virtue of the inherent flexibility of the cabin, eight, nine or even ten abreast seating is available for economy class. American Airlines MD-11 aircraft feature a nine abreast layout.** American Airlines

programs, including music, video soundtracks, and announcements from the cockpit and cabin crew. The system also included individual 5in x 5in (12.7cm x 12.7cm) colour monitors. The passenger service system provides a multiplexed control for reading lights and flight attendant call. The addition of three panels (located in the forward, mid and aft workstations) enables the crew to determine exact seat locations of passengers making attendant calls. Today individual in-seat audio-video systems are generally installed in first and business class. TV-monitors are placed throughout the cabin for passenger safety briefing, aircraft route and position information and, in economy class, also for the showing of movies. Further cabin features may include on-board telephones, live satellite-television, power hookups at individual seats for the use of laptops and in-flight gambling.

Not only passenger comfort was taken care of; extra crew comfort could also be provided. Besides the optional cockpit crew rest area adjacent to the cockpit, two cabin rest area options were offered for use by the cabin and cockpit crew on long range flights. First, the so-

called 'Skybunk' of which two can be installed on the port and/or starboard side in the central overhead area aft of the adjacent galley complex and which are accessible by steps. Furthermore, a large secluded rest container was available providing space for five bunks. Although normally located in the central section of the passenger cabin adjacent to the aft galley area, the unit can be installed in several cabin locations.

With the new Combi McDonnell Douglas offered yet another aircraft which was designed for extraordinary flexibility. The combi aircraft features a huge160in x 102in (4.06m x 2.59m) cargo door in the rear port side fuselage and can be equipped to handle four, six, eight or ten cargo pallets in combination with a one, two or three class passenger configuration. The flexibility allows the operator to select a different cargo/passenger split and take advantage of route or directional changes. Furthermore, the Combi can also be converted to an all-passenger layout for seasonal changes. A trained ground crew can change between any of the pallet configurations during an eight-hour shift. The standard combi version provides loading

of six 88in x 125in (2.23m x 3.18m) or 96in x 125in (2.44m x 3.18m) pallets. The MD-11C with the maximum ten pallets installed has a cargo volume of 10,904ft^3 (309m^3). As an option, the Combi also has the capability of transporting a spare DC-10 or MD-11 engine in the rear of the cabin. For absolute safety, Class C fire detection and extinguishing systems have been installed in the main deck cargo area.

The Convertible Freighter offers the possibility of an all passenger- or all cargo-configuration. As is the case with the regular MD-11 passenger aircraft, numerous seating arrangements are available for the CF variant. The main deck cargo loading area can handle as many as 34 88in x 108in (2.23m x 2.76m) cargo pallets, or up to 26 of the larger 96in x 125in (2.44m x 3.18m) size. The aircraft also has a location for an engine transport at the forward starboard side of the main deck. The total main deck cargo volume amounts to 14,508ft^3 (411m^3). The pallets are loaded through the large 140in x 102in (3.56m x 2.59m) main deck cargo door in the forward port side fuselage. Although the standard cargo management is a non-powered system, optional steerable powered rollers at the doorway and fixed powered rollers throughout the cargo area could be installed for improved loading and faster turnaround. The conversion time from passenger to freighter aircraft is 2.25 days and the reverse conversion can be accomplished in 4 days. The Convertible Freighter offers increased profitability through capturing the peaks of both the passenger and cargo market.

Lower compartments

All variants of the MD-11 have three baggage and cargo compartments in the lower fuselage consisting of a forward, centre and an aft compartment. The forward compartment can accommodate 18 LD3 or 9 full-width LD6 containers, or 6 88in x 125in (2.23m x 3.18m) respectively 6 96in x 125in (2.44m x 3.18m) pallets. The maximum volume of this compartment is 2,844ft³ (80,53m³). The containers or pallets are loaded through a 104in x 66in (2.64m x 1.68m) cargo door.

The centre compartment can handle 14 LD3 containers which are loaded through the standard door which measures 70in x 66in (1.78m x 1.68m). If the optional larger cargo door is installed 4 96in x 125in pallets or alternatively 2 LD3 and 4 88in x 125in pallets can be loaded. The first airline to order the optional larger cargo door, which has the same measurements as the forward compartment door, was Martinair Holland. Other cargo handling airlines, like World Airways and Lufthansa Cargo, opted for this door for greater flexibility in cargo loading. KLM also ordered the larger door for its ten passenger aircraft. The total internal centre compartment volume is 2,212ft³ (62,64m³). The volume of the bulk-only aft compartment is 510ft³ (14,44m³). The aft compartment door measures 30in x 36in (76cm x 91cm).

The total containerised capacity of the lower compartments, including the bulk-only aft section, is 5,566ft³ (158m³). This volume increases to 6,850ft³ (194m³) if bulk cargo is loaded in the forward and centre compartments.

The sophisticated cargo handling system of the MD-11 permits a swift loading and unloading of the cargo in the forward and centre compartments. A powered handling system in either compartment moves containers laterally in or out of the door, and longitudinally within the compartment. The system is joystick-operated

---

STANDARD

The diagram shows a selection of the multiple passenger configurations available for the wide-body airliner.
McDonnell Douglas

Two-Class – 323 Passengers

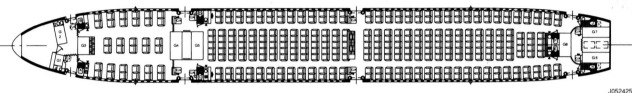

J052425
VG110061-19

| First | 34 Seats, 42/41-in. Pitch |
| Economy | 289 Seats, 33/34-in. Pitch |

OPTION

Three-Class – 298 Passengers

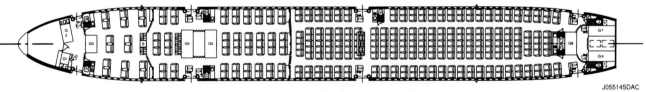

J055145DAC
VG110061-19

First	16 Seats, 60-in. Pitch
Business	56 Seats, 38-in. Pitch
Economy	226 Seats, 32-in. Pitch

OPTION

All Economy – 409 Passengers

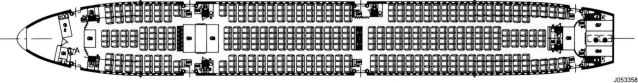

J053358

409 Seats, 30/31/32-in. Pitch

Above left: The MD-11 Combi version has a huge 160in x 102in (4.06m x 2.59m) cargo door in the rear port side fuselage. McDonnell Douglas

Below: Although the Combi aircraft is normally operated in a six pallet configuration, main deck flexibility allows the transport of up to ten pallets. McDonnell Douglas

Above: The forward lower compartment can be loaded with LD3, LD6 or pallets of different sizes. Federal Express Corporation

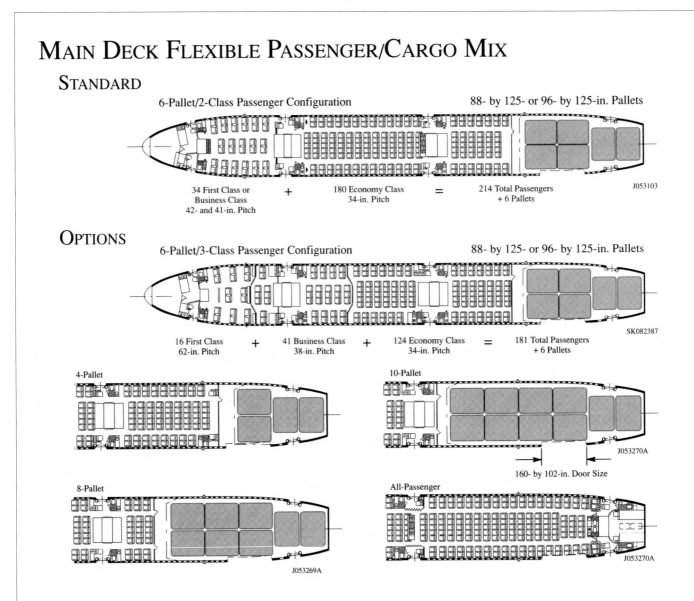

MAIN DECK FLEXIBLE PASSENGER/CARGO MIX

STANDARD

6-Pallet/2-Class Passenger Configuration — 88- by 125- or 96- by 125-in. Pallets

34 First Class or Business Class 42- and 41-in. Pitch + 180 Economy Class 34-in. Pitch = 214 Total Passengers + 6 Pallets

J053103

OPTIONS

6-Pallet/3-Class Passenger Configuration — 88- by 125- or 96- by 125-in. Pallets

16 First Class 62-in. Pitch + 41 Business Class 38-in. Pitch + 124 Economy Class 34-in. Pitch = 181 Total Passengers + 6 Pallets

SK082387

4-Pallet

10-Pallet

J053270A

160- by 102-in. Door Size

8-Pallet

J053269A

All-Passenger

J053270A

by only one person standing on the ground handling equipment located at the forward and centre cargo doors. All cargo doors are hinged at the top and open outwards and upwards. They are opened and closed electrically and, if necessary, can also be operated manually.

For ease of loading and unloading the door sills are below the compartment floor. Omni-directional rollers are located at the doorway floor area to allow the lateral and longitudinal movement of the containers or pallets. The area is itself equipped with self-retracting powered rollers which move the containers or pallets through the doorway. Instead of pneumatic brakes, the powered rollers feature integral electric brakes. Furthermore, anti-rollout restraint latches are installed at the doorway. Each compartment has five rows of roller conveyors, adequately spaced to support either LD3, LD6 or pallets, installed in the cargo floor away from the door area. By means of powered loading and unloading shuttles the containers are moved from and toward the doorway area. In case of a power or component failure, the systems can be disengaged to permit manual loading and unloading. The highly efficient cargo handling design ensures operations at all times.

It should be noted that MDC planned the so-called 'Panorama Deck' for the MD-11 in the early stages of the development programme. The option was once more offered to the air-

The MD-11CF can be operated in an all passenger- or all cargo-configuration. The convertible freighter has a large 140in x 102in (3.56m x 2.59m) main deck cargo door.
McDonnell Douglas

lines as the MD-11D variant in 1993. (See 'MD-11 Variants' on page 95) The 70ft (21.2m) long compartment, located in the lower forward fuselage, would have provided seating for up to 94 economy passengers. This variant was seen as an alternative especially for charter operators who did not need the forward lower compartment for cargo space.

The Pure Freighters

Towards the end of the DC-10 production, Douglas built the last commercial version of the aircraft, the pure freight DC-10-30F, of which Federal Express had ordered ten examples. In the case of the MD-11 programme, the freighter was part of the aircraft family from the beginning. Not surprisingly, since a world cargo traffic forecast at the time predicted a growth by 7.4% over the next twenty years. In 1993, the worldwide freighter fleet included just over 1,000 aircraft, 13.8% of these were large freighters, aircraft such as the DC-10-30F, MD-11F and the Boeing 747-200F and 747-400F capable of carrying payloads of 80 tons or more. Both McDonnell Douglas and Boeing predicted in 1994 that by the year 2014 large freighters would make up nearly 33% of all dedicated freighters. That meant there would be a need for more than 600 additional large freighters over the next twenty years. At the end of 1999, the world freighter fleet consisted of 1,676 aircraft of which 318 were large freighters. As demand for new large freighters grew, cargo operators increasingly turned to the MD-11F. The aircraft with its long range, high payload capability and low operating costs, met operators' needs in a wide range of growing intercontinental markets. The MD-11F requires 25% less fuel per ton/kilometer than the Boeing 747-200F.

Federal Express was the launch customer for the freighter version. As is evident from early photographs the first aircraft was built as a kind of half freighter/half passenger aircraft for flight test purposes and publicity photos. After the flight testing was completed, N111MD went through the so-called RFD (Refurbish For Delivery) programme, and became a full freighter for FedEx.

The all-cargo configuration provides a freight carrying space in the cabin of 144ft (43.9m) in length and has a floor area of 2626ft^2 (238.7m^2). The total cargo volume of the freighter amounts to 22,380ft^3 (641m^3); 15,530ft^3 (447m^3) on the main deck and 6,850ft^3 (194m^3) on the lower deck. Compared to the DC-10 freighter, which has a total cargo volume of 17,096ft^3 (484m^3), the MD-11 freighter offers over 25% more cargo volume. The MD-11 freighter has a weight limited gross payload 202,100 lb (91,670kg) versus the maximum 163,000 lb (73,397kg) of a DC-10-30 freighter.

On the main deck the MD-11 freighter has a maximum standard pallet capability of 26 88in x 125in (2.23m x 3.18m), 26 96in x 125in (2.44m x 3.18m) or 34 88in x 108in (2.23m x 2.74m) pallets. The aircraft also offers the possibility of loading the large 96in x 196in (2.44m x 4.98m) or 96in x 238.5in (2.44m x 6.06m) pallets in combination with standard-size pallets. The maximum stack height on the main deck is 98.25in (2.5m).

As is the case with the Combi and Convertible Freighter variants, an engine transport device can be accommodated on the main deck. Pallets are loaded through the 140in x 102in (3.56m x 2.59m) large forward cargo door.

Following Boeing's decision to stop MD-11 production, airlines were unable to order any

additional passenger or freighter MD-11 aircraft. Some operators have decided to replace their MD-11 passenger aircraft with 767s, 777s, Airbus A340s and other types. So far, all passenger aircraft replaced have been converted to freighters. Like American Airlines, Swissair decided to phase out the aircraft type and the MD-11s of both airlines will all be operated as freighters by FedEx within the next few years. Gemini Air Cargo also added converted MD-11 freighters to its extensive DC-10 freighter fleet.

The conversion includes the modification of the main deck floor and the installation of a main deck cargo door and a pallet-handling system. A modified air-conditioning system and smoke/fire detection systems are also installed. A standard cargo barrier net separates the freight section from the area behind the cockpit, which houses a galley, a toilet and seating capacity for two passengers. In August 1997, a solid aluminium rigid cargo bulkhead (RCB) was introduced in place of the barrier net. Commissioned by McDonnell Douglas prior to the merger with Boeing, the bulkhead is produced by Tolo of Irvine, California, and

offered to DC-10, MD-10 and MD-11 freighter operators. The optional RCB is based on Tolo's patented Grid-Lock technology and consists of a 10in (25.4cm)- thick interlocking bonded aluminium sandwich structure supported at 18 locations on the fuselage shell and 10 locations on the main deck floor. The design resulted in the most weight-efficient cargo barrier in the world, as measured in pounds of cargo per pound of barrier. The closed-cell panel weighs 1498 lb (680kg) and fulfils the FAA requirement of withstanding 200,000 lb (90,800kg) accelerated at 9g. The RCB frees the space forward of the net that is otherwise kept clear to allow for stretching during an emergency landing. The extra space can be used for more baggage stowage or additional crew seats. The RCB incorporates an access door with a viewing window on the left side of the fuselage, a decompression panel on the right side, and a complete smoke barrier. Compared with nets, the RCB offers operators more space for cargo and additional crew as well as higher allowable main deck cargo loads. The installation requires the relocation of the electrical equip-

ment, adding 40ft³ (1.2m³) additional stack height. Not surprisingly, FedEx was the first operator to order the bulkheads, replacing the nylon barrier nets. (See Chapter Six)

In March 1999, The Boeing Company announced the official launch of Boeing Airplane Services (BAS), a subsidiary dedicated to post-delivery modification and engineering services for commercial aircraft. Besides engineering design and installation, performance improvements, aircraft recovery and repair services, the portfolio of products includes passenger to freighter conversions. The first MD-11 modified at the Boeing Airplane Services' facility in San Antonio, Texas, was delivered to Korean Air in November 1999. Boeing Airplane Services' Wichita Modification Center completed its first MD-11 conversion, another Korean Air aircraft, in December 1999.

Freighter conversions are not only undertaken in the USA but also in Europe and the Near East. Finmeccanica/Alenia subsidiary Aeronavali in Italy has been a McDonnell Douglas partner since 1985 when the first DC-8 was converted into full freighter configuration. The

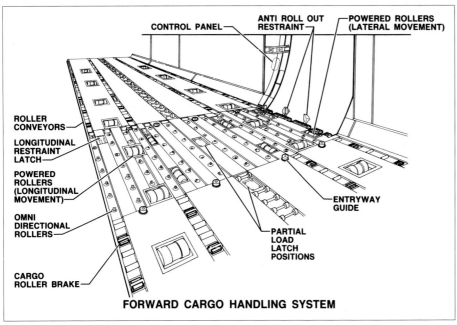

ROLLER CONVEYORS
LONGITUDINAL RESTRAINT LATCH
POWERED ROLLERS (LONGITUDINAL MOVEMENT)
OMNI DIRECTIONAL ROLLERS
CARGO ROLLER BRAKE
CONTROL PANEL
ANTI ROLL OUT RESTRAINT
POWERED ROLLERS (LATERAL MOVEMENT)
ENTRYWAY GUIDE
PARTIAL LOAD LATCH POSITIONS

FORWARD CARGO HANDLING SYSTEM

Above left: **LD3 containers can be loaded through the standard centre lower compartment door. The optional larger door shown provides greater flexibility in cargo loading.** Heiko Hauptreif

Above right: **Because of its tapered shape, the aft cargo compartment only accommodates bulk cargo. It is also used for the shipment of pets, small animals and crew baggage.** Reiner Geerdts

Left: **Schematic of the standard container and pallet handling system, forward lower cargo compartment.** McDonnell Douglas

DC-8 program, with a total of 47 aircraft converted, was so successful that McDonnell Douglas and Finmeccanica/Alenia Aerospazio signed a license for the freighter conversion of DC-10 aircraft by its subsidiary Aeronavali in 1990. Besides the regular DC-10 conversions, Aeronavali is supporting Boeing Airplane Services with its MD-11 and MD-10 passenger-to-freighter conversion programme. Conversions are performed at the company's facilities in Venice, Naples and Brindisi, Italy.

Israel Aircraft Industries (IAI) in Tel Aviv also is among the companies in the international Boeing network of modification and engineering facilities to provide retrofit packages for Boeing commercial aircraft. The company's Bedek division completed its first modification, a China Eastern Airlines MD-11, in December 1999.

The MD-11 freighter is the world's most advanced tri-jet freighter, an aircraft definitely fulfilling all operators' requirements.

State-of-the-art Systems

McDonnell Douglas equipped the new tri-jet with state-of-art systems to assure a reliable, safe operation and offer maximum passenger comfort.

MDC selected Sundstrand Corporation, a major supplier in the commercial and military aerospace power generation field, to supply the electrical power generating system for the MD-11. (Sundstrand was acquired by United Technologies Corporation in 1999 and combined with Hamilton Standard, forming subsidiary Hamilton Sundstrand). Original power requirements for MDC's new wide-body called for a system that included a 75/90 kiloVolt Ampere (kVA) integrated drive generator (IDG) mounted to each of the tri-jet's engines, resulting in a 270 kVA output. Six months into the development, the MD-11 team decided that a higher output would be necessary.

Sundstrand engineers set aside the four-pole 75/90 kVA IDGs and designed and built a 100/120 kVA unit incorporating the latest two-pole generator technology. The two-pole rotor is substantially smaller and allows the generating system to meet the higher power requirements while essentially retaining the same size and weight. Another innovation was Sundstrand's 'no break' power system, which supports the MD-11 advanced avionics on the flightdeck. The system allows load shifting from ground power to the aircraft's main engines without power interruption. This feature permits the flight crew to save time by setting cockpit settings on the ground. Without the 'no break' system, the settings would be lost during transfer to aircraft power.

The auxiliary power unit (APU) was supplied by AlliedSignal's Garrett division. The 90 kVA 700-4E gas turbine engine is the same as the 700-4B which was designed specifically for the DC-10 by Garrett AirResearch. However, control has been improved by the installation of a fully digital electronic control unit. The APU is

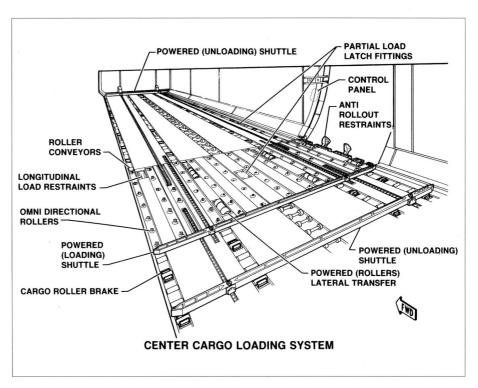

CENTER CARGO LOADING SYSTEM

Schematic of the standard container and pallet handling system, centre lower cargo compartment. McDonnell Douglas

installed in an unpressurised section of the lower fuselage forward of the cabin pressure bulkhead. The advantage of the APU is the supply of electrical power and compressed air for operation of the air conditioning system and power to start the engines without being dependent on external power equipment for normal operation of the aircraft systems.

In the unlikely event of a loss of the primary power sources in flight, the MD-11 has two additional emergency power sources. First, the Saft 50 AH aircraft battery which provides at least 30 minutes of system power for a safe flight and landing. Secondly, the aircraft is equipped with a Marquardt air driven generator (ADG). The ADG is located in the forward starboard fuselage and when extended provides up to 25 kVA long term emergency electrical power.

Three separate, parallel, continuously operating hydraulic systems provide power to operate flight control surfaces, wheel brakes, nose wheel steering and landing gear. Hydraulic pressure for each system is provided by redundant pumps driven by each engine. Primary flight control surfaces are divided into segments and hydraulically powered in such a manner that loss of any one system does not significantly affect aircraft control during any phase of the flight including approach and landing. This fail-safe philosophy played an important role in the design of the MD-11's systems.

The Aircraft Pneumatic System controls the air quantities and pressures necessary for the operation of the air conditioning system, wing

ice protection system, cross-engine starting and various other air-using systems.

The sophisticated air conditioning system permits the temperature control in four different zones: cockpit, forward, centre and aft cabin. Hot air from the pneumatic system distribution manifold is supplied to each of the three refrigeration units, so-called air cycle machines, where it is cooled and then distributed to the different zones. The cabin temperature for the different zones is controlled by switches located at the cockpit's overhead panel and can furthermore be adjusted at the forward left flight attendant panel. Thus passenger comfort is greatly enhanced as the separate temperature control eliminates uncomfortable temperature variations which could result from unbalanced passenger loads between compartments. Fresh air supplied to the passenger cabin is changed every three minutes – an impressive ventilation rate. The APU provides exceptional cooling while the aircraft is on the ground.

The cabin pressure is maintained at sea level pressure conditions at flight altitudes up to 22,000ft (6,705m). Over 22,000 and up to 42,000ft (12,801m) the system creates a cabin altitude of less than 8,000ft (2,438m). Although manual control is provided, the system will automatically control cabin pressure throughout the flight once the destination airport elevation and its barometric settings are selected. Uncomfortable pressure changes are virtually eliminated by the advanced system.

Cockpit oxygen is supplied to the crewmembers masks from a conventional high pressure oxygen cylinder. However, the MD-11 passenger oxygen system is unique. Located above the passenger seats, the system consists of a chemical oxygen generator, a starting mechanism, supply hoses and regular passen-

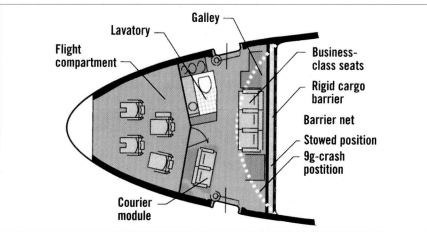

Top: **The MD-11F, the pure freight version, is equipped with the same size cargo door as installed on the convertible freighter.** Werner Krueger – Lufthansa Cargo

Above right: **The interlocking bonded aluminium sandwich structure of the rigid cargo barrier.** The Boeing Company

Above left: **The rigid cargo barrier and the nylon barrier net installation.** The Boeing Company

Left: **The impressive main deck of a MD-11 freighter with the cargo barrier net installed.** McDonnell Douglas

ger oxygen masks with reservoir bags. The lavatories, galleys and flight attendant stations are similarly equipped. The system automatically deploys the masks when the cabin altitude is more than 14,500ft (4,350m) and, once activated, each individual generator supplies 15 minutes of oxygen. Since the oxygen system is a self-contained unit, it completely eliminates the need for distribution lines, high-pressure oxygen cylinders and regulators. The system offers considerable weight reduction to conventional oxygen systems, and maintenance is reduced to a minimum.

McDonnell Douglas' experience in commercial transport automatic approach systems and in manned space flight made it possible that a fully integrated flight guidance and control system could be developed. The sophisticated flight control and automatic flight control systems provide for the excellent characteristics of the MD-11. The system's design goal was fulfilled when the MD-11 was certified for Category IIIb fail-operational automatic landings.

The Category IIIb certification allows the crew to approach and land with a visibility of down to 100yd (90m) and zero altitude decision height, ensuring all-weather landing performance.

Fuel

Fuel for the MD-11 is contained in three integral tanks within the wing and outboard fuselage, the auxiliary tank in the wing centre section and the horizontal tail with a total fuel capacity of 38,615 gallons (146,174 litres). The fuel system normally supplies fuel from the tank in each wing to the adjacent engine on that wing. The tank that delivers the fuel to the tail engine is composed of the two inboard sections of both wings. In this way, the shortest tank-to-engine supply is ensured. The tail tank, which has a capacity of 2000 gallons (7,570 litres), is installed in the horizontal stabiliser. Besides adding to the total fuel capacity which increases the aircraft's range, the control of the fuel quantity at this position gives better control of the aircraft's centre of gravity , thus reducing trim drag and increasing fuel economy. When necessary fuel from the tail tank is moved forward to the centre auxiliary tank. The fuel system features a fully automatic operation through the fuel system controller (FSC) which maintains the fuel feed and the transfer of tail tank fuel for centre of gravity control.

For extended range operations, one or two supplemental fuel tanks can be installed in the lower forward compartment. The fuel capacity can so be increased by a total of 3,000 gallons (11,355 litres).

The MD-11 uses two adjacent fuel receptacles in each wing for refuel operations. For normal fuelling operations the receptacles in the right wing are used. However, if necessary, the aircraft can be refuelled simultaneously on both sides. A refuel control panel which controls the fuel system servicing is located on the right wing.

Undercarriage

The MD-11's undercarriage arrangement is similar to that of the long range DC-10 Series 30 and 40 aircraft. The main wing mounted undercarriage units have four wheels and retract inboard where they are stored in a well beneath the cabin floor. Commonality being one of the design characteristics, the right and left main gear assemblies are interchangeable with minor changes.

Whereas the freighter aircraft main gear struts are normally equipped with a single chamber oleo pneumatic shock strut, most passenger aircraft obtained dual chamber struts for more dampening. However, the question arose whether pilots or passengers could even tell the difference between landings with dual or single chamber struts. Besides that the single chamber is much simpler to service; another advantage of the single chamber strut is that it is about 66 lb (29.9kg) lighter than the dual chamber strut. After McDonnell Douglas had delivered about 130 MD-11s it was decided that the serviceability and weight savings of the single chamber strut more than offset the additional dampening of dual chamber strut.

The nose and the twin bogie centreline gear retract forward into the fuselage wheel wells. The maximum nose wheel steering angle is 70° right or left of the centre. Although not a stan-

dard procedure, the MD-11 crew may opt for the centre gear to remain in the retracted position when operating at light gross weights.

The landing gear doors, which are normally closed when the aircraft is on the ground, can be opened without the use of tools for servicing and maintaining equipment located in the wheel wells.

While the nose wheel is similar to the one on the DC-10-30/40, the main gears feature larger Bendix 24in- (61cm-) diameter wheels with carbon fibre brakes. Besides offering a longer brake life than a comparable steel brake, the carbon fibre brake weighs 1,500 lbs (680kgs) – or about seven passengers – less than a traditional brake.

The MD-11 disposes of dual hydraulic systems for its brakes and the nose wheel steering. Anti-skid control is incorporated in both brake systems. All MD-11s are equipped with an automatic braking system. With selectable minimum, medium and maximum deceleration rates, the system greatly reduces the pilot workload and increases overall break performance.

The diagram shows the multiple variations of container and pallet configurations for the MD-11F. McDonnell Douglas

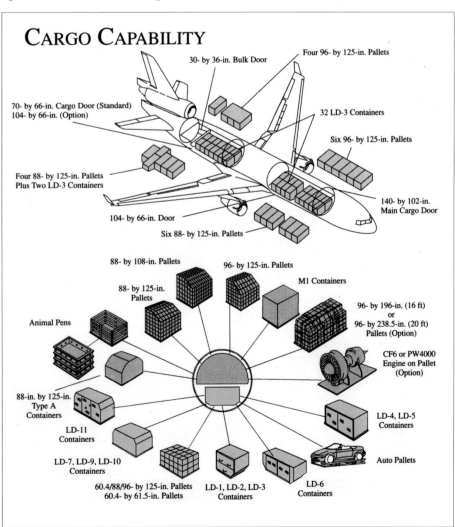

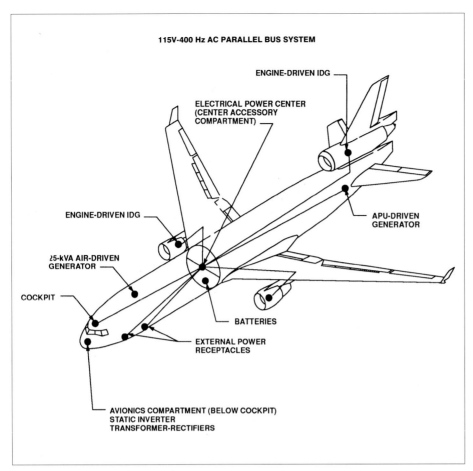

115V-400 Hz AC PARALLEL BUS SYSTEM

ENGINE-DRIVEN IDG

ELECTRICAL POWER CENTER
(CENTER ACCESSORY
COMPARTMENT)

APU-DRIVEN
GENERATOR

ENGINE-DRIVEN IDG

25-kVA AIR-DRIVEN
GENERATOR

COCKPIT

BATTERIES

EXTERNAL POWER
RECEPTACLES

AVIONICS COMPARTMENT (BELOW COCKPIT)
STATIC INVERTER
TRANSFORMER-RECTIFIERS

Electrical power system. McDonnell Douglas

The 90 kVA 700-4E auxiliary power unit (APU) was supplied by Garrett, a division of AlliedSignal. AlliedSignal

KC-10B and KMD-11 Tanker/Transport

With the KC-10A McDonnell Douglas provided the US Air Force with a versatile workhorse which has proven itself during worldwide missions since the first delivery in 1981. The Royal Netherlands Air Force can be considered as the 'launch customer' of the KDC-10. Based on the DC-10-30CF, the KDC-10 conversion programme may well attract other air forces to obtain a reliable tanker/cargo aircraft.

Once more proving the versatility of its products, McDonnell Douglas followed up on the KDC-10 programme with a military version of the MD-11: the KMD-11.

McDonnell Douglas offered the same advanced tanker technology for conversion of new commercial MD-11s into tanker/cargo aircraft for future air force operations. Besides the extra range, the KMD-11 offered an increase of 35,000 lb (15,876kg) in maximum take-off weight and 8,400 lb (3,810kg) in fuel load over the KC-10A.

It should be noted that during the development of the MD-11 McDonnell Douglas already proposed a tanker/transport version of the new tri-jet in 1987, named the KC-10B.

Several hundred Boeing KC-135 Stratotankers and other specialist role versions are in service with the USAF and other air forces and it will only be a matter of time that a replacement for these ageing aircraft will be required. With no serious rival on the market, certainly not as far as performance is concerned, McDonnell Douglas again held all the trumps. Although Boeing maintained that there was a place for this aircraft in the new product line, the later decision to stop the MD-11 production also meant the end of the KMD-11 programme.

Planned KMD-11 Specification –
Where differing from the MD-11

Dimensions		
Cargo door	160in x 102in	4.06m x 2.59m
Weights		
Max take-off	625,000 lb	283,500kg
Empty*	281,500 lb	127,688kg
Max fuel load	347,600 lb	157,671kg
Max cargo load	169,800 lb	77,021kg

*Tanker configuration with supplemental fuel tanks, centreline boom, wing pods, no cargo handling equipment.

Opposite top: **Artist's impression of a KMD-11 showing McDonnell Douglas' plans for a future tanker/cargo aircraft.** McDonnell Douglas

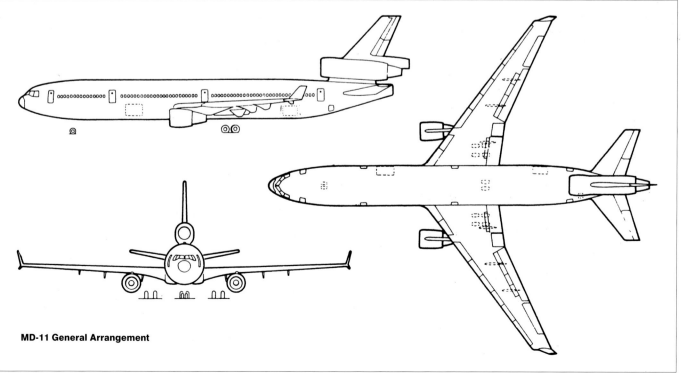

MD-11 General Arrangement

MD-11 General Specifications

	MD-11P		MD-11C		MD-11CF		MD-11F	
Capacity								
Passengers	250-410		181-214		350-410 (pass)			
Cargo Holds – main deck	–		6 pallets [a]		14,508ft³ (freight)		15,530ft³	
	–		6 pallets [a]		411m³ (freight)		447m³	
– lower deck [b]	6,850ft³	194m³	6,850ft³	194m³	6,850ft³	194m³	6,850ft³	194m³
Dimensions								
Wingspan	169.5ft	51.70m	169.5ft	51.70m	169.5ft	51.70m	169.5ft	51.70m
Length overall with								
General Electric engines	201ft 4in	61.40m	201ft 4in	61.40m	201ft 4in	61.40m	201ft 4in	61.40m
Pratt & Whitney engines	200ft 11in	61.28m	200ft 11in	61.28m	200ft 11in	61.28m	200ft 11in	61.28m
Height overall:	57.8ft	17.60m	57.8ft	17.60m	57.8ft	17.60m	57.8ft	17.60m
Wing area								
Including winglet	3,648ft²	339m²	3,648ft²	339m²	3,648ft²	339m²	3,648ft²	339m²
Sweepback	35°		35°		35°		35°	
Landing gear								
Tread (main wheels)	34.7ft	10.60m	34.7ft	10.60m	34.7ft	10.60m	34.7ft	10.60m
Wheel base (fore and aft)	80.8ft	24.60m	80.8ft	24.60m	80.8ft	24.60m	80.8ft	24.60m
Engines								
Three engine options for all models	3 x GE CF6-80C2D1F turbofan		3 x P&W PW4460 turbofan		3 x P&W PW4462 turbofan			
Take-off thrust	61,500 lb	273kN	60,000 lb	266kN	62,000 lb	275kN		
Delivery data								
Max. take-off weight [c]	630,500 lb	285,990kg	630,500 lb	285,990kg	630,500 lb	285,990kg	630,500 lb	285,990kg
Max. landing weight:	430,000 lb	195,045kg	458,000 lb	207,745kg	481,500 lb [d]	218,405kg [d]	481,500 lb [d]	218,405kg [d]
Max. zero fuel	400,000 lb	181,437kg	430,000 lb	195,045kg	451,300 lb	204,706kg	451,300 lb	204,706kg
Operator's empty weight	286,965 lb	130,165kg	288,885 lb	131,036kg	289,965 lb (pass)	131,526kg	251,149 lb	113,919kg
					254,372 lb (freight)	115,381kg		
Fuel capacity (volume)	38,615gal	146,174 litres	38,615gal	146,174 litres	38,615gal	146,174 litres	38,615gal	146,174 litres
Fuel capacity (weight)	258,721 lb	117,354kg	258,721 lb	117,354kg	258,721 lb	117,354kg	258,721 lb	117,354kg
Weight limited payload	113,035 lb	51,272kg	141,115 lb	64,009kg	161,335 lb (pass)	73,180kg	200,151 lb [e]	90,787kg [e]
					196,928 lb (freight) [e]	89,325kg [e]		
Performance								
Maximum level flight speed at 31,000ft, all models	588 st. mph, M.87							
	511 n. mph, 945km/h							
FAA take-off field length (max take-off weight) [f]	10,220ft	3,115m	10,220ft	3,115m	10,220ft	3,115m	10,220ft	3,115m
FAA landing field length (max landing weight)	6,950ft	2,118m	7,330ft	2,234m	7,620ft	2,323m	7,620ft	2,323m
Design range (FAR int'l reserves)								
Statute miles	7,865 [g]		7,730 [i]		7,865 (pass) [g]	4,540 (freight) [h]	4,540 [h]	
Nautical miles	6,840 [g]		6,720 [i]		6,840 (pass) [g]	3,950 (freight) [h]	3,950 [h]	
Kilometers	12,655 [g]		12,435 [i]		12,655 (pass) [g]	7,310 (freight) [h]	7,310 [h]	
Statute Miles	8,300 [g][j]		6,600 [k]		–		–	
Nautical Miles	7,220 [g][j]		5,740 [k]		–		–	
Kilometers	13,355 [g][j]		10,620 [k]		–		–	

[a] Pallet dimensions: 88in x 125in (2.23m x 3.18m) or 96in x 125in (2.44m x 3.18m)
[b] Bulk capacity. Containerised capacity is 32 LD3 containers, or 5,566ft³ (517m³)
[c] Optional take-off weight (standard is 602,555 lb / 273,319kg)
[d] Optional landing weight (standard is 471,500 lb / 213,872kg)
[e] Including Tare Weight
[f] Take-off with optional PW 4462 engines

[g] 298 passengers with baggage, 3-class configuration
[h] Weight limited payload
[i] 183 passengers with baggage, 3-class configuration plus 6 main deck freight pallets
[j] With 3,000 US gallon (11,355 litres) supplemental fuel tank
[k] Space limited payload

Above: **The MD-11 undercarriage is similar to the DC-10-30/40 arrangement with two main gears and one centreline gear.** Reiner Geerdts

Right: **The dual-wheel nose gear retracts forward.** Heiko Hauptreif

Bottom right: **Like the nose gear, the centre twin bogie retracts forward.** Reiner Geerdts

Bottom: **The four-wheel main gear retracts inwards.** Reiner Geerdts

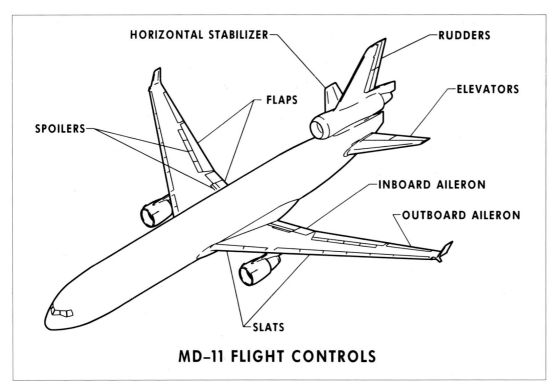

Flight control surfaces.
McDonnell Douglas

HORIZONTAL STABILIZER

RUDDERS

FLAPS

ELEVATORS

SPOILERS

INBOARD AILERON

OUTBOARD AILERON

SLATS

MD-11 FLIGHT CONTROLS

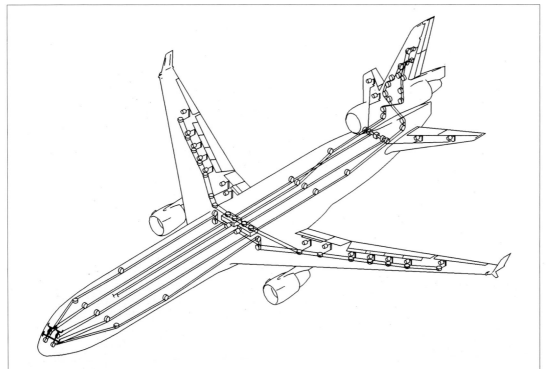

Flight control cable diagram.
McDonnell Douglas

Fuel storage. McDonnell Douglas

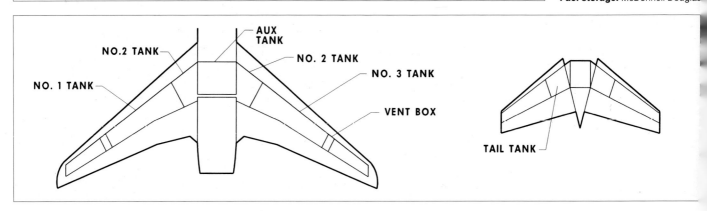

AUX TANK

NO.2 TANK

NO. 2 TANK

NO. 1 TANK

NO. 3 TANK

VENT BOX

TAIL TANK

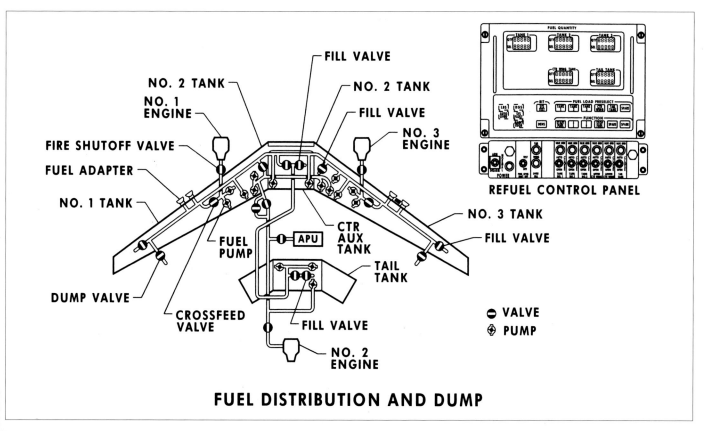

FUEL DISTRIBUTION AND DUMP

Labels in diagram:
FILL VALVE
NO. 2 TANK
NO. 2 TANK
NO. 1 ENGINE
FILL VALVE
FIRE SHUTOFF VALVE
NO. 3 ENGINE
FUEL ADAPTER
NO. 1 TANK
NO. 3 TANK
FILL VALVE
FUEL PUMP
CTR AUX TANK
DUMP VALVE
TAIL TANK
CROSSFEED VALVE
FILL VALVE
NO. 2 ENGINE
VALVE
PUMP
REFUEL CONTROL PANEL
FUEL QUANTITY

Fuel Distribution and Dump. McDonnell Douglas

Below: **Refuelling from an underground pipeline.** Swissair

McDonnell Douglas MD-11 Cutaway Drawing Key

1 Radome
2 Weather radar scanner
3 ILS glideslope aerials
4 Pitot heads
5 Front pressure bulkhead
6 Radome hinge points
7 Windscreen wipers
8 Electrically heated windscreen panels
9 Overhead systems switch panel
10 Maintenance engineering panel
11 Observer's seat
12 First Officer's seat
13 Instrument panel shroud
14 Captain's seat
15 Electronic Flight Instrumentation System (EFIS), six colour CRT displays
16 Underfloor avionics equipment bay
17 Floor hatch access to avionics bay
18 Optional second observer's seat
19 Crew wardrobe
20 Cockpit bulkhead doorway
21 Conditioned air delivery ducting
22 Sidewall galley units, port and starboard
23 Curtained entry lobby
24 Forward cabin doorway, port and starboard
25 Cabin attendant's folding seat
26 Nose undercarriage wheel bay
27 Air conditioning system intake ducts
28 Nosewheel steering jacks
29 Twin nosewheels, forward retracting
30 Torque scissor links
31 Nosewheel leg doors
32 Air conditioning packs (two port and one starboard)
33 Sidewall toilet compartments, port and starboard
34 Central galley unit
35 Conditioned air distribution ducting
36 Overhead baggage lockers
37 First-class passenger cabin, 6-abreast
38 Cabin window panels
39 Fuselage lower lobe skin panelling
40 Outline of cargo door on MD-11F and CF version
41 Mid-cabin entry door, port and starboard
42 Mid-cabin galley unit
43 ATC aerial
44 Sidewall toilet compartments, port and starboard
45 Forward freight hold door
46 Door actuating motor
47 Forward underfloor freight hold, capacity 2,844ft³ (80.5m³)

48 LD3 baggage containers, 18 in forward hold
49 Cabin air outflow valve
50 Freight conditioned air ducting
51 Glassfibre/Kevlar wing root fillet fairing
52 Tourist-class passenger cabin, nine-abreast
53 Cabin wall insulating blankets
54 Engine bleed air ducting to air conditioning plant
55 Main electrical distribution panels
56 Hydraulically actuated slat cable drive unit
57 Wing centre-section carry-through
58 Centre section integral fuel tank, with bag tank beneath
59 Centre section skin panels
60 Floor beam construction
61 Centre section cabin doorway, port and starboard
62 Centre fuselage frame and stringer construction
63 Anti-collision light
64 Starboard wing integral fuel tank
65 Fuel system piping
66 Inboard leading-edge slat segment
67 Thrust reverser cascades, open
68 Starboard engine nacelle
69 Intake duct acoustic lining
70 Nacelle strakes
71 Nacelle pylon
72 Outboard slats hydraulically-actuated cable drive
73 Pressure refuelling connections
74 Wing skin panelling
75 Wing stringers
76 Outboard integral fuel tankage
77 Slat guide rails
78 Outboard leading-edge slat segments
79 Starboard navigation light
80 Starboard upper winglet
81 Tail navigation and strobe lights
82 Fixed portion of trailing edge
83 Outboard, low-speed aileron
84 Aileron hydraulic actuator
85 Fuel jettison pipe
86 Outboard double-slotted flap segment
87 Articulated flap vane and guide rails
88 Outboard spoiler panels
89 Spoiler hydraulic actuators
90 Flap hydraulic jacks

91 External flap hinges
92 Inboard, high-speed aileron
93 Hydraulic actuator
94 Inboard spoiler
95 Inboard double-slotted flap segment
96 VHF aerial
97 Pressure floor above wheel bay
98 Starboard main undercarriage wheel bay
99 Mainwheel door hydraulic jack
100 Hydraulic reservoir, triple system
101 Seat mounting rails
102 Dual ADF aerials
103 Rear cabin air ducting
104 Cabin roof trim and lighting panels
105 Overhead baggage lockers
106 Passenger service units
107 Rear cabin passenger seating
108 LD3 baggage containers, 14 in rear hold
109 Rear freight hold door and actuator
110 Rear underfloor freight hold, 2,212cu. ft (62.6m³)
111 Freight hold bulkhead
112 Cabin wall trim panelling
113 Rear seat rows
114 Central toilet compartments, two
115 Central galley unit
116 rear galley units, port and starboard
117 Rear pressure bulkhead
118 Sloping fin spar attachment frames
119 HF aerial
120 Centre engine intake ducting
121 Intake lip hot air de-icing
122 Starboard trimming tailplane
123 Fin root fillet
124 Intake duct ring frames
125 Fin attachment joint
126 Starboard elevator
127 Rudder actuator cable drive
128 Fin spar and rib construction

129 VOR localiser No1 aerial
130 Fin tip aerial fairing
131 VOR localiser No 2 aerial
132 Rudder horn balance
133 Static dischargers
134 Double-acting rudder upper segment
135 Rudder mass balance
136 Rudder hydraulic actuators
137 Lower rudder segment rib construction

138 Centre engine mounting beam
139 Bleed air pre-cooler
140 Pylon tail fairing
141 Core engine, hot-stream, exhaust nozzle
142 Fan air, cold stream, exhaust duct
143 Translating cowl thrust reverser
144 Thrust reverser cascades
145 Centre General Electric CF6-80C2D1F turbofan engine
146 Engine nacelle pylon structure

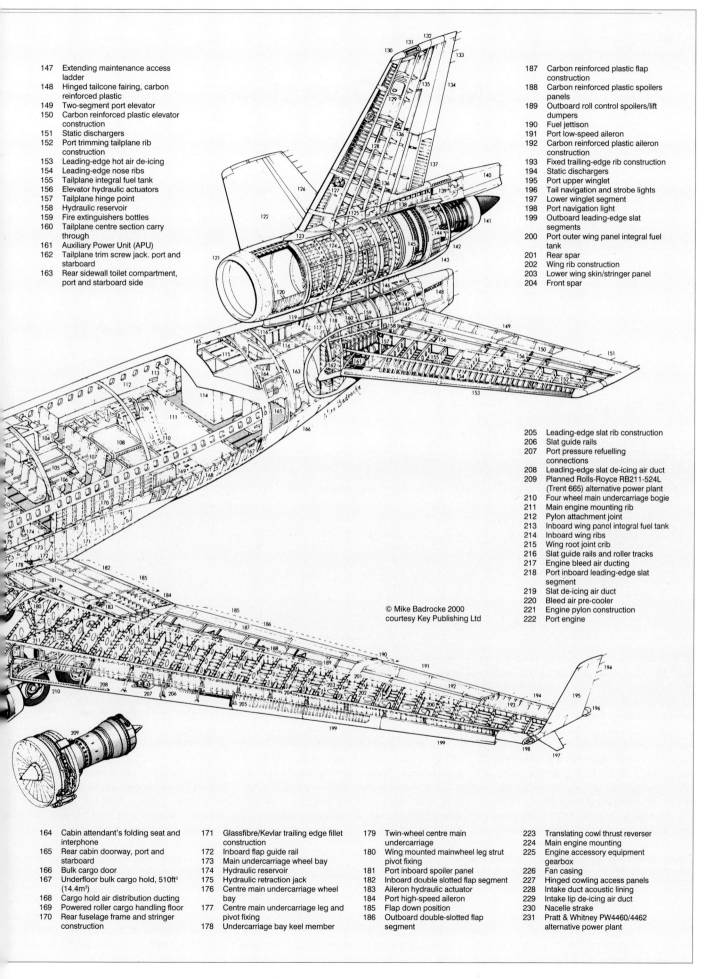

147 Extending maintenance access ladder
148 Hinged tailcone fairing, carbon reinforced plastic
149 Two-segment port elevator
150 Carbon reinforced plastic elevator construction
151 Static dischargers
152 Port trimming tailplane rib construction
153 Leading-edge hot air de-icing
154 Leading-edge nose ribs
155 Tailplane integral fuel tank
156 Elevator hydraulic actuators
157 Tailplane hinge point
158 Hydraulic reservoir
159 Fire extinguishers bottles
160 Tailplane centre section carry through
161 Auxiliary Power Unit (APU)
162 Tailplane trim screw jack. port and starboard
163 Rear sidewall toilet compartment, port and starboard side

187 Carbon reinforced plastic flap construction
188 Carbon reinforced plastic spoilers panels
189 Outboard roll control spoilers/lift dumpers
190 Fuel jettison
191 Port low-speed aileron
192 Carbon reinforced plastic aileron construction
193 Fixed trailing-edge rib construction
194 Static dischargers
195 Port upper winglet
196 Tail navigation and strobe lights
197 Lower winglet segment
198 Port navigation light
199 Outboard leading-edge slat segments
200 Port outer wing panel integral fuel tank
201 Rear spar
202 Wing rib construction
203 Lower wing skin/stringer panel
204 Front spar

205 Leading-edge slat rib construction
206 Slat guide rails
207 Port pressure refuelling connections
208 Leading-edge slat de-icing air duct
209 Planned Rolls-Royce RB211-524L (Trent 665) alternative power plant
210 Four wheel main undercarriage bogie
211 Main engine mounting rib
212 Pylon attachment joint
213 Inboard wing panel integral fuel tank
214 Inboard wing ribs
215 Wing root joint crib
216 Slat guide rails and roller tracks
217 Engine bleed air ducting
218 Port inboard leading-edge slat segment
219 Slat de-icing air duct
220 Bleed air pre-cooler
221 Engine pylon construction
222 Port engine

© Mike Badrocke 2000
courtesy Key Publishing Ltd

164 Cabin attendant's folding seat and interphone
165 Rear cabin doorway, port and starboard
166 Bulk cargo door
167 Underfloor bulk cargo hold, 510ft³ (14.4m³)
168 Cargo hold air distribution ducting
169 Powered roller cargo handling floor
170 Rear fuselage frame and stringer construction

171 Glassfibre/Kevlar trailing edge fillet construction
172 Inboard flap guide rail
173 Main undercarriage wheel bay
174 Hydraulic reservoir
175 Hydraulic retraction jack
176 Centre main undercarriage wheel bay
177 Centre main undercarriage leg and pivot fixing
178 Undercarriage bay keel member

179 Twin-wheel centre main undercarriage
180 Wing mounted mainwheel leg strut pivot fixing
181 Port inboard spoiler panel
182 Inboard double slotted flap segment
183 Aileron hydraulic actuator
184 Port high-speed aileron
185 Flap down position
186 Outboard double-slotted flap segment

223 Translating cowl thrust reverser
224 Main engine mounting
225 Engine accessory equipment gearbox
226 Fan casing
227 Hinged cowling access panels
228 Intake duct acoustic lining
229 Intake lip de-icing air duct
230 Nacelle strake
231 Pratt & Whitney PW4460/4462 alternative power plant

Chapter Three

MD-11 Operators

Although the majority of the MD-11s built were passenger aircraft, the freighter version played an important role from the start of production.
George Hall/Clay Lacy - Lufthansa Cargo

Over ten years have gone by since the first MD-11 entered service. During the production period McDonnell Douglas/The Boeing Company delivered new aircraft to 23 customers. Following the cessation of production of the aircraft, some of the original customers have decided to sell their MD-11s and replace them with aircraft such as the Boeing 747-400, 767-300/400, 777-200/300, Airbus A330 and A340. The majority of these displaced MD-11s will be converted to full-freighters.

In this chapter, specific MD-11 operations by user airlines are defined. Airlines are given in alphabetical order by 'operating' name and abbreviation (if widely used to refer to the carrier). Operators that ordered the aircraft type, or announced their intention to operate them, but in the end failed to start MD-11 operations are also detailed. Additionally, airlines that 'name' their aircraft are given in tabulated form. Brief details of major accidents and write-offs are also given. No attempt has been made to list all the individual aircraft operated by the large users, as this material is readily available elsewhere. (See the Bibliography, page 4) However, delivery details and present status of each MD-11 built are made available in the Chapter Four.

With ever-changing 'corporate identities', all MD-11 liveries used by the operators over the years are described and every effort has been made to illustrate them. This includes 'one-off' and 'celebration' schemes that may have only been applied for a brief time. An index of IATA and ICAO codes of the airlines appears on page 87.

Aer Lingus

Aer Lingus inaugurated transatlantic services from Dublin and Shannon to New York and Boston with leased Lockheed Super Constellations. The Constellations remained in service until December 1960 when the Boeing 720 was introduced. In 1970 the first of three 747s operated by the airline was added to the fleet. The last 747 was retired in 1995. Transatlantic flights from Dublin, Shannon and Belfast to Boston, Chicago, New York, Newark and Los Angeles are now conducted with Airbus A330s; presently a total of seven A330s are operated.

Aer Lingus wet-leased a World Airways MD-11 for the first time from May until December 1998. The aircraft was used on services between Ireland and the USA and carried the attractive livery of the Irish airline. This paint scheme consists of a dark green cabin roof, divided by a twin light green and blue cheatline from the white lower fuselage.

A white 'Aer Lingus' title is applied above the forward passenger windows. The company's emblem is the famous Irish shamrock which was placed in a bright green colour on the tail section, winglets and wing engines of MD-11 N272WA. The aircraft was named after *St. Kilian/Cilian*, Irish monk and Bishop. The same aircraft was again in seasonal use with Aer Lingus in 1999, 2000 and 2001 wearing the airline's full colour scheme.

Aero Lloyd

The German private carrier was established in December 1980 and started charter flights to destinations in the Mediterranean with a fleet of Sud-Aviation SE.210 Caravelle aircraft in March 1981. Aiming at the charter market in the USA and the Far East, the airline ordered two MD-11s for delivery in 1992 through the ADO Finance Company in Switzerland. It also held options on a further two aircraft. Unfortunately the plans for long haul charter flights were abandoned and subsequently the orders were cancelled. Presently the airline operates with a fleet of Airbus A320s and A321s.

The artist's impression depicts a MD-11 in the former Aero Lloyd livery. A broad cheatline below the passenger windows consisted of horizontal yellow, orange and red bands, interrupted by a large blue 'Aero Lloyd' title, on a white upper fuselage. The striping and title were repeated on the white tail fin. The company's 'A' logo was placed above the passenger windows at the forward entry doors.

AIR ALM

Air ALM is the national carrier of the Netherlands Antilles. Besides inter-island services within the Caribbean, the airline operates flights to North and South America with a fleet of Bombardier Dash 8-300s and McDonnell Douglas MD-80s. In July 2000, Air ALM signed an agreement with Belgian carrier City Bird to conduct flights between Amsterdam and Curacao; twice-weekly non-stop flights between the two cities started in December 2000. The contract ended in March 2001. A City Bird MD-11 in a 36 business and 335 economy seats cabin layout is used on the transatlantic service. The aircraft carried the full City Bird livery without additional titles.

Top: **World Airways N272WA, on lease to Aer Lingus, displays the attractive livery of the Irish carrier.** Malcolm Nason

Above: **German charter airline Aero Lloyd had ordered two MD-11s for long range operations. The artist's impression shows the aircraft in the airline's former livery.** McDonnell Douglas

Left: **At Kuala Lumpur Subang Airport, World Airways MD-11, N278WA, operating Hadj flights for Air Asia.** World Airways

Below: **Artist's impression of a MD-11 in the colourful livery of Air Europe. The UK tour operator was the only airline to order the aircraft with Rolls-Royce engines.** McDonnell Douglas

AirAsia

This Malaysian carrier was founded in December 1993 and the airline's first flight took place in November 1996 between Kuala Lumpur and Pattaya, Thailand, with a leased Boeing 737. The carrier conducts domestic scheduled services from Kuala Lumpur Subang Airport. Based on request, the airline also offers scheduled charter flight to various destinations.

Air Outre Mer

Air Outre Mer started operations in May 1990 with a scheduled service from Paris to St Denis de la Réunion using DC-10 equipment. At the end of 1991 the fleet consisted of three Series 30s. The carrier had ordered four PW4460-powered MD-11s for delivery during 1994 and 1995 (serial number 48534 through 48537 assigned). In January 1992 the carrier took over Minerve and the name Air Outre Mer was changed to AOM French Airlines. The result of the merger was a total order for seven MD-11s; however none of these orders were taken up. AOM French airlines today operates with a fleet of eleven MD-83s and thirteen DC-10-30s. In February 1999, the SAirGroup acquired a 49% stake in the airline.

The MD-11 artist's impression displays the simple Air Outre Mer livery. An all-white fuselage and tail were the background for a blue 'Air Outre Mer' title and winged red and blue 'AOM' logo.

Air Zaire

Air Congo was founded in 1961 as the national carrier. The name Air Zaire was introduced when the country was renamed as Zaire in 1971 following the country's independence from Belgium.

The airline deployed a fleet of Fokker F.27 Friendships and Boeing 737s on its dense domestic network and to other destinations in Africa and the Middle East. For long range operations between Kinshasa to Brussels, Geneva, Paris, Rome and Zürich the carrier acquired two DC-10-30s, of which the first one was delivered on 8th June 1973. Of the two DC-8-63CFs in the carrier's fleet one example was operated as a freighter. Despite the fact that the airline was transformed into a private company in 1978, the poor financial state of the airline required a major reorganisation. As part of this, the second DC-10 was sold to British Caledonian Airways in 1985.

The carrier ordered two MD-11s for delivery in September 1992 and November 1993 respectively. However the order was cancelled and the aircraft, serial numbers 48529 and 48530, were not built.

To replace the two Boeing 737s, Air Zaire had also placed an order for three McDonnell Douglas MD-82s for delivery during the 1990s.

During March and April 1999 AirAsia leased two MD-11 aircraft from World Airways for Hadj pilgrim flights between Kuala Lumpur Subang Airport and Jeddah. The aircraft, N277WA and N278WA , did not carry the airline's own colourful livery but displayed simple 'AirAsia' titles on the fully white fuselage while the white 'Tabung Aji' title and logo of the Malaysian Hadj foundation within a black square was placed on the tail fin.

Air Europe

The airline was founded by British company ILG (International Leisure Group) in 1978. Operations for major UK tour operators started with a fleet of Boeing 737-200s. The rapid development of the carrier as a major charter airline resulted in the purchase of 737-300s and 400s and in 1983 the first Boeing 757s were brought into service. Originally operating from its London Gatwick base, the airline soon became a familiar sight at other British airports conducting flights to Mediterranean destinations.

Extending its route network, Air Europe introduced charter flights to North and Central America, the Caribbean and the Far East in 1988. The new routes and increasing passenger traffic ultimately required suitable long range equipment which led to the airline's decision in 1988 to lease two MD-11s from Mitsui and Company. The GE-powered aircraft, f/n 453 and 454, were amongst the first MD-11s built and were expected to be delivered to the airline during 1990. In February 1989, Air Europe announced an order for six MD-11s with options on a further 12 aircraft. MDC had assigned serial numbers 48506 through 48511 for the initial batch of aircraft. Following the bankruptcy of parent organisation ILG, Air Europe Ltd. ceased operations on 8th March 1991. The demise of the airline led to the irrevocable cancellation of the pending MD-11 orders and options.

The McDonnell Douglas rendering of the Air Europe MD-11 shows the aircraft in the original livery. A multiple orange and red striping, together with the 'AE' initials, started at the forward fuselage and continued up into the tail section. To underline the country of origin, the Union Flag was placed next to the black 'Air Europe' title on the upper fuselage. The black 'Air Europe' title was also displayed on the tail fin. The Rolls-Royce emblems on the wing engines show the carrier's powerplant selection.

This order was cancelled as well and the aircraft were never delivered to the African carrier. Financial losses finally forced the airline to cease operations in June 1995. Air Zaire was formally declared bankrupt by a Belgian court in October 1995.

After the airline changed its name from Air Congo into Air Zaire in 1971, a new livery was adapted as shown in the digitally enhanced photo. The country's flag colours were represented in the yellow and green pinstripes above and below the red cabin window cheatline. The company's logo, a gold winged leopard in a red circle, was displayed on the fin. The green rudder had an additional yellow-trimmed red band at the top. The company's name appeared in black letters on the upper fuselage.

Alitalia

Like many other major carriers, Alitalia selected a Douglas product for long range operations when the jet age commenced; their first DC-8s entered service in 1960. With the arrival of the 747 in 1970, Alitalia increased its passenger and cargo capacity on the North Atlantic As the 747 proved to be too large on certain routes, the airline acquired eight DC-10-30s, which

MD-11 I-DUPE *Arena di Verona*, was the first of five Combi aircraft delivered to the Italian flag carrier. The aircraft's name was changed to *Giuseppe Verdi*. McDonnell Douglas

were delivered between February 1973 and May 1975. A decision was taken to standardise on a pure 747 fleet and all DC-10s were sold between 1982 and 1986. Alitalia nevertheless remained a McDonnell Douglas wide-body customer when the carrier became a launch customer for the MD-11. The airline was the first and would remain the only customer to order the MD-11 combi. A total of five examples of this version as well as three full-passenger aircraft were delivered between November 1991 and June 1994. All eight Alitalia MD-11s are powered by GE CF6-80C2D1F engines. Both the full-passenger and combi aircraft offer seating for 30 'Magnifica' business class passengers, whereas in economy class respectively 253 and 174 seats have been installed. In 1966 Alitalia founded a new low-cost, high-competition company – Alitalia Team. The division today operates over sixty aircraft which are excluded from the Alitalia fleet. The MD-11 aircraft have also been transferred to the Alitalia Team fleet.

The corporate fleet consists of aircraft produced by the world's leading manufacturers, Airbus Industrie, Boeing and former McDonnell Douglas. Currently Alitalia operates a fleet of A300, A320, A321, 747-200, 767, MD-82 and MD-11 aircraft.

The Alitalia livery represents the colours of the national flag. A broad dark green cheatline starts as a wedge at the nose and partly sweeps up into the tail section to form the superimposed green and red company's 'A' logo. This logo is repeated on the winglets. The white fuselage displays a large 'Alitalia' title

which, in a smaller form, is shown beside each cabin door. The individual name given to each MD-11 aircraft is placed above the forward entry doors. Since the deployment with Alitalia Team, a red and white 'Team' logo has been placed alongside the 'Alitalia' title on the cabin roof.

Because Alitalia decided for an early delivery of MD-11 I-DUPU in August 1992, the aircraft was delivered by the manufacturer with a bare metal fuselage with regular 'Alitalia' titles applied on the upper fuselage and the company's logo on the winglets. The tail section however was painted in full colours.

I-DUPA	*Teatro alla Scala*, renamed *Gioacchino Rossini*
I-DUPB	*Valle dei Templi*, renamed *Pietro Mascagni*
I-DUPC	*V. Bellini*
I-DUPD	*G. Donizetti*
I-DUPE	*Arena di Verona*, renamed *Giuseppe Verdi*
I-DUPI	*Giacomo Puccini*
I-DUPO	*Canal Grande*, renamed *Nicolo Paganini*
I-DUPU	*Ponte Vecchio*, renamed *Antonio Vivaldi*

American Airlines

Over the years the world's second-largest airline has had a tremendous influence on the US aviation industry. Besides the DC-3, the airline has also determined the design of famous aircraft such as the DC-4, DC-7, Convair 240,

Lockheed L-188 Electra, Convair 990 and last but not least the DC-10. On 25th January 1959, American Airlines became the first airline to offer transcontinental jet service between New York and Los Angeles with Boeing 707 equipment. The expansion of the route network and an increase in passenger traffic led to the acquisition of the Boeing 747 in 1970.

During a ceremony at Long Beach on 29th July the following year, American Airlines and its competitor United Airlines took delivery of the first DC-10 aircraft, for which both airlines had been the most important launch customers. The airline introduced its first transatlantic service to London in May 1982.

New international services were inaugurated which necessitated the acquisition of a suitable long-range aircraft. In February 1989, American ordered and optioned 50 MD-11s (respectively 8 and 42 aircraft). The carrier was able to take early delivery of three aircraft which had been ordered by British Caledonian but were cancelled after its takeover by British Airways. Because of contractual obligations these aircraft were refurbished at Marshall's of Cambridge in the UK. The first MD-11 arrived on 1st February 1991 and a further four aircraft were delivered during that year. The excessive fuel burn experienced during proving flights, resulting in a range deficiency, and system malfunctions forced the airline to ground its first aircraft and delay delivery of further examples until all problems were corrected by McDonnell Douglas. The carrier's MD-11s were all powered by GE CF6-80C2D1F engines and originally had a three-class cabin layout, seating 16 first, 66 business and 163 economy passengers. While different seat configurations were adapted later, the airline currently offers an Atlantic cabin arrangement of 18 first, 35 business and 203 economy seats. The Pacific arrangement offers seating for 18 first, 52 business and 163 economy passengers.

Although American Airlines had changed a further 11 options into firm orders, the 19th and last aircraft was delivered in September 1993, the fate of the MD-11 in the airline's fleet had been sealed. All aircraft will be taken over by FedEx and converted to MD-11Fs. In January

Alitalia took early delivery of MD-11 I-DUPU *Antonio Vivaldi*. **The aircraft was delivered with a bare metal fuselage but with a fully painted tail section and winglets, and an 'Alitalia' title on the cabin roof.** Dario Cocco

Alitalia MD-11 I-DUPO *Nicolo Paganini* **was transferred to the carrier's low-cost division. The red and white 'TEAM' logo has been placed alongside the 'Alitalia' title.** Dario Cocco

The early artist's impression depicts the American Airlines 'MD-11' with a highly-polished tail section. McDonnell Douglas

American Airlines MD-11 LuxuryLiner, N1751A, showing the airline's famous livery with the light grey tail section. American

American Airlines MD-11 N1750B at Frankfurt in 1994. After being sold to FedEx the aircraft was lost at Subic Bay, Philippines, on 17th October 1999. Author's collection

Bottom right: **At John F Kennedy International Airport, New York, AVIANCA, N278WA, on lease from World Airways.** Bill Hough

1996, the first MD-11 was handed over and at the time of writing eleven aircraft are already in service with the express carrier. The remaining eight aircraft will have been transferred by 2002.

A contract was closed in November 1996 between the airline's parent company, AMR, and Boeing which foresees that only Boeing products will be bought for the next 20 years. While it is planned to retain the Airbus A300-605R fleet, American intends to phase-out all Fokker and all other McDonnell Douglas aircraft.

Currently American Airlines has a fleet of over 700 aircraft, consisting of A300-600s, 737s, 727s, 757s, 767s, 777s, Fokker 100s, MD-11s and MD-80s.

The American Airlines livery dates back to 1969. A triple blue, white and red cheatline is applied on the natural metal fuselage with a large red white-outlined 'American' title on the cabin roof.

The MD-11 is named 'LuxuryLiner' in American service and this title is shown below the forward entry doors. The company logo, a red and a blue letter 'A' together with the blue scissor eagle, is displayed on the light grey tail fin. The early artist's impression, based on a DC-10 photograph, shows the aircraft with a highly-polished tail section used on American's aircraft before the current grey tail scheme was introduced.

AVIANCA

AVIANCA (Aerovias Nacionales de Colombia) entered the jet age with the acquisition of two Boeing 720 aircraft in November 1961. The jet fleet was expanded with further examples of the type as well as 707s. In November 1976 the first Boeing 747 was placed into service on the carrier's international routes.

Today the airline operates a diversified fleet of aircraft, consisting of Fokker 50s, 757s, 767s, MD-83s and a single 727. To cover increased passenger traffic on its New York route during the year's end holiday season the airline has leased additional wide-body equipment in the past years.

World Airways MD-11 N278WA was operated for the Colombian carrier from 14th December 1998 until 28th January 1999. Unfortunately the aircraft did not wear the airline's attractive red and white paint scheme. A simple red 'Avianca' and a black 'Columbia' title was displayed on the upper white fuselage. Thin dark blue striping between the cabin doors were a leftover from the paint scheme used on its previous lessee, El Al. Conforming with the airline's own livery a diagonal red 'Avianca' title was placed on the tail section.

British Airways

Following the merger of British Overseas Airways Corporation (BOAC) and British European Airways (BEA), British Airways started operations as a unified airline in 1974. Long

range operations were conducted with Boeing 707/747 and Vickers Super VC-10s. BA took delivery of its first Lockheed TriStar in 1974 and took over British Caledonian Airways in December of that year. With the takeover of the UK's second largest airline BA inherited orders for Airbus A320 and McDonnell Douglas MD-11 aircraft placed by BCAL. BA would go on to accept delivery of the A320s, the first Airbus type in the airline's fleet, but the MD-11 order was a different matter altogether. Ignoring the supersonic operations, BA at the time operated a fleet of 747 and L-1011 aircraft on long distance flights. This fleet was complemented by eight former BCAL DC-10-30s, some of which would remain in service until 1999. Although BA considered different options to bring the MD-11 into service, a decision against the aircraft was taken in favour of the Boeing 767-300 which entered service in 1990. Delivery of the initial three MD-11 aircraft also had originally been scheduled to take place during 1990. The aircraft were subsequently sold to American Airlines enabling the US carrier to deploy the MD-11 in early 1991.

In 1990 McDonnell Douglas started a presentation campaign of its planned MD-12X tri-jet program to the airline industry. MDC envisaged BA as a possible launch customer for the aircraft, conceived as a direct competitor

The beautiful former livery of British Airways is depicted in this MD-11 artist's impression. McDonnell Douglas

Artist's rendering of how a British Caledonian Airways MD-11 would look in the extremely attractive livery of once Britain's largest independent carrier. McDonnell Douglas

to the Boeing 747-400 and 777. Again, the Seattle-based manufacturer won over MDC when BA placed an order for 777s in 1991.

Besides its seven Concorde aircraft, BA today operates a modern long range fleet consisting of Boeing 747-236B, 747-436, 767-336 and 777-236 airliners.

The British Airways MD-11 artist's rendering show the aircraft in the airline's former distinctive livery. The top of the fuselage was pearl grey with midnight blue 'British Airways' lettering at the front. The midnight blue belly had a symbolised dark red 'Speedwing' which extended as a cheatline to the rear of the aircraft. The colours of the Union Flag appeared above the rear engine while the white crown highlighted the blue tail fin. The wing-mounted engines were also kept in blue.

British Caledonian Airways

British Caledonian Airways was founded on 30th November 1970 after British United Airways had been taken over by charter carrier Caledonian Airways. As a result of government policy, Britain's largest independent carrier

was awarded the routes to South America, West and Central Africa in 1976 and was thus looking for a large capacity aircraft and decided to purchase DC-10-30s. At the time the airline operated a fleet of Vickers VC-10 and Boeing 707 aircraft on international routes. Between March 1977 and April 1981, eight DC-10-30s were delivered. Further wide-body aircraft operated by BCAL included the Airbus A310-200 and the 747-200. Long range services were extended to North America, Africa, the Middle and Far East.

Later long range expansion plans, which included further destinations in North and South America as well as the Far East, led to the order of a new generation wide-body airliner: the MD-11. BCAL placed an initial order for three aircraft of the type on 3rd December 1986, weeks before the MD-11 program was officially launched on 30th December. The airline also was a launch partner for the A320 with an initial order for seven aircraft. The A320 would have been a replacement for its ageing BAC One-Eleven aircraft.

However in 1988, after financial difficulties, the ailing airline was taken over by one of its strongest competitors, British Airways. While

the A310s had already been sold in May 1986, the fleet of eight DC-10s and four 747s was transferred to the new owner. Whereas BA took delivery of the A320s ordered, the order for the MD-11 aircraft was not taken up (see British Airways).

The MDC artist's impression shows the extremely attractive livery of British Caledonian: a golden cheatline started below the nose and was separated from the blue upper cheatline by a white pinstripe. Bold black 'British Caledonian' titles and the Union Flag were placed on the upper white fuselage. The most remarkable part of the paint scheme was the dark blue tail with the gold lion rampant. The company was often referred to as BCAL, this lettering together with a shield appeared on the wing-mounted engines.

China Airlines

China Airlines (CAL) was established in Taipei, Republic of China on 16th December 1959. The carrier was appointed national airline of the republic in 1965. International services to Saigon (now Ho Chi Minh City) with Lockheed

Constellations were started in 1966. The airline acquired two new Boeing 707s at the end of 1969 and flights to San Francisco via Tokyo and Honolulu were initiated in early 1970. Entering into service in 1975, the 747 was the first wide-body aircraft to be introduced in the China Airlines fleet.

China Airlines ordered four MD-11s from the manufacturer which were delivered between October 1992 and December 1993. Actually the first MD-11, N489GX, was on lease from GATX and entered service with CAL in September 1992 but was returned to the leasing company in February 1993. After having served with World Airways, the aircraft once more became a part of the fleet when a four year lease was concluded in October 1997. CAL's MD-11s are equipped with P&W PW4460 engines. The cabin has a 34 Dynasty business class and 270 economy passenger configuration. The same configuration was used on aircraft leased to subsidiary Mandarin Airlines.

Three MD-11s were leased to Mandarin Airlines and were operated in the latter carrier's livery. See Mandarin Airlines for paint scheme details.

The carrier lost an MD-11 (f/n 518), B-150, at Hong Kong's Chek Lap Kok Airport on 22nd August 1999. The aircraft, on a China Airline's flight from Bangkok to Taipei with a scheduled stop in Hong Kong, crashed on the runway while a landing was attempted in a tropical storm. The aircraft carried the Mandarin Airlines markings.

With the expansion of the airline's international scheduled passenger and cargo network the wide-body fleet rapidly increased. Currently the carrier operates a fleet of four MD-11s, one 747-209B and 13 747-409s on its long range passenger network which include destinations such as Amsterdam, Dallas, Frankfurt, Honolulu, Los Angeles, New York, San Francisco and Tokyo. Cargo services are currently operated with a fleet of five 747 freighter aircraft. China Airlines has ordered seven A340-300s for delivery during 2001 and 2002. A total of 13 747-409Fs (SCD) will be delivered between 2000 and 2007. With the introduction of the A340, the MD-11 aircraft will be phased out. Three aircraft (f/n 449, 546 and 558) have been sold to FedEx and will be converted to freighters during 2001.

The MD-11s were delivered by McDonnell Douglas in CAL's former paint scheme. A triple

Top right: China Airlines MD-11, B-150, was the first of four aircraft ordered to be delivered to the Taiwanese carrier. The aircraft is shown in the original paint scheme. McDonnell Douglas

Centre right: At Frankfurt International Airport, B-153 displays the attractive China Airlines colour scheme introduced in 1995.
Author's collection

Below: The China Eastern Airlines MD-11 artist's impression displays the proposed positioning of the airline's titles on the forward fuselage section. McDonnell Douglas

blue, white and red cheatline was applied on the upper white fuselage. This arrangement was repeated diagonally on the winglets and the tail fin which also showed the national flag. The 'China Airlines' title in Chinese and English were placed on the cabin roof.

With the presentation of a new corporate identity on 7th October 1995 an attractive livery was introduced. The aircraft feature a mainly white fuselage with a wide dark lilac and dark blue band starting underneath the nose running down diagonally to the lower light lilac fuselage section. A combination of the four colours is shown on the winglets. A 'China Airlines' title, together with a white and pink 'We blossom every day' logo, is located on the forward upper fuselage. The company's new pink 'plum blossom' logo is positioned on the tail fin.

China Cargo Airlines

On 30th July 1998 China Eastern Airlines announced the establishment of a new cargo subsidiary, following approval from the Civil Aviation Administration of China (CAAC). The operation, named China Cargo Airlines, is a joint venture with China Ocean Shipping, which holds a 30% stake, while China Eastern owns the remaining shares. Operations started in October 1998 with China Eastern's single MD-11F, which was transferred to the new

One of five passenger aircraft delivered, B-2171 shows the current paint scheme of China Eastern Airlines. McDonnell Douglas

China Eastern Airlines acquired one freighter aircraft. B-2170 was delivered in October 1991. McDonnell Douglas

Although a Memorandum of Understanding for the purchase of six MD-11s was signed by China Southern Airlines, no aircraft were delivered to the airline. McDonnell Douglas

MD-11 OO-CTB *Albatros* showing City Bird's beautiful dark green livery. McDonnell Douglas

cargo carrier. A further two China Eastern MD-11 passenger aircraft have been converted to the freighter role. Besides domestic freight services, cargo flights are conducted to international destinations which, amongst others, include Beijing, Brussels, Chicago, Hong Kong, Osaka, Paris, Seattle and Tokyo. The main base of China Cargo Airlines is Shanghai Hongqiao International Airport. At the time of writing the freighter aircraft carry the parent company's livery. See China Eastern Airlines below for details.

China Eastern Airlines

Following a State Council directive, the Civil Aviation Administration of China (CAAC) separated its governmental, administrative and regulatory role from the commercial airline operations that were being conducted by the CAAC and its regional administrators.

After separation from the CAAC, China Eastern Airlines started its own operations in 1988. At the time the airline's fleet consisted of McDonnell Douglas MD-82s, Airbus A310s and BAe 146s. The airline was an early customer for the MD-11 and placed an order for five passenger and one freighter aircraft in January 1989. The aircraft were delivered between 1991 and 1993 and allowed the airline to offer passenger services to Europe and the USA. Early destinations included Brussels, Chicago, Los Angeles, Madrid and Seattle. The MD-11F also permitted the carrier to start full cargo flights to Europe and the USA. All aircraft were delivered with P&W PW 4460 engines. The passenger aircraft have a seating arrangement for 44 first and 270 economy class passengers.

In September 1998 China Eastern Airlines signed an agreement with Boeing's Long Beach Division to convert two of its passenger aircraft into freighters for its cargo subsidiary. The conversion of the first aircraft was completed in December 1999. Ultimately, the remaining three China Eastern MD-11 passenger aircraft will be transferred to China Cargo Airlines after conversion to freighters. The carrier plans to replace the aircraft with five additional Airbus A340s.

As well as a dense domestic network, the airline has strongly developed its international operations. International destinations presently include Bangkok, Chicago, Fukuoka, Hong Kong, Los Angeles, Madrid, Munich, Nagasaki, Nagoya, Okayama, Osaka, Paris, San Francisco, Seoul, Singapore, Sydney and Tokyo. The current wide-body passenger fleet consists of ten A300-605Rs, five A340-300s and three MD-11s.

The simple livery displays triple red, gold and dark blue cheatlines extending from the front to the rear of the fully white fuselage. 'China Eastern' titles in English (blue) and Chinese (red) are placed on the upper fuselage. On the freighter aircraft a large 'Cargo' title is placed on the tail engine.

World Airways N273WA was one of three MD-11s leased from the US carrier. City Bird *Seagull* displays the livery based on a white fuselage.
Nicky Scherrer – VIP Photoservice

The company's logo, a white stylised bird within a red and dark blue circle, is displayed on the white tail fin. On the MD-11 aircraft this logo is also placed on the winglets.

China Southern Airlines

After the reorganisation of the CAAC, China Southern Airlines was established as an independent carrier in 1991 and is a member of the Southern Airlines Group. Formerly known as the CAAC Guangzhou Regional Administration, the carrier already operated Western-built aircraft in the mid-eighties. Seven 737-200s were in service at the time.

Envisaging international operations, the airline signed a Memorandum of Understanding (MoU) for the acquisition of six MD-11s as early as 3rd July 1988. While serial numbers 48462 through 48467 were allocated, the deal failed to materialise and the aircraft were never built.

The airline today operates an extensive fleet of A320s, 737s and 757-200s on its domestic network. In 1995 China Southern became the first Chinese airline to place the 777 into service.

The MD-11 artist's rendering shows the planned livery of China Southern Airlines. A fivefold of light blue, golden, dark blue, golden and light blue bands started at the nose section and became thinner towards the middle of the forward fuselage. The same scheme was repeated in reverse on the rear fuselage and tail section. The Chinese and English 'China Southern' titles, respectively in dark and light blue, were placed next to the national flag on the upper fuselage. The airline's white logo was displayed on the light blue tail fin.

City Bird

City Bird was founded by Victor Hasson in 1996 and is a subsidiary of City Hotels, S.A. The airline took delivery of its first MD-11 on 13th December 1996. Until the start-up of its own operations on 27th March 1997, City Bird leased the aircraft to STAR Europe.

The carrier leased three MD-11 aircraft from World Airways. While N271WA and N273WA were operated on short term lease, N280WA was with City Bird from June 1997 until March 1998, when the airline's second MD-11 was delivered. A third example joined the fleet in April 1998.

Two of the carrier's MD-11s had GE engines while one was powered by P&W PW4460 engines.

Two aircraft, OO-CTS and OO-CTC, were leased to Sabena in April and May 1998 respectively and operated for the Belgian flag carrier until March 2001. See Sabena for more details.

The airline's international scheduled network includes the destinations Las Vegas, Los Angeles, Mexico City, Miami, Orlando and San Francisco. City Bird further operates charter flights to Cuba, the Dominican Republic, Guadeloupe, Kenya, Mexico and Venezuela. The MD-11 operated by the airline itself had a two-class 371 seat configuration, 36 Royal Eagle business and 335 Colibri economy passengers. City Bird ceased MD-11 operations at the end of April 2001. For long range services City Bird currently operates two 767-300ERs

Although the carrier planned to acquire two MD-11 freighters for dedicated cargo operations to Asia, South America and the USA, two Airbus A300C4-605Rs were ordered in 1998 and delivered in July and August 1999 respectively.

The airline chose an attractive, extraordinary livery which consisted of a dark green upper fuselage and tail section. The lower part of the fuselage and wing engines were kept in a medium grey colour.

A huge white 'City Bird' and a smaller 'The Flying Dream' title were placed on the forward section. The company's yellow and white 'bird' logo was incorporated in the 'City Bird' title and was also displayed on the tail fin and winglets. The Belgian and European Community flags were displayed on the tail engine. The aircraft on lease from World Airways featured a white upper fuselage with dark green 'City Bird' and 'The Flying Dream' titles. The company logo was placed on the white tail fin and grey winglets.

OO-CTB *Albatros*
OO-CTC *Seagull* (also used on N273WA and N280WA)
OO-CTS *Cormorant*

Crossair

Crossair is a subsidiary of SAirLines and member of the SAirGroup. The carrier leased a 257-seat MD-11 from partner Swissair from June until October 1997 for its weekly service between Zürich and Palma de Mallorca. It replaced a 156-seat MD-83 during that period. The aircraft was operated in the full Swissair livery.

Delta Air Lines

Delta Air Lines was a jet leader among the world's airlines, becoming the first airline to introduce the DC-8 in 1959, the Convair CV-880 in 1960 and the DC-9 in 1965.

Although several 747s and DC-10s were operated during the seventies, Delta would standardise its long range fleet on the Lockheed TriStar. However, route network expansion in the late eighties and early nineties required an aircraft more capable than the L-1011. On 22nd September 1988, Delta signed an order for nine MD-11s with options on a further 31 aircraft. Altogether 15 aircraft from this order would be delivered to the carrier between March 1992 and February 1998. However, two aircraft, f/n 453 and f/n 454, originally destined for Air Europe, were leased from Mitsui & Company, enabling Delta to commence MD-11 operations in December 1990, thus becoming (after Finnair) the second airline to place the aircraft in scheduled passenger service. These two leased aircraft remained in service until December 1993. Although these were GE powered, Delta selected the P&W PW4460 engine for its own MD-11 fleet. The MD-11s originally featured a three-class layout in different versions. Since 1999 the cabin has been configured with seating for 50 Business-Elite and 210 or 219 economy passengers.

In March 1997 the airline announced a long term loyalty contract to purchase airliners only from the Seattle-based manufacturer for the next 20 years. After the Boeing-McDonnell Douglas merger in August 1997, the Boeing Company announced in November 1997 that production of the MD-80 and MD-90 would be terminated when production commitments

MD-11 N892DL was one of two GE powered aircraft delivered to Delta Air Lines in 1990. The attractive livery was changed in 1997. McDonnell Douglas

Delta Air Lines MD-11 N812DE *The Centennial Spirit* **showing the very striking 1996 Olympic Games colour scheme.** Derek Hellmann

Additional 'The official airline' and '1996 Olympic Games' titles were placed on all other Delta Air Lines aircraft during the period. Author's collection

MD-11 N802DE was the first aircraft to obtain the new Delta Air Lines livery introduced in 1997. Exavia

ended. The MD-11 would suffer the same fate. Although the acquisition of a substantial numbers of both the MD-11 and MD-90 had been planned by Delta, Boeing's decision forced the airline to rethink its fleet planning and the retirement of both aircraft types will be accelerated. The fleet of TriStars and MD-11s will be replaced by 767-400s and 777-200s. The long range aircraft fleet currently consists of MD-11s, L-1011s, 767s and 777-200s.

All but one of the MD-11 aircraft were delivered in the attractive livery which remained unchanged for a long period of time until the introduction of a new paint scheme in April 1997.

The name 'delta' originating from the Mississippi river delta, the company's logo is a dark blue and red delta. This logo, known as the 'widget', appeared on the forward fuselage and on the tail section. The lower part of the fuselage was natural metal, the upper part was white with a wide dark blue line over the windows and a red pinstripe above the latter. The sloping 'Delta' lettering appeared on the upper forward fuselage and on the rear engine.

For the 1996 Centennial Olympic Games in Atlanta, Georgia, MD-11 N812DE obtained a special colour scheme and was appropriately named *The Centennial Spirit*. The tri-jet transported the Olympic flame on a historic 7,000 mile flight from Athens, Greece, to Los Angeles, California, for the start of the 1996 Torch Relay. The aircraft was delivered new to Delta on 8th April 1996 at the Long Beach plant from where it started its flight to Athens. The very attractive livery was applied by the McDonnell Douglas paint shop staff. The forward section of the fuselage is kept in white with streaks in red, white and red flowing from the front to the rear. The dark blue 'Delta' and light blue 'Air Lines' titles are placed alongside the airline's logo on the upper section. The dark blue aft fuselage displays a white 'Atlanta' and '1996' title with the colourful Olympic torch logo in between. A white 'Official Airline 1996 Olympic Games' title is placed underneath the 'Atlanta' title: The enlarged torch flames and light blue star of the Olympic logo are displayed on the dark blue tail section.

This Olympic scheme was also applied to 767-232 N102DA which was named *The Spirit of Delta*. A 'The official airline, 1996 Olympic Games' title together with the Olympic The torch logo was placed at the forward fuselage section on all other Delta aircraft.

A new livery, introduced on 10th April 1997, was first applied to 767-322ER N190DN.

The first MD-11 aircraft to receive the new paint scheme was N802DE. The new dark blue 'Delta' and light blue 'Air Lines' titles alongside the Delta logo were taken over from the 1996 Olympic aircraft scheme. A dark blue cheatline started at the nose section and extended over the windows to the rear of the aircraft. At the beginning this cheatline was offset by thin red striping. This combination was repeated on the wing engines as well as the tail section. A white

'Delta' title was placed on the tail engine.

Within only three years of the introduction of the latter paint scheme the airline unveiled another livery and a new visual identity. On 22nd March 2000 a 777, N863DA, was rolled out at a ceremony at Hartsfield Atlanta International Airport, featuring the new livery. As part of the new identity the words 'Air Lines' were removed from its logotype and only the name 'Delta', alongside an updated and softer version of the triangular 'widget' logo, is placed on the white upper fuselage. The livery features a dramatic change to the tail of Delta's aircraft, which displays a ribbon-like design in a colourful and vibrant dark blue and red, with the addition of the lighter blue that was previously used for the words 'Air Lines'. The wing engines are ringed in dark blue and red. The new visual identity was designed by the airline industry's leading branding consultancy Landor and Associates. At the time of writing none of the MD-11 aircraft had taken on the new livery.

El Al Israel Airlines

The Israeli flag carrier operates scheduled passenger flights to destinations in Africa, Asia, Canada, Europe, the Middle East and the USA. All-cargo services are conducted with 747F equipment to destinations in Asia, Europe and the USA. The airline currently operates with an all-Boeing aircraft fleet consisting of different types of the 737, 747, 757, 767 and 777.

To boost its long-haul fleet, the carrier introduced MD-11 services for the first time with an aircraft leased from World Airways. The aircraft was operated from June until October 1998 on

routes from Israel to various points in the USA, supplementing the airline's own Boeings 747s and 767s. The aircraft, N278WA, was operated in a white upper and bare metal lower fuselage with thin dark blue striping between the cabin doors. The light and dark blue 'El Al' title in English and Hebrew was placed next to the Israeli flag on the cabin roof. Light and dark blue striping was applied to the winglets. The dark blue Star of David, between two dark blue stripes, was applied on the white tail fin. During 1999 and 2000 the carrier again leased World Airways MD-11s; N277WA, which was operated in 2000, featured a smaller 'El Al' title above the passenger windows between the forward doors.

Emery Worldwide Airlines

Although the company was founded as Emery Air Freight in 1946, it did not start its own airline operations until 1980. From the airline's main base at Dayton, Ohio, and its US hubs, air freight and package delivery services are conducted to destinations in the USA and Canada. Overseas services are flown to the airline's hub at Brussels National Airport, Belgium.

El Al Israel Airlines leased World Airways MD-11 N278WA in 1998. The aircraft displays the large 'El Al' titles. Rolf Wallner

World Airways MD-11 N277WA was operated by the Israeli carrier in 2000. Small 'El Al' titles were applied on the forward cabin roof. Author's collection

Artist's impression showing the planned 'Evergreen' livery for Taiwan's carrier EVA Airways. McDonnell Douglas

EVA Air MD-11 B-16101 displays the colourful 'globe and compass' tail section paint scheme. McDonnell Douglas

To underline the co-operation with Air Nippon, additional 'ANK' and 'joint service' titles were placed on the fuselage of EVA Air passenger aircraft in 1998. Euro Aviation Slides

EVA Air operates nine MD-11 freighter aircraft. N105EV is shown. McDonnell Douglas

Over the years the airline's own Douglas DC-8 fleet has grown tremendously and currently includes two -54Fs, seven -62Fs, nine -63Fs, ten -71Fs and sixteen -73Fs. The carrier bought five former Continental DC-10-10s which were converted to the freighter role. The first two aircraft entered service in 1999. In 2000 Emery Worldwide acquired its first two DC-10-30Fs. Further wide-body aircraft will eventually replace part of the ageing DC-8 fleet.

Since 1999 Emery Worldwide has been operating a World Airways MD-11F N274WA on a long term lease on the Dayton, Ohio - Brussels route. The aircraft is operated in full World Airways livery without any additional titles.

EVA Airways

This airline was founded in March 1989 by Evergreen, the world's largest container shipping company. Although the name 'Evergreen' was considered for Taiwan's first private international carrier, the plan was dropped since Evergreen International Airlines, Mc Minnville, Oregon, already was an established cargo carrier operating under the same name. The 'EVA' name was created from the first two letters of

The first MD-11F delivered to launch customer Federal Express was N602FE. The aircraft is shown in the original eye-catching purple and white livery. McDonnell Douglas

'Evergreen' and the first letter of 'Airways'. Operations started on 1st July 1991 with three Boeing 767-300s on the routes to Bangkok, Manila, Hong Kong and Seoul. The following year the airline acquired its first 747-400s. EVA Air became a McDonnell Douglas customer with an order for MD-11 passenger and freighter aircraft. A total of twelve MD-11s, three passenger and nine freight examples, were delivered between August 1994 and August 1999. In common with the majority of the MD-11 operators, the airline selected the GE CF6-80C2D1F engine for the aircraft. The passenger version is flown in a 24 Super Class, 83 Evergreen Deluxe and 168 economy seating arrangement. As well as the twelve MD-11s, the carrier currently operates with a fleet four 767-200s, five 767-300s and fifteen 747-400s.

The artist's impression shows the original livery proposal consisting of only a green 'Evergreen' title and compass logo, respectively placed on the completely white fuselage and tail fin. Fortunately this uninspiring scheme was

not adopted, which can also be attributed to the name change as described above.

The airline introduced a simple yet attractive livery with a thin orange and green striping on the upper section of the fully white fuselage. The green 'EVA AIR' title in English and Chinese is placed next to the forward entry doors. The freight aircraft carry an additional green 'Cargo' title. A small 'Evergreen Group' title is shown below the cockpit section. The company 'globe and compass' logo is applied on the green tail section which is accentuated by orange striping. This green and orange scheme is also shown on the winglets. To underline the co-operation with ANK Air Nippon of Tokyo, an additional dark blue 'ANK' and green 'joint service' title was placed on the fuselage of the passenger aircraft in 1998.

Federal Express Corporation

Federal Express Corporation, generally known as FedEx, is the world's largest parcel and document carrier. Not surprisingly, Memphis, Tennessee, where FedEx has its headquarters, retained its position of the world's busiest cargo hub again in 2000. In 1980 the first three,

ex-Continental, DC-10s were brought into service. With the purchase of Flying Tigers in 1989, the DC-8 and 747 equipment of the latter carrier was added to the ever growing fleet of 727 and DC-10 aircraft. FedEx was the only carrier to have ordered the DC-10-30F and a total of ten were delivered by MDC between January 1986 and October 1988.

FedEx was one of the launch customers for the MD-11 and the first carrier to order the MD-11F freighter version. The first aircraft was handed over during a ceremony at Long Beach on 29th May 1991. The following month, on 27th June, FedEx took delivery of MD-11F N601FE which was actually the first aircraft built (f/n 447). The aircraft was originally one of the five aircraft used in the certification program and was registered as N111MD during that period. McDonnell Douglas would deliver a total of 22 aircraft to the freight carrier between May 1991 and June 1999. Whereas the first 19 aircraft were fitted out with GE CF6-80C2D1F engines, FedEx selected the P&W PW4462 powerplant for the last three aircraft delivered during 1999.

To increase capacity, FedEx is acquiring additional passenger MD-11 aircraft, which after conversion to freighters, will be added to

the fleet. So far, eleven ex-American aircraft have been delivered while the airline's remaining eight examples will follow in 2001 and 2002. Furthermore, three former-China Airlines MD-11s will join the fleet during 2001. Following Swissair's decision to standardise on an all-Airbus fleet, the carrier's 19 MD-11s will be disposed of and will enter service with FedEx between 2002 and 2004. In June 1999, the Boeing Company announced it signed a Letter of Intent to supply passenger-to-freighter modification services for these aircraft for FedEx by Boeing Airplane Services.

The carrier has lost two of its MD-11Fs. Aircraft N611FE (f/n 553) crash-landed at Newark International Airport, NJ, on 31st July 1997 and was subsequently destroyed by fire. It was the first MD-11 to be involved in a fatal accident. On 17th October 1999 N581FE (f/n 450) was destroyed when the aircraft, arriving from Shanghai, overshot the runway at Subic Freeport International Airport, Philippines. This aircraft was originally used as the fourth test aircraft (N411MD) by the manufacturer before it

Top: **FedEx MD-11F N601FE in the current and striking livery of the parcel and document carrier.** Federal Express Corporation

Centre: **FedEx MD-11F N583FE 'Panda One' transported two giant pandas from China to Washington, DC in December 2000. The aircraft also displays the new 'FedEx Express' titles on the forward fuselage.** Exavia

Left: **Artist's rendering showing the proposed light grey belly livery for Finnair's MD-11.** McDonnell Douglas

Opposite: **Finnair was the first airline to take delivery of an MD-11. OH-LGA shown was the first MD-11 to be brought into passenger service.** McDonnell Douglas

was delivered to American Airlines in May 1991. It was acquired by FedEx in February 1997 and, after conversion to freighter, entered service in May 1997.

In 1994 newly-ordered Airbus A300-605Fs as well as the first converted ex-Lufthansa A310s joined the fleet. Also in 1994 Federal Express changed its brand name to 'FedEx' and a new livery and corporate identity were introduced.

In September 1996, McDonnell Douglas and Federal Express Corporation announced the launch of the MD-10 program. During 1997, FedEx entered into agreements with American Airlines and United Airlines to acquire 53 DC-10s, spare parts, aircraft engines and other equipment, and maintenance services in exchange for a combination of aircraft engine noise reduction kits and cash. Delivery of these aircraft began in 1997 and will continue through 2001. Following the reconfiguration to freighters, the aircraft, together with other sisterships, will be converted to MD-10 status. (see Chapter Six) Additionally, the two airlines may exercise options through 31st December, 2003, requiring FedEx to purchase up to 29 additional DC-10s along with aircraft engines and equipment.

FedEx today maintains a fleet of jet aircraft that includes 727s, A300-605Fs, A310s, DC-10s, MD-10s and MD-11s. It should be noted that some of the DC-10 fleet are passenger aircraft which still have to be converted to the freighter role.

The original eye-catching livery featured a purple and white livery with a white and orange cheatline. A large white 'Federal' title was placed on the purple upper fuselage and an orange 'Express' title on the white lower fuselage. This livery stayed until 1994 when the current paint scheme was introduced. This has a huge 'FedEx' title in purple and orange on the forward white fuselage and a small purple 'Federal Express' title underneath. The purple and orange 'FedEx' title is also applied on the wing engines while a white and orange title is placed on the tail engine. The tail section and rear part of the fuselage is kept in purple. A 'The World On Time' title is placed under the forward entry doors on both sides of the aircraft. Following a rebranding initiative in 2000, FedEx was renamed FedEx Express as a family member of the FedEx Corporation. Since then the 'Federal' in the 'Federal Express' title on the aircraft has been omitted.

Since the start-up in 1973, FedEx aircraft have been named after employees' children. These names are displayed under the port side cockpit window. Federal Express Corporation was the first service company to win the Malcolm Baldrige National Quality Award in 1990. The carrier named one of its MD-11s after the former US Secretary of Commerce, who was a strong proponent of quality management as a key to the country's prosperity and long-term strength.

In December 2000, FedEx transported two giant pandas from China to the Smithsonian Institution's National Zoological Park in Washington, DC. A large panda picture was placed on the fuselage of both MD-11 N583FE and N584FE while a smaller sticker was placed next to the forward entry doors of the aircraft. For the operation N583FE was named *Panda One,* whilst N584FE was designated for support purposes.

N581FE	*Joshua*
N582FE	*Jamie*
N583FE	*Nancy*
N584FE	*Jeffrey Wellington*
N585FE	*Katherine*
N586FE	*Dylan*
N587FE	*Jeanno*

N588FE	*Kendra*
N590FE	*Stan*
N592FE	*Joshua*
N601FE	*Christy*, renamed *Jim Riedmeyer*
N602FE	*Malcolm Baldrige 1990*
N603FE	*Elizabeth*
N604FE	*Hollis*
N605FE	*April Star*
N606FE	*Charles & Teresa*
N607FE	*Louis III*
N608FE	*Dana Elena*, renamed *Betsey*
N609FE	*Scott*
N610FE	*Marisa*
N611FE	*Cory*
N612FE	*Alyssa*
N613FE	*Krista*
N614FE	*Christy Allison*
N615FE	*Max*
N616FE	*Shanita*
N617FE	*Travis*
N618FE	*Justin*
N619FE	*Tara Lynn*
N620FE	*Grady*
N621FE	*Connor*
N623FE	*Meghan*

Finnair

In November 1966, Finnair ordered two DC-8-62CFs for long-range operations. The first DC-8 arrived in February 1969 and carried out charter flights before the first scheduled service from Helsinki to New York, via Copenhagen and Amsterdam, was inaugurated on 15th March. The first wide-body airliner in the fleet was the DC-10-30. The delivery of the first -30 took place in January 1975. A total of five examples of the type were operated. In 1986 the airline acquired two Airbus A300B4s for charter operations.

Finnair was a launch customer for the MD-11 with an order for four aircraft and was the first airline to take delivery of an MD-11; OH-LGA was presented during a ceremony held at Long Beach on 29th November 1990. The official acceptance date was 7th December 1990. After flight crew training the aircraft entered revenue service on a charter flight from Helsinki to Tenerife on 20th December 1990. The MD-11s replaced the airline's DC-10s of which the last example was phased out in May 1996. The tri-jets are powered by GE CF6-80C2D1F engines. While three aircraft are flown in a business/economy layout (respectively 28C/312Y, 28C/329Y and 35C/284Y seats), one aircraft is operated in an all-economy layout with 403 seats.

The MD-11s are used on long distance routes which include the destinations Bangkok, Hong Kong, New York (JFK), Beijing, San Francisco, Singapore, Tokyo (Narita) and Toronto.

Besides the four MD-11s, Finnair currently operates a fleet of ATR 72s, DC-9-51s, MD-82s, MD-83s, MD-87s, A319s, A321s, and 757-200s on it's short and medium range network.

The early artist's impression shows a livery proposal similar to the one used on the airline's DC-10s.

The white and blue livery originally applied to the MD-11 aircraft originated from the colours of the national flag, which in slanted form, was displayed on the tail fin. A blue cheatline extended from the cockpit to the rear of the now fully white fuselage. A blue 'Finnair' and 'Finnair MD-11' title was respectively placed on the upper fuselage and tail engine. The company's logo, a stylised letter 'F' in a blue circle, was placed below the cockpit windows.

One-off paint schemes were also applied to MD-11 OH-LGC. A publicity campaign for Japanese tourists includes a livery with the famous 'Moomin' cartoon characters. In 1995 the aircraft also obtained a special Christmas season scheme showing Santa Claus with his sleigh on the forward fuselage. Other aircraft in the fleet displayed a small Santa Claus sticker beside the second port side entry door.

In October 1997 Finnair took delivery of the first Boeing aircraft in its fleet. The 757-200 was also the first aircraft to display a new livery applied to aircraft used for charter operations. A large light blue 'Finnair' title is placed on the completely white fuselage. The white 'F' logo within a light blue circle is located underneath

Finnair MD-11 OH-LGC displays the lively 'Moomin' cartoon characters livery. Finnair

At Beijing, Finnair MD-11 OH-LGC showing the attractive 'Santa Claus' paint scheme. P J Gralla

During the Christmas season a Santa Claus sticker is placed on the fuselage of other Finnair aircraft. Author's collection

In February, 2001, the first Finnair MD-11 obtained the carrier's new livery. OH-LGA is shown on Finals for JFK International Airport, New York. Michael F McLaughlin

Garuda Indonesia operated a total of six MD-11s. The first aircraft delivered was EI-CDI. McDonnell Douglas

While on lease to Garuda Indonesia, World Airways MD-11 N271WA showing the partial colour scheme of former lessee, Malaysia Airlines. Author's collection

World Airways MD-11 N280WA was operated for the Indonesian carrier in a fully white livery with 'Garuda Indonesia' titles and logo. Pierre-Alain Petit

Garuda Indonesia leased World Airways MD-11 N272WA for the 2000 Hadj season. The aircraft carried the basic Aer Lingus colour scheme. Exavia

the cockpit windows and the logo, in reverse colours, is repeated on the tail section. The light blue at the top turns stripe-wise to a darker blue at bottom of the tail fin. The first Airbus A320 delivered to Finnair in 1999 sported a similar livery with a solid blue tail section. None of the MD-11 aircraft would wear either of these paint schemes. The airline launched a new visual identity on 1st June 2000 and the aircraft now feature a fully white fuselage with a bold blue 'Finnair' title on the upper fuselage. Having disposed of the national flag scheme, the new dark and light blue shaded tail section now displays a large stylised white letter 'F'. The cowlings of the wing engines are painted dark blue.

Garuda Indonesia

Garuda Indonesian Airways acquired its first jet aircraft, the Convair 990 Coronado, in 1963. A total of three of the type were taken delivery of. In 1965, the airline started flying to Europe, terminating at Amsterdam Schiphol Airport. The following year the first DC-8 was delivered by DAC. The first of a total of six DC-10-30s was taken into service in 1976. In 1980 the first of six 747-200s was delivered.

Increasing passenger traffic and the expansion of the route network during the eighties resulted in the acquisition of a further McDonnell Douglas product, the MD-11. Garuda Joint Venture (GJV) was established as a leasing company by Garuda and Guinness Peat Aviation (GPA) and an order for six MD-11s was placed in 1989. Three aircraft, which carried Irish registrations, were delivered in 1991 and 1992 through GJV. Although the remaining three orders were not taken up by GJV, the airline took delivery of these aircraft in 1993 on a direct lease from McDonnell Douglas. The aircraft were equipped with GE CF6-80C2D1F engines. The three-class cabin configuration included seating for 12 first, 53 business and 235 economy passengers.

The joint leasing enterprise came to an end when the first three aircraft were returned to GPA in 1996 and 1997. As a replacement Garuda took delivery of three MD-11ER aircraft, in December 1996 and in May and November

Gemini Air Cargo MD-11F N702GC *Mary* is shown after arrival at Seoul. Pierre-Alain Petit

Artist's rendering of how a MD-11F would look in the grey, yellow and brown livery of former freight carrier German Cargo. McDonnell Douglas

To augment capacity on transatlantic flights, Ghana Airways leased World Airways MD-11 N280WA. Bill Hough

Japan Airlines MD-11 JA8581 on final approach after a test flight. The aircraft had not yet received the name and logo of the *Fairy Pitta* bird species. Neither was the 'J-Bird' title applied on the tail engine. McDonnell Douglas

1997 respectively. The financial crisis in the Pacific Rim countries also had a major impact on the airline industry. As a result of a significant rationalisation all six MD-11 aircraft were returned to the leasing company, the Boeing Capital Corporation, during June and July 1998. Long distance services are currently carried out with a fleet of DC-10-30s, A330s, and 747s. The airline has a further A330 and 777 aircraft on order.

The current livery, introduced in 1985, presents an all white fuselage and dark blue tail which carries the company's bird motif logo consisting of the bird's head and five winged stripes, gradually turning from light blue to turquoise. The same symbol is repeated alongside the 'Garuda Indonesia' title on the fuselage, and in case of the MD-11 was also displayed on the winglets.

To conduct pilgrim flights to Mecca, MD-11 aircraft are frequently leased from World Airways. In these cases, 'Garuda Indonesia' titles and logo are applied to the white fuselage.

As shown, World Airways MD-11 aircraft were also operated for the Indonesian carrier in a basic Malaysia livery with added 'Garuda Indonesia' titles and logo.

Gemini Air Cargo

Gemini Air Cargo was founded in December 1995 and is based at Washington Dulles International Airport, Dulles, Virginia. The carrier initially bought seven ex-Lufthansa DC-10-30s which were converted to freighters. During its first year of operations the first three aircraft were operated by Sun Country Airlines. The carrier commenced with twice-weekly Swisscargo (the Swissair cargo division) flights from Basle to Chicago and Atlanta. On 23rd September 1996, the FAA gave Gemini Air Cargo the go ahead to start proving runs of scheduled cargo flights on the Washington, DC - Columbus - Chicago - New York JFK - Anchorage - Macau - Anchorage - New York JFK route. Upon completion of these proving flights the carrier received the FAA certificate on 22nd October 1996.

The global air company specialises in providing Aircraft, Crew, Maintenance and Insurance (ACMI) contract services for other airlines. It is the largest ACMI operator of DC-10-30F aircraft worldwide. Gemini's customers currently include Air France, Asiana, China Eastern, Emery Worldwide, European Air Transport (a subsidiary of DHL International), FedEx and Swisscargo amongst others. The cargo carrier provides services to over sixty cities and twenty-one countries on behalf of its customers. Scheduled cargo flights between the USA and the Far East are conducted under Gemini's own authority. Over the years the DC-10-30F fleet has grown to twelve aircraft. In 1999, two MD-11s, formerly operated by VARIG of Brazil, were leased from Aerfi Leasing USA after conversion to freighter aircraft, N701GC (ex PP-VOP) and N702GC (ex PP-VOQ) entered service in 2000. N702GC was converted by the Boeing Airplane Services' Modification Center in Wichita, Kansas, while N701GC underwent the conversion to freighter at Israel Aircraft Industries' (IAI) Bedek division in Tel Aviv. The carrier acquired two more MD-11s during 2000. After conversion to freighters, N705GC and N703GC entered service in December 2000 and February 2001 respectively. The aircraft had formerly been operated by Brazilian carrier VASP.

Gemini's aircraft carry a simple yet attractive paint scheme, consisting of a dark blue 'Gemini' and a yellow 'Air Cargo' title on a completely white fuselage; the tail section is kept in dark blue. In case of the MD-11F aircraft, a white 'MD-11F' title is placed on the tail engine. The tail fin and winglets display the carrier's logo. The attractive logo consists of a crate circling a globe which is encompassed by a dark blue letter 'G' and a white ring with a dark blue 'Gemini Air Cargo' title. Aircraft are named:

N701GC *Emilie*
N702GC *Mary*
N703GC *Stephanie*
N705GC *Laine*

Japan Airlines MD-11 JA8580 *Tufted Puffin*, the first of ten aircraft delivered to the Japanese airline. Japan Airlines

German Cargo Services

German Cargo Services was founded in March 1977 as a Lufthansa subsidiary serving the freight charter market. GCS started worldwide operations with four Boeing 707-330Cs which were replaced by two Douglas DC-8-73AFs and three DC-8-73CFs in 1984. McDonnell Douglas considered GCS a potential customer for the MD-11 freighter version and made early proposals to the carrier which however at that time did not materialise. On 30th November 1994 the transformation of GCS to Lufthansa Cargo AG took place.

The McDonnell Douglas artist's impression shows the freighter aircraft in the light grey fuselage livery with a dark brown 'German Cargo' title on the forward section. The yellow tail fin displays the company's dark brown 'crate' logo.

Ghana Airways

The Ghanaian flag carrier started operations on 15th July 1958 with a scheduled service from Accra to London, utilising Boeing 377 Stratocruiser aircraft on lease from BOAC. In 1965 the airline acquired two Vickers VC-10s for use on the long range network.

The first wide-body aircraft, a DC-10-30, was delivered to the airline on 25th February 1983. Currently Ghana Airways operates three examples of the type. The aircraft are used on the long distance flights to Düsseldorf, Harare, Johannesburg, London, New York and Rome. From October 1994 until the end of March 1995 the airline operated an MD-11 on lease from World Airways which was mainly used on the airline's New York route.

The Ghana Airways livery shows the colours of the national flag, red, yellow and green on the triple cheatline while the Ghanaian flag itself is placed on the tail fin. On the airline's DC-10 aircraft, all three engines display the emblem of the company and black 'Ghana Airways' title appear above the cheatlines on the white upper fuselage.

During the short term lease to Ghana Airways, World Airways MD-11 N280WA displayed only a black 'Ghana Airways' on the completely white fuselage and the airline's logo on the tail engine.

Japan Airlines – JAL

Japan Airlines' ties with the Long Beach manufacturer go back to 1954 when it started transpacific services from Tokyo to San Francisco with Douglas DC-6s. The DC-8 was introduced in on the airline's long range routes in 1960. Over the years the carrier operated an extensive fleet of DC-8s. The international route network was expanded rapidly and by 1965 included the European destinations Copenhagen, Frankfurt, Hamburg, London and Paris. In 1970 JAL took delivery of its first 747s.

The airline ordered twenty DC-10-40s and the wide-body tri-jet entered service in 1976. As a replacement for the DC-10 fleet, JAL evaluated both the Airbus A340 and McDonnell Douglas MD-11. In the end a decision in favour of the MD-11 was taken and in March, 1990, the airline signed up for twenty aircraft, ten firm orders and ten options. As had been the case with the DC-10, JAL selected Pratt & Whitney as the engine supplier. Although the ten ordered aircraft were delivered between November 1993 and March 1997, the remaining options were not taken up. The MD-11s have a two-class cabin layout with four different configurations within the fleet: 38C/262Y, 65C/168Y, 67C/168Y and 66C/198Y seats. The airline's long range fleet further includes 747s, 767s, 777s. The phase-out of the DC-10s started in late 1997. In November 2000, JAL announced that the MD-11s will be replaced by 767s and 777s. The aircraft will be traded in to Boeing

Additional logo and title of 'World City Expo Tokyo '98' on MD-11 JA8583 *Golden Eagle*. Fred Lerch

MD-11 JA8582 *Red-Crowned Crane* with 'Official Airline for Nippon Love Goal' sticker at Hong Kong Kai Tak. Author's collection

The Japan Airlines J Bird motifs are illustrated in this set of cards. They relate to the individual MD-11s in the aircraft registration sequence set out on the opposite page. Japan Airlines

and leave the airline's fleet between 2002 and 2004. After conversion of the aircraft into cargo configuration, Boeing will deliver the freighters to UPS Airlines.

The present livery, introduced in 1989, features a white fuselage with a red and grey cheatline on the forward section with large 'JAL' lettering. A small 'Japan Airlines' title is placed beside the second entry doors. The tail emblem consists of a rising sun formed by the spread wings of a red crane, called the 'Tsuru', with white 'JAL' letters. The ten MD-11 aircraft are named after endangered bird species. The MD-11 therefore is generally called 'J Bird' and this title is shown on the tail engine. The attractive bird motifs and names are placed on the fuselage, with the motifs repeated on the inside and outside of the winglets.

A 'We support Unicef' title and Unicef emblem are positioned above the passenger windows on the rear fuselage. Over the years further small titles and emblems have been applied commemorating special events, eg football world championship 'Official Airline for Nippon Love Goal' in 1997 and 'World City Expo Tokyo 98'.

JA8580	*Tufted Puffin*
JA8581	*Fairy Pitta*
JA8582	*Red-Crowned Crane*
JA8583	*Golden Eagle*
JA8584	*Okinawa Rail*
JA8585	*Hodgson's Hawk Eagle*
JA8586	*White Stork*
JA8587	*Pryer's Woodpecker*
JA8588	*White Tailed Eagle*
JA8589	*Rock Ptarmigan*

Jugoslovenski Aerotransport – JAT

The Yugoslav national airline's first step in the direction of international flights was made in 1970 when JAT purchased the Boeing 707. Initially charter flights were operated to Australia, Canada and the USA. With further examples of the type being acquired, scheduled flights to Baghdad, Moscow, New York and Sydney were offered.

The carrier ordered two DC-10-30s to replace the 707s; the first aircraft was delivered on 8th December 1978 with another of the type following on 14th May 1979. Further DC-10 aircraft were leased from Air Afrique, Finnair, Sabena and World Airways. With the addition of the DC-10s to the fleet, the development of the international route network was greatly accel-

Artist's impression of Jugoslovenski Aerotransport - JAT MD-11 with the English 'Yugoslav Airlines' title on the starboard fuselage. McDonnell Douglas

KLM replaced its DC-10 fleet with MD-11s. Still carrying the manufacturer's US registration N6202D, the first aircraft is shown during a test flight. McDonnell Douglas

erated. By the end of the eighties international services were also offered to Chicago, Cleveland, Detroit, Los Angeles, Montreal and Toronto. After having evaluated competing aircraft, the Airbus A340 and Boeing 767, the airline decided to renew its wide-body fleet with MD-11s. An order for three aircraft was placed in 1988, with an option on a further two examples. The war in former Yugoslavia and international sanctions placed on the Federal Republic of Yugoslavia led to the interruption of international flights for two and a half years and the grounding of almost the entire fleet. Between June 1992 and October 1994, the airline operated only domestic flights. These events put a stop to the airline's development and resulted in the cancellation of the MD-11 orders.

The MD-11 artist's rendering shows the airline's colour scheme at the time the order for the new wide-body aircraft was placed. The blue, white and red cheatline on a white upper fuselage represented the colours of the national flag. The 'JAT' logo was placed on the blue tail fin and red 'Yugoslav Airlines' titles appeared on the forward starboard fuselage.

KLM Royal Dutch Airlines

KLM – Koninklijke Luchtvaart Maatschappij is the world's oldest scheduled airline still operating under its original name. The first long range jet aircraft, the DC-8, was introduced in 1960

and would remain the workhorse on international routes until the mid-seventies. A total of 30 DC-8 aircraft of different series were operated. The first 747 was delivered in 1971 and the first DC-10 followed in 1972. A total of eleven DC-10-30s were delivered between 1972 and 1975.

From DC-2 to DC-10 all Douglas and McDonnell Douglas commercial aircraft types have flown in the different KLM liveries.

The airline's long-term experience with the excellence of the McDonnell Douglas products contributed to the decision to purchase the MD-11 as a replacement for the DC-10 aircraft in the fleet. On 23rd March 1990 contracts for an order for ten MD-11s, with options for another five of the type, were signed at the KLM head office in Amstelveen. This order was the largest ever in KLM history. Unfortunately the options for five more MD-11s were not exercised. With the introduction of the MD-11 into the airline's fleet, KLM ceased DC-10 operations in 1994. KLM selected the GE CF6-80C2D1F power plant for its MD-11s. The cabin configuration includes 37 world business class seats (with satellite telephone at every seat) and 260 tourist class seats (satellite telephones available in various locations).

The MD-11 fleet is deployed to destinations in North America (Memphis, Montreal), Central and South America (eg Aruba, Caracas, Quito, Lima), the Near East (Cairo), the Far East (eg Sapporo, Nagoya) and Africa (eg Dar Es Salaam and Nairobi).

At the time of writing the wide-body fleet further includes 767-306s (ER), 747-206Bs (SUD),
747-306s, 747-406s as well as 747-206B converted freighter aircraft for its cargo division.

Delivery was taken of the first MD-11 during
a ceremony at Long Beach on 7th December
1993; this ceremony also marked the achieve-
ment of sixty years of business relations between
KLM and Douglas/McDonnell Douglas. PH-KCA
Amy Johnson was the only aircraft delivered in
full KLM livery, albeit with a bare metal lower
fuselage which was painted light grey within
days after the arrival of the aircraft at Schiphol
Airport. The remaining eight aircraft were delivered bare-metal with a corrosion protection
coating, except for the rudder which has to be
painted prior to being installed and balanced,
and was completed in the full livery in the carrier's modern paint facilities.

The MD-11s carry the distinctive and attractive livery of the airline. The deep blue window
line separates the prominent light blue cabin
roof from a white cheatline below the windows.
The lower fuselage is kept in a light grey colour.
The KLM logo, existing of the letters 'KLM' and
a stylised crown, appear in white on the forward
cabin roof. The company logo, this time in light
blue, is also displayed on the white tail section,
on the inboard and outboard cowlings of the
wing mounted engines and on the winglets.

The name of the aircraft and the 'Royal Dutch
Airlines' title are shown at the front of the white
cheatline, while the title 'The Flying Dutchman'
is located in front of the last cabin door.

Since 1993 the 'Seal of Partnership' has
been applied on the cabin roof of all KLM aircraft to underline the co-operation with Northwest Airlines. During test flights with the first
aircraft, N6202D, registered PH-KCA upon
delivery, the 'Seal of Partnership' stickers were
omitted.

The third aircraft, PH-KCC, was delivered in
July 1994 at the time of the football world championship in the USA and a sticker for the Dutch
team was placed on the forward fuselage
showing a football player with a ball and the
word 'aanvallen' (attack).

KLM celebrated its 75th anniversary in October 1994 and McDonnell Douglas decorated

PH-KCE with a special birthday message when it was delivered the following month. Part of the corrosion protection coating had been removed and besides the light blue KLM logo and red '75 years' title, the sentence 'gefelici-eerd met het jubileum' (congratulations on the anniversary) and 'Douglas Aircraft' were applied on the bare metal surface. McDonnell Douglas also painted the complete tail section showing the full KLM logo.

On 27th June 1995 KLM made the inaugural flight from Amsterdam to Memphis, Tennessee. On this occasion the aircraft, PH-KCF was temporarily named 'Elvis 1' and a large photo of famous 'King of Rock & Roll' Elvis Presley was placed in front of the second port side door.

When the last KLM MD-11, PH-KCK, departed Long Beach for Amsterdam on 25th April 1997, it featured a large sticker with the emblem of the Anaheim 'Mighty Ducks' ice hockey team and the names of the flight crewmembers and the acceptance team. It had become a custom for the acceptance team to attend a sports game and have a dinner with McDonnell Douglas and supplier personnel on the occasion of each MD-11 delivery. The last delivery coincided with a play of the Anaheim 'Mighty Ducks' which explains the club's logo sticker on the aircraft. The appropriate callsign on the delivery flight was 'Mighty Duck'. For this flight the aircraft carried the name Christine Teszler, at the time assistant to former MD-11 Fleet Captain Rob Snoeks. It should be noted that one aircraft was leased to VASP and delivered directly to the Brazilian carrier upon completion at the Long Beach plant in November 1995. The aircraft, PP-SPM, returned to the KLM fleet in August 1998 and was re-registered PH-KCI.

All KLM MD-11s have been named after women famous in their fields:

PH-KCA *Amy Johnson*
        (British aviation pioneer)
PH-KCB *Maria Montessori* (Italian
        physician and educational)
PH-KCC *Marie Curie* (French chemist)
PH-KCD *Florence Nightingale* (English
        nurse and philanthropist)
PH-KCE *Audrey Hepburn*
        (American actress)
PH-KCF *Annie Romein* (Dutch historian)
PH-KCG *Maria Callas* (Greek/American
        soprano)
PH-KCH *Anna Pavlova* (Russian ballerina)
PH-KCI *Moeder Theresa/Mother Theresa*
        (Albanian religious)
PH-KCK *Ingrid Bergman* (Swedish actress)

Korean Air

Korean Air Lines started international services with two ex-Eastern Air Lines Boeing 720s in September 1969 and February 1970 respectively. The first 707 was delivered in 1971. Korean Air Lines received its first two 747s in 1973. The international network was expanded and at the time included Hong Kong, Honolulu, Los Angeles, Osaka and Paris.

The rapid growth of the Korean economy also influenced the expansion of the country's flag carrier. Further wide-body aircraft joined the fleet in 1975, the Airbus A300B4 and the McDonnell Douglas DC-10-30. A total of five aircraft of the latter type were operated by the airline. In 1984 the name of the airline was changed to Korean Air. The airline ordered five MD-11 passenger aircraft to replace the DC-10 fleet. Korean Air was an early customer for the new tri-jet and the PW 4460 powered aircraft were delivered between January 1991 and October 1992.

The cabin accommodated 20 first, 30 business and 223 economy class passengers. With an ever increasing fleet of passenger-747s and the need for additional cargo aircraft in the mid-nineties, the decision was taken to convert three MD-11s to the freighter role. HL7372 entered service as a freighter in June 1995, to be followed by HL7373 in March 1996 and HL7374 in August 1997. The two remaining passenger aircraft, HL7371 and HL7375, were converted to freighters in 1999.

The carrier lost one of its MD-11 freighter aircraft when HL7373 (f/n 490), en route from Shanghai Hongqiao Airport to Seoul, crashed after shortly after take-off from the Chinese airport on 15th April 1999.

Presently Korean Air operates scheduled passenger and cargo services to destinations in Asia, Australia, Europe, the Middle East and the USA. The carrier's wide-body fleet consists of A300-622, A330, 747, 747F, 777 and the MD-11F aircraft.

With the introduction of the name 'Korean Air' in 1984, a new livery was presented which is still eyecatching against the many 'white bodies'. A light blue upper fuselage with a silver cheatline and light grey underside form the remarkable paint scheme. The company's logo, known as the 'Taeguk', is on the tail section and also forms the 'O' in the dark blue 'Korean Air' title on the forward fuselage. To mark a tourist promotion campaign a 'Visit Korea '94' title and logo were placed on the upper aft fuselage. The converted MD-11 freighter aircraft display 'Korean Air Cargo' titling.

Douglas sent a special message on MD-11 PH-KCE on occasion of the 75th anniversary of the Dutch airline in 1994. A J Altevogt

MD-11 PH-KCF, temporarily named *Elvis 1*, is shown taxiing out at Amsterdam Schiphol Airport on the inaugural flight to Memphis, Tennessee, on 27th June 1995. Note the US and Dutch flags in the cockpit windows. KLM

LTU International Airways

This airline was founded as Lufttransport Union on 20th October 1955; the present name LTU was adopted in 1956. The first wide-body aircraft, the Lockheed L-1011 TriStar, arrived in 1973 and over the years a total of eleven aircraft of the type were in service with the German charter carrier. A fleet renewal programme included the purchase of four MD-11s which were delivered to the airline between December 1991 and March 1993. The plan further included the acquisition of A330-300, 757-200 and 767-300ER aircraft. The LTU MD-11s were powered by P&W PW 4460 engines. An all-economy cabin layout provided seating for 409 passengers. The aircraft were deployed on the airline's scheduled and charter services to Cancun, Fort Myers, Los Angeles, New York, Orlando, Miami, Montego Bay, Phoenix, Puerto Cana, Puerto Plata, Santo Domingo, Isla Margarita as well as to destinations within Europe and North Africa.

A major reorganisation was announced in July 1997 and the SAirGroup became a majority stockholder. The rationalisation included the sale of the four MD-11s to Swissair. The aircraft were delivered to the Swiss airline in October and November 1998. At the time of writing the airline's fleet consists of A320-200s, A330-300s, 757-200s and 767-300ERs.

The MD-11s sported the current livery of the airline. A broad white cheatline, extending from the front to the rear, was placed on the upper red fuselage. A red 'LTU' title was positioned on the cheatline aft of the cockpit windows. The tail section was red except for the front engine cowling which was kept in white and displayed a small black 'TriJet' title. A large black 'LTU' title appeared on the tail fin. The light grey wing engines featured a red 'LTU' and black 'TriJet' title.

Before departure from Long Beach, KLM's last MD-11, PH-KCK *Christine Teszler***, is shown with the KLM acceptance team and McDonnell Douglas West Ramp employees.**
McDonnell Douglas

Close up of the Anaheim *Mighty Ducks* **ice hockey team sticker with the names of the MD-11 crew, the acceptance and technical team on KLM's last MD-11, PH-KCK. Shown are amongst others: former MD-11 Fleet Captain Rob Snoeks (top row, third from left), Captain Jan Keesen (top row, fourth from right), First Officer Jan Louwerse (top row, third from right) and Flight Engineer Henk Pijpstra (bottom row left).**
McDonnell Douglas

Open house in hangar 11 at KLM's Schiphol base on 10th October 1999, celebrating the carrier's 80th anniversary. MD-11 PH-KCB *Maria Montessori* **is parked beside a Douglas DC-2 of the Dutch Dakota Association.** KLM

At high altitude, Korean Air HL 7372 shows impressive vapour trails. McDonnell Douglas

Korean Air HL 7374 displays 'Visit Korea '94' title and logo. Author's collection

The attractive paint scheme of Korean Air stands out amongst the increasing trend towards 'white-body' aircraft. MD-11F HL 7372 is shown with additional 'Cargo' title. Euro Aviation Slides

LTU took delivery of its first MD-11, D-AERB, in 1991. The carrier's four MD-11s were transferred to Swissair in 1998. McDonnell Douglas

Lufthansa Cargo

As well as being the first European airline to place the Boeing 747 into passenger service in 1970, Lufthansa was the launch customer for the 747 full freighter and the world's first airline to commence operations with the type in April 1972. Lufthansa Cargo AG became an independent company within the Lufthansa Group on 1st January 1995. The fleet at the time consisted of ten 747 freighter aircraft formerly operated by the parent company and five ex-German Cargo Services DC-8-73Fs. (See German Cargo Services) A 'thinking in new directions' programme not only include new services, products, partners, and alliances, but also a new aircraft in the fleet, the MD-11 Freighter.

The airline ordered eight aircraft of the type which were delivered during 1998 and 1999. Six options were exercised to become firm orders and these aircraft were delivered in 2000 and 2001.

The world's largest cargo carrier took delivery of the 200th and last MD-11 built, f/n 646, on 25th January 2001. The last MD-11 to leave the Long Beach site was handed over on 22nd February 2001. This actually was the penultimate aircraft (f/n 645) which had been used in flight testing of the Honeywell Pegasus 920 flight management system. During 2000, the Lufthansa Board of Directors approved the purchase of a further three passenger aircraft, to be converted to freighters for the cargo division. At the time of writing no decision had been taken from which carrier the aircraft will be purchased.

It is of interest to note that contrary to the usage of an initial of the manufacturer in the registration of Lufthansa aircraft (eg D-ABTA for Boeing, D-AIGH for Airbus Industrie and, formerly, D-ADCO for McDonnell Douglas aircraft), the MD-11 aircraft registrations include the letters LC for Lufthansa Cargo. The MD-11 freighters are powered by GE CF6-80C2D1F engines. In addition to the fourteen MD-11Fs Lufthansa Cargo currently operates ten Boeing 747-200Fs.

The carrier has its main hub at the Lufthansa Cargo Center, Frankfurt/Main Airport. The international hubs are located at Nairobi, Miami,

Moscow, Sao Paulo and Sharjah. Worldwide scheduled and charter freight flights are operated.

During a presentation ceremony at Long Beach on 25th June 1998 the first two MD-11 aircraft were delivered. In honour of Lufthansa officials involved in signing the MD-11 order, the Douglas Product Division had placed their names on the fuselages.D-ALCA carried the names of Wilhelm Althen, chairman of the executive board of Lufthansa Cargo, and Klaus Schlede, chairman of the Lufthansa supervisory board, respectively on the port and starboard side. The names of Karl-Heinz Steinke, head of finance Lufthansa Cargo, and Jean-Peter Jansen, former head of corporate purchasing and properties management of the Lufthansa Group, respectively appeared on the port and starboard side of the second aircraft, D-ALCB. These names were removed upon arrival at Frankfurt/Main Airport. When Lufthansa Cargo accepted the third aircraft on 13th August 1998, D-ALCC was temporarily named after the company's vice president of network development Karl-Ulrich Garnadt during the delivery ceremony. The names of the Dohse brothers, who piloted the aircraft to Germany, were placed on the fuselage of D-ALCF upon delivery on 26th August 1999. The name of Dirk Dohse, former head of Lufthansa Cargo flight operations, appeared on the port side while the name of his brother Bjoern, former MD-11 Fleet Captain, was displayed on the starboard side of the aircraft.

The carrier's livery is based on that of the Lufthansa passenger aircraft. A large dark blue 'Lufthansa Cargo' title appears on the forward white upper fuselage. The lower part of the

Lufthansa Cargo MD-11F D-ALCD was the fourth of fourteen aircraft of the type delivered to the German cargo giant. George Hall/Clay Lacy – Lufthansa Cargo

Artist's impression shows a special 'Service Revolution' livery, which unfortunately was not applied to an MD-11 aircraft in service. Lufthansa Cargo

The last MD-11 built, f/n 646, entered service with Lufthansa Cargo in January 2001. MD-11 D-ALCN is seen at Frankfurt/Main Airport. Author's collection

Opposite page:

The last MD-11 delivery. Lufthansa Cargo MD-11 D-ALCM taxiing in under it's own power behind the Boeing Color Guard for the delivery ceremony at Long Beach on 22nd Feburary, 2001. The banner in the foreground appropriately displays 'Celebrating 30 Years of Trijet Production . . . And Many More Years of Service in the Future'. The Boeing Company

On approach to Hong Kong's Kai Tak International Airport in 1996, World Airways N271WA displays the full livery of Malaysia Airlines. Harald M Helbig

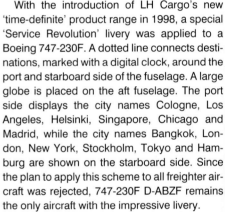

fuselage is kept in light grey. The dark blue tail displays the company logo, a stylised blue crane in a yellow circle. This motif in dark blue is repeated on the nose section. An 'MD-11 Freighter' title is placed behind the forward entry doors.

With the introduction of LH Cargo's new 'time-definite' product range in 1998, a special 'Service Revolution' livery was applied to a Boeing 747-230F. A dotted line connects destinations, marked with a digital clock, around the port and starboard side of the fuselage. A large globe is placed on the aft fuselage. The port side displays the city names Cologne, Los Angeles, Helsinki, Singapore, Chicago and Madrid, while the city names Bangkok, London, New York, Stockholm, Tokyo and Hamburg are shown on the starboard side. Since the plan to apply this scheme to all freighter aircraft was rejected, 747-230F D-ABZF remains the only aircraft with the impressive livery.

With the introduction of MD-11 freight services to the Far East in 1998, the area marketing office published a poster showing an artist's rendering of a MD-11F in a similar livery. The 'Service Revolution' scheme connected the cities of Bangkok, Penang, Singapore, Manila and Sydney.

Malaysia Airlines

Malaysian Airline System (MAS) commenced international services to Amsterdam, Frankfurt, London and Zürich in 1974, using Boeing 707 equipment. The first wide-body in the airline's fleet was the DC-10-30 of which three were delivered by the manufacturer between August 1976 and February 1981. During 1990 another three -30s were acquired. Over the years additional -30CFs were leased from World Airways for the cargo division MAShargo. 1982 marked the arrival of the carrier's first 747s. In October 1987 MAS introduced a new corporate identity which besides a new livery included the name change to Malaysia Airlines, although the abbreviation MAS remained the same.

The strong ties with World Airways led to the introduction of the MD-11. The first aircraft three passenger and one freighter versions were leased from the US carrier in 1994.

The Airbus A330 was chosen as a replacement for the DC-10 and a total of ten aircraft were delivered in 1995. After the last of four aircraft was transferred to World Airways, MAS officially ceased DC-10 operations on 8th March 1996.

International destinations within Asia, to Australia, Europe and the USA are served by a large fleet of A330s, 777-200s and 747-400s. The MASkargo division's fleet consists of two 737-300Fs, two 747-200Fs and one 747/300F.

The paint scheme, introduced in 1987, features an all-white upper half with a twin red and blue cheatline which widens at the tail section. The name 'Malaysia' appears on the upper fuselage, while the 'Kalantan Kite' motive is retained on the tail fin and winglets, if mounted. In case of cargo operations, a 'MASkargo' title is displayed on the cabin roof. The livery was also carried by the MD-11s during long term leases. During short term lease periods, the 'Malaysia' or 'MASkargo' titles and 'Kalantan Kite' logo were simply placed on the totally white fuselage and tail fin of the World Airways aircraft.

Mandarin Airlines MD-11 B-152 on approach to Hong Kong's Kai Tak International Airport. Reiner Geerdts

Artist's impression of a Martinair Holland MD-11CF displaying the aircraft with a 'Martinair Holland' title and both forward and rear cargo door. McDonnell Douglas

Martinair Holland was the first carrier to take delivery of the MD-11CF. The first Convertible Freighter built is shown with test flight registration N90187. McDonnell Douglas

Martinair MD-11CF PH-MCS with '40 years in the air' title. Author's collection

The Dutch carrier also operates two full-freight aircraft. MD-11F PH-MCU is shown here at Amsterdam Schiphol Airport.
Nico G J Roozen

In celebration of its 40th anniversary, the carrier also applied the '40 years in the air' title on the MD-11 freighter aircraft.
Nico G J Roozen

still is the company's official name, the title 'Holland' was dropped from the aircraft in 1995.

In 1973 the first of four DC-10-30CFs ordered was delivered. The decision to select the Convertible Freighter version permitted the carrier to operate in the lucrative cargo field.

Further wide-body aircraft were acquired; two Airbus A310-203s (one full passenger and one combi aircraft) arrived in 1984, followed by the first 747-21AC (SCD) in February 1987.

The A310s were replaced by Boeing 767-31A (ER) aircraft and a further modernisation of the fleet was put in place when Martinair chose the MD-11 as the replacement for its remaining three DC-10s. Based on its more than positive experience with the DC-10-30CF, Martinair was the first carrier to order the MD-11CF offered by McDonnell Douglas and so became the launch customer for the Convertible Freighter version of the aircraft. The first of four MD-11CFs was delivered in December 1994. If used in the passenger configuration, 24 Star business and 344 tourist class seats are available in the wide-body cabin.

With the continuing expansion in cargo operations Martinair took delivery of a MD-11F in October 1996 while a second full freighter aircraft joined the fleet in December 1998.

Unlike parent company KLM, Martinair selected the PW4462 engine for their MD-11 fleet.

In addition to the four MD-11CFs and two MD-11Fs, the airline currently operates two 757s, six 767s and three 747s. Martinair conducts passenger charter flights to destinations in Asia, Canada, the Caribbean, the Mediterranean, South America and the USA. Cargo flights are flown to worldwide destinations.

The carrier's livery shows a white upper fuselage with a wide red cheatline extending from the nose to the tail section and a bare metal lower fuselage. A large black 'Martinair' title is positioned above the passenger windows. An additional 'Cargo' title is added on the freighter aircraft. At the time of negotiations between the carrier and McDonnell Douglas for the acquisition of the MD-11 the 'Martinair Holland' title was still in use, as can be seen on the artist's impression. The rendering shows the aircraft with both a front and aft cargo door. This proposal from Martinair was presented to the manufacturer but was rejected because of the weight penalty for the added aft cargo door.

Mandarin Airlines

Mandarin was established on 1st June 1991. Operations to Australia started in October 1991 with a single Boeing 747SP, on lease from China Airlines. The carrier became wholly owned by China Airlines in December 1992. With the extension of the network, eg Amsterdam, Vancouver and Zürich, further CAL MD-11 and 747 aircraft were leased. The first MD-11 entered service in July 1993 with four of the type being operated from November 1995 onwards. One Mandarin MD-11 was lost in an accident at Hong Kong's International Airport on 22nd August 1999 while operating a flight for parent company China Airlines. (see China Airlines.)

On 8th August 1999 Mandarin Airlines was officially merged with Formosa Airlines taking over domestic services previously provided by the latter carrier. Following the merger the three MD-11 aircraft were returned to the parent company and at the time of writing Mandarin operates one 747-400 and international services from Taipei to Chiang-Mai, Kuantan, Saipan and Yangon.

Mandarin's livery is based on a white upper and light grey lower fuselage. A dark and a light blue cheatline, respectively above and below the passenger windows, extend from the front to the rear of the aircraft. The dual lines are also placed on the winglets. The 'Mandarin' title in English and Chinese appears above the cheatlines on the upper fuselage. The company's emblem is the gyrfalcon. The graceful golden 'bird' logo is placed on the dark blue tail fin in the form of a stylised 'M'.

Martinair Holland

In May 1958 J Martin Schroeder founded his own airline Martin's Luchtvervoer Maatschappij which started operations under the name Martin Air Charter (MAC). In 1964, KLM acquired 25% of Martin's Air Charter while other shares were sold to Koninklijke Nedlloyd NV (Royal Nedlloyd NV). Over the years the stakes in Martinair became equally divided between the latter companies.

In 1968 the name of the company was changed to Martinair Holland. Although this

and surrounding structure. The first MD-11, PH-MCP, was also the first newly delivered aircraft without the former 'Holland' title on the fuselage. The red company logo is placed on the tail fin and a black 'Martinair' title on the tail engine. A smaller logo and title are repeated on the wing engines and in case of the MD-11 aircraft also on the winglets. All aircraft proudly carry the McDonnell Douglas logo at the top of the tail fin. Martinair celebrated its 40th anniversary in May 1998 and an appropriate '40 years in the air' title was placed on the forward upper fuselage of all aircraft.

Minerve

This French airline was founded in 1975 as a helicopter operator and in 1982 commenced charter flights to worldwide destinations, also serving the French colonies in the Pacific and the West Indies with two former JAL DC-8-50s. Over the years the fleet rapidly expanded and in 1991 consisted of MD-83, DC-8-62, DC-8-73, DC-10 and 747 aircraft.

The carrier had placed an order for two PW4460-powered MD-11s in September 1988 and for a further example in June 1989. The aircraft were planned to be delivered during 1991, 1993 and 1994 respectively and were destined to replace the DC-8s and DC-10s on the carrier's long range routes. Serial numbers assigned for the aircraft were 48481 (built for American Airlines), 48526 and 48625 (last two serial numbers not built). However, on 1st January 1992 Minerve merged into AOM Air Outre Mer, which then became known as AOM French Airlines.

The artist's impression shows an MD-11 in the original Minerve colour scheme. A large red 'Minerve' title and four cheatlines in burgundy, white, blue and red on a white fuselage formed the first livery.

The tail displayed the white goddess Minerve in a red and blue circle. It should be noted that the artist's impression does not show the quadruple cheatlines on the wing mounted engines as well as the 'Minerve' title as they were displayed on the DC-10s operated by the carrier at the time.

The artist's impression shows a Minerve MD-11 in the airline's early livery. McDonnell Douglas

While on lease to Monarch Airlines, World Airways MD-11 N277WA displayed a simple black title and logo of the British charter carrier on the upper white fuselage and tail fin. Author's collection

Digitally enhanced photo of how a Nigeria Airways MD-11 would look in the airline's former livery. Michael F McLaughlin

World Airways MD-11CF N275WA shows a large 'Philippines' title. Collection Eddy Gual

Monarch

British charter carrier Monarch started operations to European destinations in 1968. Charter flights to the USA commenced in 1988. In March 1996 the airline acquired the first McDonnell Douglas product, a DC-10-30. This aircraft was delivered new to Zambia Airways in 1984 and remained with that carrier until it ceased operations in 1994. The aircraft is presently used on the London-Gatwick and Manchester routes to Orlando, Florida, Montego Bay, Jamaica and the Far East.

The present network includes destinations in the Mediterranean, Egypt, East Africa, the Caribbean, the USA and Asia. Furthermore, ski charter flights are carried out to Munich, Switzerland and Austria in winter.

Today, the long range fleet consists of the sole DC-10, four Airbus A300-605Rs and two A330-243s.

To add capacity for its long range operations, Monarch leased a World Airways MD-11. The aircraft, N273WA, accommodating 407 economy passengers, entered service on 21st May 1998 on the Manchester - Sanford, Florida route and was returned to World Airways on 14th October 1998. At that time it was replaced by sistership N277WA. In 1999 Monarch again used a World Airways MD-11, this time N278WA. Unlike the other Monarch aircraft with the striking broad yellow and black cheatlines on a white fuselage, the leased aircraft carried only the black 'Monarch' title on the forward fuselage and the crowned 'M' company logo on the tail fin.

Nigeria Airways

Nigeria Airways acquired the first of three Boeing 707s in May 1971, entering service on the Lagos-London route. Route expansion led to the purchase of the DC-10-30; the first aircraft was delivered in October 1976 while the second example was added to the long range fleet in October the following year. A third Series 30 was delivered in July 1989. For use on its dense African network the airline bought four Airbus A310-200s which were delivered during 1983 and 1984.

Nigeria Airways ordered a single MD-11 passenger aircraft for delivery in December 1991.

Philippines MD-11CF N276WA displays a sticker commemorating the 100th anniversary of the Republic of the Philippines. Collection Eddy Gual

At Frankfurt, Philippines MD-11ER N278WA is shown with a small 'Philippines' title. M Kaspczak

Sabena MD-11 OO-CTS in the carrier's 1993 paint scheme. McDonnell Douglas

'Flying together with Swissair' titling, as shown on OO-CTS, marks the partnership with the Swiss carrier. Nicky Scherrer – VIP Photoservice

Financial problems however forced the airline to reduce costs and to suspend unprofitable routes. This resulted in a fleet reduction and also in the cancellation of the MD-11 order.

International flights are operated with the sole DC-10 aircraft. A British Airways 747-200, in the new Nigeria Airways livery, was leased from and jointly operated by the British carrier from December 1999 until August 2000.

Being the national carrier, the colours of the national flag are reflected in the former livery as shown in the digitally enhanced photo. The white upper fuselage had two green cheatlines with a green 'Nigeria Airways' title, the lower fuselage finish was natural metal. The company logo, a large green letter 'N' encompassing a white circle with a green falcon, appeared on the white tail fin.

Philippine Airlines / Philippines

Philippine Airlines (PAL) started international services across the Pacific with a newly acquired Douglas DC-8-53 in June 1962. Further examples of the four-engined jetliner were bought or leased and in 1969 the airline began European services to Amsterdam, Frankfurt and Rome. PAL commenced DC-10-30 operations with two aircraft leased from KLM in 1974, replacing the DC-8s on the European flights. Two new -30s were delivered in 1976 and 1980 respectively. In 1986 Boeing 747s started replacing the DC-10s.

To supplement the PAL long range fleet, World Airways operated several MD-11 aircraft in 1996 and 1997 on the airline's international routes which at the time included Frankfurt, Paris and Vancouver, amongst others. The airline's current long distance fleet consists of eight A330-300s, two A340-300s and four Boeing 747-400s.

The present Philippines livery was introduced in 1987. It features a pure white fuselage with a boldfaced dark blue 'Philippines' title and the company logo above the forward passenger windows. The colours of the national flag, red, white and blue are represented in a stylised form on the tail fin. The blue section on the fin is highlighted by a superimposed yellow rising sun. During their deployment with PAL the World Airways MD-11s carried the full livery of the Philippine airline. The 'Philippines' title was applied in a thin or boldface lettering. A special sticker '1896-1996', commemorating the 100th anniversary of the Republic of the Philippines, was placed underneath the cockpit windows.

Sabena

The Belgian national carrier's first wide-body aircraft, the 747 and the DC-10, entered service in 1971 and 1973 respectively. Sabena was the first European carrier to introduce the DC-10-30CF, taking delivery of the first aircraft in September 1973. Another four were ordered and by 1980 the airline operated all five -30CFs. The last -30CF originally owned was sold in November 1994, however the airline leased two Lufthansa -30s the same year to supplement other wide-bodies in the fleet. The carrier officially ceased DC-10 operations when the leasing contract of the last Lufthansa aircraft expired in April 1997. On 4th May 1995 Sabena and Swissair signed a co-operation agreement and following approval of the agreement by the European Commission in July of that year the SAir Group acquired 49.5% of Sabena's shares.

At the end of October 1997 Sabena and City Bird agreed to co-operate in the operation of scheduled flights between Brussels and Johannesburg, Nairobi, New York, Montreal and Sao Paulo. These flights were operated with two City Bird MD-11s, all seats of which were sold to Sabena as a wet lease agreement. City Bird MD-11s OO-CTS and OO-CTC entered service in April and May 1998 respectively. The aircraft had a 48 business and 249 economy class seating configuration. From the start of the 2000 winter flight schedule one MD-11 was operated on the Brussels - Bamako, Mali - Conakry, Guinea - Brussels route. The other aircraft was used on the Johannesburg route. Sabena's own long range fleet currently consists of A330s and A340s.

The former Sabena livery, based on a completely white scheme, was introduced in 1993. A huge 'Sabena' title in a very light shade of blue was accompanied by a small dark blue 'Sabena' title on the fuselage. Changes in the tail section included the restyled letter 'S' in a dark blue circle on the fin and the display of the Belgian and European Community flags on the tail engine (DC-10 aircraft at the time). To emphasise the partnership with Swissair, 'Flying together with Swissair' titles were applied on the rear fuselage at the end of 1995.

Both City Bird MD-11s took on the basic colour scheme as described above. Shortly after being placed into service 'Flying together with Swissair' titles were added. In June 1998 an additional 'operated by City Bird' title was placed under the cockpit windows of both aircraft. Sabena celebrated its 75th anniversary in 1998 and a stylised '75' 1923-1998 sticker was applied on all aircraft. In December 1998 Sabena introduced a new paint scheme. The huge 'Sabena' lettering on the fully white fuselage is dark blue. The 'Sabena-S' is placed in a white and blue open circle on the dark blue tail. The 'S' logo is repeated on the wing engines which are also kept in dark blue.

On aircraft equipped with winglets, these are decorated with the 'L'oiseau de Ciel' ('Skybird') painted for the airline by Belgian artist Magritte. As a member of the *Quali*flyer Group, Sabena adapted the 'blue belly' livery in early 2001. This livery was however not applied on the MD-11 aircraft. The leases for both aircraft were terminated in March 2001 and the aircraft returned to City Bird.

Artist's impression of an MD-11F in Saudi Arabian Airlines' former paint scheme. McDonnell Douglas

Saudi Arabian MD-11F HZ-ANA in the current, very attractive, livery. McDonnell Douglas

World Airways conducted Hadj flights with MD-11 N272WA in a basic Aer Lingus livery during 1999. The Starboard side displays Arabic titles. Exavia

The port side of MD-11 N272WA with English titles. Exavia

Saudi Arabian Airlines

In 1962 Saudi Arabian Airlines purchased two Boeing 720s, thus becoming the first airline in the Middle East to operate commercial jet airliners. The route network expanded vastly and the first two Boeing 707-320s were delivered in 1968. With the adoption of a new livery in 1971 the company name 'Saudia' was adopted. The first wide-body aircraft ordered by Saudia was the Lockheed L-1011 TriStar which entered service in 1975; a total of 18 of the type saw service. The airline started Boeing 747 services in 1977. During the 1980s and 1990s cargo flights were operated with leased Douglas DC-8-63Fs/CFs and Boeing 747s.

During 1995 the airline signed orders for 61 new aircraft from McDonnell Douglas and Boeing. These included 29 MD-90-30 passenger and four MD-11F freighter aircraft. The first of each aircraft type (MD-11F, MD-90, 747-400 and 777-200) ordered were presented to the carrier during a ceremony at Everett, Washington, on 22nd December 1997. The remaining three MD-11Fs were delivered during December 1997 and January 1998. The carrier selected the GE CF6-80C2D1F powerplant for the MD-11Fs.

emblem of a Swiss canton which was placed on the forward section of the polished belly below the dark brown cheatline. In 1991 a special sticker with a 'growing' Swiss cross and '700th Anniversary of the Swiss Confederation' was applied on all aircraft alongside the 'Swissair' title to commemorate the event.

In May 1994 Swissair introduced a new livery. MD-11 HB-IWN *Basel-Land*, delivered in August of that year was the first MD-11 to carry the new colour scheme. The fully white upper fuselage features a large red 'Swissair' title while the lower part is kept in bare metal finish. The canton's emblem is placed on the white fuselage below the forward passenger windows. No changes were made to the livery of the tail section. Starting September 2000, Swissair also applied the company's Swiss flag logo on the winglets of several MD-11 and A330 aircraft. However this application was short-lived and disappeared with the introduction of a new livery in October.

On 24th October 2000, the first Swissair aircraft, an Airbus A321, entered service with the new *Quali*flyer Group livery. This paint scheme includes a blue lower fuselage with an additional white 'The *Quali*flyer Group' title and logo. In addition to the Swissair and Crossair aircraft, all aircraft of the other *Quali*flyer Group members (Sabena, AOM French Airlines, TAP Air Portugal, amongst others) should eventually carry the blue belly paint scheme.

In order to conduct scheduled flights to Taiwan and avoid political complications with the People's Republic of China, Swissair introduced the Swissair Asia service. On 7th April 1995 the first scheduled flight from Zürich to Taipei, Taiwan by Swissair Asia took place. Currently two MD-11s carry the Swissair Asia colour scheme. On both the former and current livery a large light grey 'Asia' title was/is added to the red 'Swissair' title on the upper fuselage. The tail fin displays a white Chinese character with the meaning 'Switzerland' and 'happiness'. On the Swissair Asia aircraft the canton emblems are omitted.

There were paint scheme divergences on occasion of two special events. On the 11th and 12th October 1994, MD-11 HB-IWG *Valais/Wallis* transported the Munich Philharmonic Orchestra on a special flight (SR2044) from Zürich to Taipei, Taiwan. The return flight (SR2045) was routed Abu Dhabi-Munich. For political reasons – the relations between Taiwan and China – the white cross was removed from the tail section.

In June 1998 the Swiss carrier transported the Argentinean delegation for the football world championship in Paris, France from Buenos Aires via Sao Paulo and Geneva to Paris. The aircraft involved in the operation was MD-11 HB-IWL *Appenzell a.Rh*. On this occasion the red 'Swissair' title was replaced by a small black 'Argentina' title, the Argentinean flag and a football. HB-IWG and HB-IWN are both currently wearing SR Asia livery.

HB-IWA	*Obwalden*
HB-IWB	*Graubünden*
HB-IWC	*Schaffhausen*
HB-IWD	*Thurgau*
HB-IWE	*Nidwalden*
HB-IWF	*Vaud*
HB-IWG	*(Valais/Wallis)*
HB-IWH	*St Gallen*
HB-IWI	*Uri*
HB-IWK	*Fribourg*
HB-IWL	*Appenzell a.Rh.*
HB-IWM	*Jura*
HB-IWN	*(Basel-Land)*
HB-IWO	*Schwyz*
HB-IWP	*Basel-Land*
HB-IWQ	*Valais/Wallis*
HB-IWR	*Bern*
HB-IWS	*Ticino*
HB-IWT	*Basel*
HB-IWU	*Luzern*

MD-11 HB-IWN displays the Swissair Asia livery based on the 1994 paint scheme. Rolf Wallner

The Swissair Asia logo was applied to the winglets in late 2000. Swissair Asia MD-11 HB–IWN is seen at Zurich Airport. Rolf Wallner

For the special Munich Philharmonic Orchestra flight the Swiss cross was removed on MD-11 HB-IWG *Valais/Wallis*. Rolf Wallner

The Argentinean delegation was transported on MD-11 HB-IWL *Appenzell a.Rh.* in 1998. Special stickers were applied above the forward passenger windows. Rolf Wallner

Thai Airways International

During 1975 and 1976 THAI leased three DC-10-30s from KLM, UTA and Air Afrique to replace the DC-8s operated on the long haul routes. The following year the airline took delivery of the first two of its own -30s. These two aircraft were sold to SAS in February 1987 and leased back by the airline until the delivery of two -30ERs in December of that year. Another of the type joined the fleet in May 1988. With a surge in air travel to Thailand and around the world, the airline made the decision to upgrade its fleet with more wide-body aircraft. The first Airbus A300B4s were delivered at the end of 1977 and the 747 was introduced two years later.

On 1st April 1988, THAI and its parent company, TAC, merged into a single airline bringing together domestic and international operations. THAI was formally registered as Thai Airways International Public Company Limited on 20th May 1994.

THAI was a launch customer of the MD-11 and ordered four aircraft to replace the DC-10s in the airline's fleet. The first aircraft was delivered in June 1991. Although an order for a further three aircraft had been placed at the time, the airline decided against an expansion of the tri-jet fleet and the aircraft were never built. The MD-11s are equipped with GE CF6-80C2D1F engines. The cabin is configured to seat 10 Royal first, 42 Royal executive and 233 economy passengers.

THAI's current wide-body fleet consists of A300-600s, A330-300s, 777-200s/300s, 747-300s/400s and the MD-11s. The international network includes destinations in Australia, Europe, the Far East, the Middle East, New Zealand and the USA.

THAI's current attractive colour scheme designed by Walter Landor and Associates was introduced in 1975. Based on a pure white fuselage, two dark purple cheatlines are separated by a light purple one and accentuated by gold pinstriping. The cheatlines flow out of a stylised orchid. The same motif is superimposed on the tail section followed by the 'Thai' title. As the carrier became a member of the Star Alliance in 1997, the Star Alliance logo has since been placed between the cockpit windows and forward doors.

In 1998 the Tourism Authority of Thailand started an 'Amazing Thailand' tourist promotion campaign. The campaign's logo, consisting of a stylised golden eye and the years 1998 and 1999 on a black background, was added on the upper fuselage of the Thai aircraft.

To commemorate the 72nd birthday of the country's monarch, King Bhumibol Adulyadej, on 5th December 1999, two aircraft, 747-400 HS-TGJ and A330-300 HS-TEK were completely repainted with a graphic rendition of the 'Suphannahong', the Royal Barge. All other aircraft in the THAI fleet displayed a 'The King's 72nd Celebration' title and royal emblem on the upper fuselage. It is of interest to note that in Chinese culture significant birthdays occur on cycles of 12 years with the sixth cycle, the 72nd, being the most important.

HS-TMD *Phra Nakhon*
HS-TME *Pathumwan*
HS-TMF *Phichit*
HS-TMG *Nakhon Sawan*

TransAer International Airways

This Irish carrier was founded in 1991 as Translift Airways and started operations in February 1992 with DC-8 equipment. In May 1997 the name was changed to TransAer International Airways. The airline operated ad hoc charters and wet-leased aircraft for tour operators and for charter as well as scheduled airlines throughout Europe and the USA, but ceased operations in October 2000. At that time the fleet consisted of eleven Airbus A320 and seven A300B4 aircraft.

A World Airways MD-11 was leased to the airline from 9th July until 1st September 1999. The aircraft, N278WA, was operated in an all white colour scheme without any titles.

UPS Airlines

In 1987 United Parcel Service received authorisation from the FAA to operate its own aircraft, thus becoming an official airline. Until then various carriers such as Evergreen International Airlines, Merlin Express, Orion Air, Ryan International Airlines and Interstate Airlines had

The striking livery of Thai Airways International on MD-11 HS-TME *Pathumwan*. McDonnell Douglas

MD-11 HS-TMD *Phra Nakhon* **with 'Amazing Thailand' sticker above the rear passenger windows.** Harald M Helbig

At Munich, MD-11 HS-TMG *Nakhon Sawan* **displays a 'The King's 72nd Celebration' title on the cabin roof.** Harald M Helbig

UPS Airlines MD-11 freighter aircraft will feature the carrier's classic 'Pullman' brown livery with the golden UPS logo on the tail fin and winglets. UPS Creative Media

USAFRICA Airways

USAfrica Airways was founded in 1993 as an international scheduled passenger and cargo airline. Although it was originally planned to start services with DC-10-30 equipment leased from Continental Airlines, operations with an MD-11, leased from American Airlines, commenced on 3rd June 1994 on the carrier's sole route Washington Dulles International Airport - Johannesburg, via Cape Verde Islands for a fuel stop. During its short period of existence USAfrica deployed two American Airlines MD-11s, N1757A and N1758B, which were configured with 238 seats in three classes of service. The aircraft were returned to American Airlines when operations were suspended on 3rd February 1995. USAfrica filed for Chapter 11 bankruptcy protection on 8th February 1995. Although a restart was planned, the carrier did not resume operations.

The MD-11s sported a natural metal fuselage with a red cheatline and a large white-outlined dark blue 'USAFRICA' title on the forward upper section. The tail and wing engines were kept in a light grey colour. The dark blue tail section displayed the red company logo which was also placed on the dark blue winglets. During their short time of deployment with USAfrica both aircraft carried the name of the airline's Chief Operating Officer, Edward R Bolton, under the cockpit windows.

VARIG – Viacao Aérea Rio-Grandense, SA

In 1960 VARIG introduced a scheduled jet-service to New York with Boeing 707 equipment; this aircraft type which would remain the backbone on long range services for years to come. The Brazilian carrier started DC-10 operations with three -30s in 1974. Further examples were acquired and a total of 12 were in the fleet by 1981. VARIG withdrew the six remaining DC-10 passenger aircraft from service in March 1999

In 1986 the airline became one of the launch customers for the MD-11 by ordering six of the type; these were delivered in 1991, 1992 and 1993. The fleet further expanded when three former Garuda aircraft were added in December 1996 and April and September 1997 respectively. A further six aircraft, formerly operated by the Indonesian carrier, were leased from Boeing Capital Corporation in 1998 and 1999. This number includes three

operated flights on behalf of UPS. An extensive fleet of 727s, DC-8-71s and -73s, 757-24APFs and 747-123s was operated from the start. The carrier was the launch customer for both the 757-24APF (All Parcel Freighter) and the 767-300F, the latter having entered service in 1995. UPS ordered 30 Airbus A300-622Fs in 1998 for increased airlift on domestic routes and the first aircraft were delivered in 2000. A further 60 aircraft of the type were ordered in January 2001.

On 2nd November 2000 the carrier announced that it had selected the MD-11 as its next long-range wide-body jet freighter. Over the next four years, UPS will acquire 13 preowned MD-11s from Boeing, to be delivered between 2001 and 2004. The 13 aircraft include ten former-JAL and three ex-VASP MD-11s. The agreement also includes options for 22 additional MD-11s. If exercised, the optional aircraft will be delivered between 2005 and 2010.

Under terms of the agreement, Boeing will convert the aircraft from passenger aircraft to freighters. Boeing Airplane Services and UPS selected ST Aviation Services (SASCO), Singa-

pore, to modify the thirteen aircraft. In addition to the freighter conversions, UPS also has chosen SASCO to perform concurrent maintenance work on the aircraft.

UPS's main air hub is located at Louisville International Airport, Kentucky. Serving more than 200 countries and territories, UPS is one of the world's largest express carriers and package delivery companies. The current 238 aircraft fleet consists of A300-622Fs; 727Fs, Cs and QCs; 757-24APFs; 747-100/200Fs; 767-300Fs and DC-8-71/73Fs.

The livery of the UPS aircraft is based on a white fuselage with a Pullman railroad brown cheatline flowing up and encompassing the tail section. The corporate identity dates back to the late 1920s when all UPS vehicles were painted the now-familiar brown colour. A large brown 'United Parcel Service' title is placed on the upper fuselage. The carrier's golden logo, consisting of the letters 'ups' within a shield and a ribboned parcel, decorates the tail. At the time of writing UPS had not as yet taken delivery of an MD-11 freighter.

MD-11ER aircraft. GE CF6-80C2D1F engines power all aircraft in the fleet. With the arrival of the last two -11ERs, two regular -11s were returned to leasing company GECAS. After conversion to freighters these aircraft entered service with Gemini Air Cargo. The MD-11s offer a 12 first, 49 business and 221 tourist class seating arrangement. Besides offering an extensive domestic and South American network, the airline provides scheduled passenger and cargo services to North and Central America, Europe, South Africa and the Far East.

The wide-body fleet currently comprises ten MD-11s, three MD-11ERs, 12 767-200ERs/300ERs and five 747-300s. The VARIG Cargo division has a fleet of five 727 freighters and three DC-10-30Fs.

The former livery dates back to 1955 and was only changed once, in 1960, when the Icarus motif on the tail was substituted by a mariner's compass. A broad light blue cheatline with twin white pinstripes started at the nose and extended to the rear of the aircraft. A large 'VARIG' title was displayed over the wings on the white upper fuselage which also showed the black 'Brazil' title and national flag at the front section. A small blue Icarus logo in a white circle was located on the blue cheatline between the aft cockpit window and forward entry door.

The white and blue compass, together with a small black 'VARIG' title were placed on the tail fin while a red 'MD-11 Intercontinental' title was shown on the tail engine. The lower fuselage was kept in the bare metal finish.

In October 1996 VARIG unveiled a new livery, replacing the still-attractive former scheme. This livery features an overall white fuselage with deep blue lower section. The engines and the tail – which displays a redesigned golden and white compass logo – are also deep blue. An elegantly written, golden 'Brasil' title is added to the blue 'VARIG' lettering on the upper fuselage. In 1998 VARIG joined the Star Alliance (other members at the time were Air Canada, Lufthansa, SAS, Thai and United) and, additionally, the logo of the alliance has since been placed between the cockpit windows and the forward doors.

Prior to the football world championship in 1998, VARIG MD-11 PP-VPP obtained a striking, special livery. Exavia

VASP PP-SOZ was the second MD-11 delivered to the Brazilian carrier. The aircraft is now operated by VARIG. McDonnell Douglas

On occasion of the inaugural service to Osaka in 1996, MD-11 PP-SPK was christened Kasato Maru**, the name of the ship on which the first Japanese emigrants arrived in Brazil in 1908.** Author's collection

Commemorating the 500th anniversary of the discovery of Brazil, all VASP aircraft gained a special sticker on the nose section. Exavia

Prior to the 1998 football world championship in France MD-11 PP-VPP received a special colour scheme.The colours of the national flag were represented by a broad green and yellow diagonal band across the fuselage, separating the white front and deep blue rear sections. Beside the three emblems of the CBD (Confederacao Brasileira Desportos – Confederation of Brazilian Sports) and the emblem of the CBF (Confederacao Brasileira de Futebol – Confederation of Brazilian Football) below the forward passenger windows, the title 'Transportadora official da Selecao Brasileira de Futebol' (Official carrier of the Brazilian football team) was applied. Four golden and four deep blue stars were placed over the CBD and CBF emblems respectively.

The four stars and years, sweeping up from the belly into the tail section, indicate the football world championship victories of the Brazilian team: 1958 in Sweden, 1962 in Chile, 1970 in Mexico and 1994 in the USA. It is of interest to note that a 737-3K9, PP-VOZ, was also decorated in this colourful scheme.

VASP – Viacao Aérea Sao Paulo, SA

VASP was founded in 1933 and was one of the first airlines to offer scheduled services. The airline over the years developed into the nation's second largest and, following privatisation, started its first international service in 1990.

For that purpose the airline leased two DC-10-30s which were returned to the leasing companies in November 1992. The first two MD-11s arrived in February and March 1992 and over the years the fleet grew to a total of nine examples of the type. All aircraft were equipped with GE CF6-80C2D1F engines. The airline selected a 325 passengers seat configuration consisting

of ten first, 21 executive and 294 economy class seats.

MD-11 PP-SPM was delivered to KLM as PH-KCI in November 1995 and sub-leased to the Brazilian carrier the following month. The aircraft was returned to KLM in August 1998.

Financial difficulties resulted in the return of the first four MD-11s to the leasing company in February 2000 and the suspension of international destinations New York, Toronto and Los Angeles. The carrier ceased MD-11 operations when the remaining four MD-11s were withdrawn from use in late 2000. Currently a fleet of 737s and A-300s is operated. The sole DC-10-30, PP-SFB, is sub-leased to subsidiary Ecuatoriana, Ecuador.

The colour scheme features a low twin blue and black cheatline, from nose to tail, separating the white upper from the bare metal lower fuselage. Large blue 'VASP' titles are displayed between the second entry and the overwing door. The tail section, which is also kept in the blue colour, displays the stylised white company bird motif. The white motif is also placed on the blue winglets while the light grey engines show the same in blue colour.

On 27th 1996 July VASP introduced its new Sao Paulo - Los Angeles - Osaka service. The aircraft on the inaugural flight, MD-11 PP-SPK, was christened *Kasato Maru*, the name of the ship on which the first Japanese emigrants arrived in Brazil on 18th June 1908.

Celebrating the 500th anniversary of the discovery of Brazil by Portuguese explorer Pedro Alvares Cabral in 1500, a '500' year sticker together with a yellow and green 'sail' logo was applied behind the cockpit windows in 1999 to mark the occasion.

PP-SFD *Nossa Senhora Aparecida*
PP-SPK *Kasato Maru*, renamed *Luis Eduardo Magalhaes*
PP-SOW *Armando Sales de Oliveira*

VIASA – Venezolana Internacional de Aviacion SA

On 1st January 1961 VIASA was established to take over international flight operations from Avensa and Linea Aeropostal Venezolana. The airline started operations with a fleet of three Convair 880s which were replaced by two new DC-8-50s and two new DC-8-63s. The airline chose another long range McDonnell Douglas product to replace the DC-8 fleet; the first DC-10-30 was accepted by VIASA in April 1974. A total of five Series -30s were delivered by the manufacturer while a further example was leased from Iberia.

The international network included destinations in Europe, the USA and South America. During the Canadian winter season charter flights were flown to Toronto and Vancouver. The carrier ordered two MD-11 passenger aircraft which were to be delivered during 1992 Serial numbers 48524 and 48525 were assigned however, the order was cancelled and the aircraft were not built. In 1996 the fleet consisted of seven 727s and four DC-10-30s. Facing heavy losses and a lack of cash flow, VIASA was forced to cease operations on 23rd January 1997 and was liquidated in March 1997.

The artist's impression shows the MD-11 in a slightly revised version of the colour scheme used by the airline between 1979 and 1996 Instead of a single dark blue cheatline, triple cheatlines in different shades of blue, which divide the white cabin roof from the bare metal lower fuselage, are shown. The orange 'Viasa' and dark blue 'Venezuela' titles were applied above the passenger windows. A white 'Viasa' title was displayed on the orange tail engine

Fuse number	FSN	McDD config	McDD cum	Original Registration	Cust-omer	Cust cum	Model	Model cum	Engine	Assembly complete	Customer Accept	Status Config/Cust/WFU/STD/BU/L	Last/Current Registration
447	48401	MDC	1	N111MD	FX	1	11F	1	CF6-80C2	24.02.1989	27.06.1991	FX	N601FE
448	48402	MDC	2	N211MD	FX	2	11F	2	CF6-80C2	11.04.1989	29.05.1991	FX	N602FE
449	48458	MDC	3	N311MD	CI	1	11P	1	PW4460	23.05.1989	28.03.1991	CI	N489GX
450	48419	MDC	4	N411MD	AA	1	11P	2	CF6-80C2	11.08.1989	28.05.1991	11F/FX/L	N581FE
451	48420	MDC	5	N511MD	AA	2	11P	3	CF6-80C2	30.10.1989	01.02.1991	11F/FX	N582FE
452	48421	AA	3	N1752K	AA	3	11P	4	CF6-80C2	15.03.1990	22.04.1991	11F/FX	N583FE
453	48411	MDC	6	N514MD	DL	1	11P	5	CF6-80C2	18.04.1990	21.12.1990	11F/GR	N703GC
454	48412	DL	2	N892DL	DL	2	11P	6	CF6-80C2	11.05.1990	22.12.1990	11F/GR	N705GC
455	48449	AY	1	OH-LGA	AY	1	11P	7	CF6-80C2	06.06.1990	07.12.1990	AY	OH-LGA
456	48407	KE	1	HL7371	KE	1	11P	8	PW4460	27.06.1990	28.02.1991	11F/KE	HL7371
457	48408	KE	2	HL7372	KE	2	11P	9	PW4460	19.07.1990	25.01.1991	11F/KE	HL7372
458	48443	SR	1	HB-IWA	SR	1	11P	10	PW4460	06.08.1990	06.03.1991	SR	HB-IWA
459	48444	SR	2	HB-IWB	SR	2	11P	11	PW4460	05.02.1991	30.03.1991	SR	HB-IWB
460	48445	SR	3	HB-IWC	SR	3	11P	12	PW4460	19.02.1991	22.04.1991	SR	HB-IWC
461	48495	MU	1	B-2171	MU	1	11P	13	PW4460	07.03.1991	22.05.1991	MU	B-2171
462	48505	AA	4	N1757A	AA	4	11P	14	CF6-80C2	21.03.1991	02.08.1991	11F/FX	N590FE
463	48446	SR	4	HB-IWD	SR	4	11P	15	PW4460	05.04.1991	29.05.1991	SR	HB-IWD
464	48447	SR	5	HB-IWE	SR	5	11P	16	PW4460	17.04.1991	14.06.1991	SR	HB-IWE
465	48448	SR	6	HB-IWF	SR	6	11P	17	PW4460	29.04.1991	05.08.1991	SR/L	HB-IWF
466	48416	TG	1	HS-TMD	TG	1	11P	18	CF6-80C2	09.05.1991	27.06.1991	TG	HS-TMD
467	48417	TG	2	HS-TME	TG	2	11P	19	CF6-80C2	21.05.1991	15.07.1991	TG	HS-TME
468	48426	AZ	1	I-DUPA	AZ	1	11C	1	CF6-80C2	03.06.1991	27.03.1992	AZ	I-DUPA
469	48487	AA	5	N1753	AA	5	11P	20	CF6-80C2	13.06.1991	29.08.1991	11F/FX	N586FE
470	48459	FX	3	N603FE	FX	3	11F	3	CF6-80C2	25.06.1991	11.09.1991	FX	N603FE
471	48427	AZ	2	I-DUPE	AZ	2	11C	2	CF6-80C2	08.07.1991	22.11.1991	AZ	I-DUPE
472	48452	SR	7	HB-IWG	SR	7	11P	21	PW4460	18.07.1991	19.09.1991	SR	HB-IWG
473	48453	SR	8	HB-IWH	SR	8	11P	22	PW4460	29.07.1991	02.10.1991	SR	HB-IWH
474	48428	AZ	3	I-DUPI	AZ	3	11C	3	CF6-80C2	07.08.1991	12.12.1991	AZ	I-DUPI
475	48461	MU	1	B-2170	MU	2	11F	4	PW4460	16.08.1991	31.10.1991	MU	B-2170
476	48434	RG	1	PP-VOP	RG	1	11P	23	CF6-80C2	27.08.1991	11.11.1991	11F/GR	N701GC
477	48454	SR	9	HB-IWI	SR	9	11P	24	PW4460	06.09.1991	15.11.1991	SR	HB-IWI
478	48435	RG	2	PP-VOQ	RG	2	11P	25	CF6-80C2	13.09.1991	02.12.1991	11F/GR	N702GC
479	48450	AY	2	OH-LGB	AY	2	11P	26	CF6-80C2	20.09.1991	07.12.1991	AY	OH-LGB
480	48472	DL	3	N801DE	DL	3	11P	27	PW4460	27.09.1991	13.03.1992	DL	N801DE
481	48473	DL	4	N802DE	DL	4	11P	28	PW4460	04.10.1991	13.04.1992	DL	N802DE
482	48481	AA	6	N1759	AA	6	11P	29	CF6-80C2	09.01.1992	19.04.1992	11F/FX	N585FE
483	48436	AA	7	N1768D	AA	7	11P	30	CF6-80C2	27.01.1992	17.04.1992	11F/FX	N584FE
484	48484	LT	1	D-AERB	LT	1	11P	31	PW4460	25.10.1991	19.12.1991	SR	HB-IWR
485	48474	DL	5	N803DE	DL	5	11P	32	PW4460	01.11.1991	01.05.1992	DL	N803DE
486	48499	GA	1	EI-CDI	GA	1	11P	33	CF6-80C2	08.11.1991	31.12.1991	RG	PP-VPN
487	48455	SR	10	HB-IWK	SR	10	11P	34	PW4460	17.12.1991	03.02.1992	SR	HB-IWK
488	48413	VP	3	PP-SOW	VP	3	11P	35	CF6-80C2	08.01.1992	14.02.1992	RG	PP-VQL
489	48475	DL	6	N804DE	DL	6	11P	36	PW4460	17.01.1992	06.05.1992	DL	N804DE
490	48409	KE	3	HL7373	KE	3	11P	37	PW4460	27.01.1992	24.03.1992	11F/KE/L	HL7373
491	48414	VP	4	PP-SOZ	VP	4	11P	38	CF6-80C2	04.02.1992	27.03.1992	RG	PP-VQM
492	48489	AA	8	N1754	AA	8	11P	39	CF6-80C2	12.02.1992	12.03.1992	11F/FX	N587FE
493	48500	GA	2	EI-CDJ	GA	2	11P	40	CF6-80C2	20.02.1992	04.04.1992	RG	PP-VPO
494	48456	SR	11	HB-IWL	SR	11	11P	41	PW4460	28.02.1992	13.04.1992	SR	HB-IWL
495	48410	KE	4	HL7374	KE	4	11P	42	PW4460	09.03.1972	20.05.1992	11F/KE	HL7374
496	48496	MU	2	B-2172	MU	3	11P	43	PW4460	17.03.1992	22.05.1992	MU	B-2172
497	48460	FX	4	N604FE	FX	4	11F	5	CF6-80C2	25.03.1992	22.05.1992	FX	N604FE
498	48457	SR	12	HB-IWM	SR	12	11P	44	PW4460	02.04.1992	01.06.1992	SR	HB-IWM
499	48490	AA	9	N1755	AA	9	11P	45	CF6-80C2	10.04.1992	28.05.1992	11F/FX	N588FE
500	48429	AZ	4	I-DUPO	AZ	4	11C	4	CF6-80C2	20.04.1992	17.07.1992	AZ	I-DUPO
501	48418	TG	3	HS-TMF	TG	3	11P	46	CF6-80C2	06.05.1992	02.07.1992	TG	HS-TMF
502	48485	LT	2	D-AERW	LT	2	11P	47	PW4460	14.05.1992	30.06.1992	SR	HB-IWS
503	48491	AA	10	N1756	AA	10	11P	48	CF6-80C2	28.04.1992	11.06.1992	11F/FX	N598FE
504	48527	AA	11	N1758B	AA	11	11P	49	CF6-80C2	22.05.1992	08.07.1992	11F/FX	N591FE
505	48451	TG	4	HS-TMG	TG	4	11P	50	CF6-80C2	02.06.1992	31.07.1992	TG	HS-TMG
506	48437	MDC	7	N9012J	WO	1	11P	51	PW4460	09.06.1992	15.04.1993	WO	N272WA
507	48528	FX	5	N614FE	FX	5	11F	6	CF6-80C2	16.06.1992	12.11.1992	FX	N614FE
508	48430	AZ	5	I-DUPU	AZ	5	11C	5	CF6-80C2	24.06.1992	17.08.1992	AZ	I-DUPU
509	48486	LT	3	D-AERX	LT	3	11P	52	PW4460	01.07.1992	21.08.1992	SR	HB-IWT
510	48476	DL	7	N805DE	DL	7	11P	53	PW4460	10.07.1992	16.11.1992	DL	N805DE
511	48477	DL	8	N806DE	DL	8	11P	54	PW4460	20.07.1992	20.11.1992	DL	N806DE
512	48497	MU	3	B-2173	MU	4	11P	55	PW4460	27.07.1992	09.10.1992	11F/MU	B-2173
513	48501	GA	3	EI-CDK	GA	3	11P	56	CF6-80C2	04.08.1992	30.09.1992	RG	PP-VPP
514	48478	DL	9	N807DE	DL	9	11P	57	PW4460	12.08.1992	21.12.1992	DL	N807DE
515	48514	FX	6	N605FE	FX	6	11F	7	CF6-80C2	19.08.1992	29.09.1992	FX	N605FE
516	48523	KE	5	HL7375	KE	5	11P	58	PW4460	27.08.1992	27.10.1992	11F/KE	HL7375
517	48547	FX	7	N607FE	FX	7	11F	8	CF6-80C2	03.09.1992	13.10.1992	FX	N607FE
518	48468	CI	2	B-150	CI	2	11P	59	PW4460	14.09.1992	30.10.1992	CI/L	B-150
519	48469	CI	3	B-151	CI	3	11P	60	PW4460	21.09.1992	13.11.1992	CI	B-18172
520	48502	MDC	8	N9076Y	GA	4	11P	61	CF6-80C2	29.09.1992	30.09.1993	RG	PP-VQF
521	48548	FX	8	N608FE	FX	8	11F	9	CF6-80C2	07.10.1992	24.11.1992	FX	N608FE
522	48498	MU	4	B-2174	MU	5	11P	62	PW4460	14.10.1992	16.12.1992	11F/MU	B-2174
523	48404	RG	1	PP-VPJ	RG	1	11P	63	CF6-80C2	22.10.1992	30.12.1992	RG	PP-VPJ
524	48405	RG	2	PP-VPK	RG	2	11P	64	CF6-80C2	29.10.1992	30.12.1992	RG	PP-VPK
525	48518	WO	2	N271WA	WO	2	11P	65	PW4460	06.11.1992	08.03.1993	WO	N271WA
526	48550	AA	12	N1760A	AA	12	11P	66	CF6-80C2	16.11.1992	11.02.1993	11F/FX	N592FE
527	48551	AA	13	N1761R	AA	13	11P	67	CF6-80C2	24.11.1992	28.01.1993	AA	N1761R
528	48503	MDC	9	N9020U	GA	5	11P	68	CF6-80C2	04.12.1992	28.10.1993	RG	PP-VQG
529	48512	AY	3	OH-LGC	AY	3	11P	69	CF6-80C2	14.12.1992	19.02.1993	AY	OH-LGC
530	48552	AA	14	N1762B	AA	14	11P	70	CF6-80C2	22.12.1992	25.02.1993	AA	N1762B
531	48553	AA	15	N1763	AA	15	11P	71	CF6-80C2	11.01.1993	11.03.1993	AA	N1763
532	48532	RFS	1	N9093P	RFS	1	11P	72	PW4462	19.01.1993	26.08.1999	RFS	HZ-HM7
533	48538	LT	4	D-AERZ	LT	4	11P	73	PW4460	27.01.1993	13.03.1993	SR	HB-IWU
534	48431	AZ	1	I-DUPB	AZ	6	11P	74	CF6-80C2	04.02.1993	30.04.1993	AZ	I-DUPB
535	48554	AA	16	N1764B	AA	16	11P	75	CF6-80C2	12.02.1993	25.03.1993	11F/FX	N596FE
536	48479	DL	10	N808DE	DL	10	11P	76	PW4460	22.02.1993	22.06.1993	DL	N808DE
537	48596	AA	17	N1765B	AA	17	11P	77	CF6-80C2	02.03.1993	30.03.1993	AA	N1765B
538	48480	DL	11	N809DE	DL	11	11P	78	PW4460	10.03.1993	22.06.1993	DL	N809DE

Fuse number	FSN	McDD config	McDD cum	Original Registration	Cust-omer	Cust cum	Model	Model cum	Engine	Assembly complete	Customer Accept	Status Config/Cust/WFU/STD/BU/L	Last/Current Registration
539	48519	WO	3	N273WA	WO	3	11P	79	PW4460	18.03.1993	22.04.1993	WO	N273WA
540	48597	AA	18	N1766A	AA	18	11P	80	CF6-80C2	26.03.1993	14.05.1993	AA	N1766A
541	48520	MU	5	B-2175	MU	6	11P	81	PW4460	06.04.1993	20.12.1993	MU	B-2175
542	48565	DL	12	N810DE	DL	12	11P	82	PW4460	14.04.1993	22.06.1993	DL	N810DE
543	48566	DL	13	N811DE	DL	13	11P	83	PW4460	22.04.1993	22.06.1993	DL	N811DE
544	48533	RFS	2	N9020Z	RFS	2	11P	84	PW4462	04.05.1993	05.03.1999	RFS	HZ-HM8
545	48549	FX	9	N609FE	FX	9	11F	10	CF6-80C2	14.05.1993	30.06.1993	FX	N609FE
546	48470	CI	4	B-152	CI	4	11P	85	PW4460	26.05.1993	30.06.1993	CI	B-18151
547	48406	RG	3	PP-VPL	RG	3	11P	86	CF6-80C2	08.06.1993	30.12.1993	RG	PP-VPL
548	48504	MDC	10	N9076Y	GA	6	11P	87	CF6-80C2	18.06.1993	01.12.1993	RG	PP-VQH
549	48602	FX	10	N606FE	FX	10	11F	11	CF6-80C2	30.06.1993	28.07.1993	FX	N606FE
550	48598	AA	19	N1767A	AA	19	11P	88	CF6-80C2	13.07.1993	24.09.1993	AA	N1767A
551	48603	FX	11	N610FE	FX	11	11F	12	CF6-80C2	23.07.1993	25.08.1993	FX	N610FE
552	48571	JL	1	JA8580	JL	1	11P	89	PW4460	06.08.1993	29.11.1993	JL	JA8580
553	48604	FX	12	N611FE	FX	12	11F	13	CF6-80C2	20.08.1993	22.09.1993	FX/L	N611FE
554	48439	RG	4	PP-VPM	RG	4	11P	90	CF6-80C2	03.09.1993	30.12.1993	RG	PP-VPM
555	48605	FX	13	N612FE	FX	13	11F	14	CF6-80C2	20.09.1993	30.09.1993	FX	N612FE
556	48572	JL	2	JA8581	JL	2	11P	91	PW4460	04.10.1993	08.12.1993	JL	JA8581
557	48555	MDC	11	N6202D	KL	1	11P	92	CF6-80C2	18.10.1993	07.12.1993	KL	PH-KCA
558	48471	CI	5	B-153	CI	5	11P	93	PW4460	01.11.1993	11.12.1993	CI	B-18152
559	48573	JL	3	JA8582	JL	3	11P	94	PW4460	15.11.1993	04.04.1994	JL	JA8582
560	48600	MDC	12	N90178	DL	14	11P	95	PW4460	07.12.1993	15.10.1996	DL	N813DE
561	48556	KL	2	PH-KCB	KL	2	11P	96	CF6-80C2	12.01.1994	01.03.1994	KL	PH-KCB
562	48601	MDC	13	N6202S	DL	15	11P	97	PW4460	01.02.1994	08.04.1996	DL	N812DE
563	48633	WO	1	N274WA	WO	4	11F	15	PW4460	21.02.1994	31.03.1994	WO	N274WA
564	48513	AY	4	OH-LGD	AY	4	11P	98	CF6-80C2	11.03.1994	31.03.1994	AY	OH-LGD
565	48581	AZ	2	I-DUPC	AZ	7	11P	99	CF6-80C2	29.03.1994	05.05.1994	AZ	I-DUPC
566	48574	JL	4	JA8583	JL	4	11P	100	PW4460	18.04.1994	10.08.1994	JL	JA8583
567	48630	AZ	3	I-DUPD	AZ	8	11P	101	CF6-80C2	04.05.1994	10.06.1994	AZ	I-DUPD
568	48575	JL	5	JA8584	JL	5	11P	102	PW4460	08.06.1994	12.09.1994	JL	JA8584
569	48557	KL	3	PH-KCC	KL	3	11P	103	CF6-80C2	18.05.1994	24.06.1994	KL	PH-KCC
570	48542	BR	1	B-16101	BR	1	11P	104	CF6-80C2	11.07.1994	18.08.1994	BR	B-16101
571	48539	SR	13	HB-IWN	SR	13	11P	105	PW4462	24.06.1994	29.07.1994	SR	HB-IWN
572	48543	BR	2	B-16102	BR	2	11P	106	CF6-80C2	29.07.1994	13.09.1994	BR	B 16102
573	48558	KL	4	PH-KCD	KL	4	11P	107	CF6-80C2	16.08.1994	16.09.1994	KL	PH-KCD
574	48576	JL	6	JA8585	JL	6	11P	108	PW4460	01.09.1994	03.04.1995	JL	JA8585
575	48559	KL	5	PH-KCE	KL	5	11P	109	CF6-80C2	20.09.1994	18.11.1994	KL	PH-KCE
576	48415	BR	3	N103EV	BR	3	11P	110	CF6-80C2	11.10.1994	30.11.1994	BR	B-16103
577	48616	MDC	14	N90187	YM	1	11CF	1	PW4462	01.11.1994	22.12.1994	YM	PH-MCP
578	48560	KL	6	PH-KCF	KL	6	11P	111	CF6-80C2	22.11.1994	16.12.1994	KL	PH-KCF
579	48631	WO	1	N275WA	WO	5	11CF	2	PW4460	15.12.1994	02.03.1995	WO	N275WA
580	48544	BR	1	N105EV	BR	4	11F	16	CF6-80C2	13.01.1995	30.03.1995	BR	N105EV
581	48617	YM	2	PH-MCR	YM	2	11CF	3	PW4462	31.01.1995	30.03.1995	YM	PH-MCR
582	48632	WO	2	N276WA	WO	6	11CF	4	PW4460	16.02.1995	28.03.1995	WO	N276WA
583	48577	JL	7	JA8586	JL	7	11P	112	PW4460	06.03.1995	10.04.1995	JL	JA8586
584	48618	YM	3	PH-MCS	YM	3	11CF	5	PW4462	22.03.1995	03.04.1995	YM	PH-MCS
585	48561	KL	7	PH-KCG	KL	7	11P	113	CF6-80C2	12.04.1995	12.05.1995	KL	PH-KCG
586	48629	YM	4	PH-MCT	YM	4	11CF	6	PW4460	02.05.1995	23.05.1995	YM	PH-MCT
587	48545	BR	2	B-16106	BR	5	11F	17	CF6-80C2	22.05.1995	22.06.1995	BR	B-16106
588	48578	JL	8	JA8587	JL	8	11P	114	PW4460	12.06.1995	27.06.1995	JL	JA8587
589	48546	BR	3	N107EV	BR	6	11F	18	CF6-80C2	05.07.1995	30.08.1995	BR	N107EV
590	48743	MDC	15	N6203D	WO	7	11ERP	115	PW4460	16.08.1995	19.03.1996	WO	N277WA
591	48562	KL	8	PH-KCH	KL	8	11P	116	CF6-80C2	26.07.1995	31.08.1995	KL	PH-KCH
592	48744	MDC	16	N6203U	VP	1	11P	117	CF6-80C2	07.09.1995	17.11.1995	Golden Gate Leasing*	PP-SPK
593	48563	KL	9	PH-KCI	KL	9	11P	118	CF6-80C2	28.09.1995	10.11.1995	KL	PH-KCI
594	48747	FX	14	N616FE	FX	14	11F	19	CF6-80C2	19.10.1995	30.11.1995	FX	N616FE
595	48748	FX	15	N617FE	FX	15	11F	20	CF6-80C2	09.11.1995	08.12.1995	FX	N617FE
596	48745	MDC	17	N90187	VP	2	11P	119	CF6-80C2	04.12.1995	22.12.1995	5X	N798BA
597	48746	MDC	18	N9020Q	WO	8	11ERP	120	PW4460	04.01.1996	19.03.1996	Sonair	N278WA
598	48749	FX	16	N613FE	FX	16	11F	21	CF6-80C2	30.01.1996	12.03.1996	FX	N613FE
599	48579	JL	9	JA8588	JL	9	11P	121	PW4460	28.02.1996	02.04.1996	JL	JA8588
600	48766	MDC	19	N6203N	H2	1	11P	122	CF6-80C2	27.03.1996	13.12.1996	Boeing Capital Corp.*	OO-CTB
601	48768	MDC	20	N9134D	VP	3	11P	123	CF6-80C2	24.04.1996	26.06.1996	VP	PP-SFA
602	48767	FX	17	N615FE	FX	17	11F	22	CF6-80C2	22.05.1996	25.06.1996	FX	N615FE
603	48769	MDC	21	N9166N	VP	4	11P	124	CF6-80C2	24.06.1996	27.11.1996	RG	PP-VQX
604	48754	FX	18	N618FE	FX	18	11F	23	CF6-80C2	24.07.1996	22.08.1996	FX	N618FE
605	48623	DL	16	N814DE	DL	16	11P	125	PW4460	21.08.1996	14.09.1996	DL	N814DE
606	48757	YM	1	PH-MCU	YM	5	11F	24	PW4462	19.09.1996	30.09.1996	YM	PH-MCU
607	48770	FX	19	N619FE	FX	19	11F	25	CF6-80C2	17.10.1996	15.11.1996	FX	N619FE
608	48753	GA	4	PK-GIK	GA	7	11ERP	126	CF6-80C2	14.11.1996	19.12.1996	RG	PP-VQI
609	48773	MDC	22	N90187	SV	1	11F	26	CF6-80C2	16.12.1996	24.12.1997	SV	HZ-ANA
610	48774	JL	10	JA8589	JL	10	11P	127	PW4460	24.01.1997	04.03.1997	JL	JA8589
611	48540	SR	14	HB-IWO	SR	14	11P	128	PW4460	21.02.1997	11.03.1997	SR	HB-IWO
612	48564	KL	10	PH-KCK	KL	10	11P	129	CF6-80C2	21.03.1997	25.04.1997	KL	PH-KCK
613	48755	GA	5	PK-GIL	GA	8	11ERP	130	CF6-80C2	18.04.1997	24.05.1997	RG	PP-VQJ
614	48634	SR	15	HB-IWP	SR	15	11P	131	PW4462	16.05.1997	11.07.1997	SR	HB-IWP
615	48758	GA	6	PK-GIM	GA	9	11ERP	132	CF6-80C2	16.06.1997	01.11.1997	RG	PP-VQK
616	48775	MDC	23	N91566	SV	2	11F	27	CF6-80C2	15.07.1997	30.12.1997	SV	HZ-ANB
617	48776	MDC	24	N91078	SV	3	11F	28	CF6-80C2	12.08.1997	31.12.1997	SV	HZ-ANC
618	48777	MDC	25	N9166N	SV	4	11F	29	CF6-80C2	10.09.1997	09.01.1998	SV	HZ-AND
619	48778	BR	4	B-16108	BR	7	11F	30	CF6-80C2	08.10.1997	19.11.1997	BR	B-16108
620	48779	BR	5	B-16109	BR	8	11F	31	CF6-80C2	05.11.1997	22.12.1997	BR	B-16109
621	48541	SR	16	HB-IWQ	SR	16	11P	133	PW4462	05.12.1997	22.12.1997	SR	HB-IWQ
622	48624	DL	17	N815DE	DL	17	11P	134	PW4460	15.01.1998	20.02.1998	DL	N815DE
623	48756	H2	2	OO-CTS	H2	2	11P	135	CF6-80C2	12.02.1998	30.03.1998	Boeing Capital Corp.*	OO-CTS
624	48780	H2	3	OO-CTC	H2	3	11P	136	PW4460	13.02.1998	17.04.1998	Boeing Capital Corp.*	OO-CTC
625	48781	LH	1	D-ALCA	LH	1	11F	32	CF6-80C2	09.04.1998	25.06.1998	LH	D-ALCA
626	48782	LH	2	D-ALCB	LH	2	11F	33	CF6-80C2	07.05.1998	25.06.1998	LH	D-ALCB
627	48783	LH	3	D-ALCC	LH	3	11F	34	CF6-80C2	05.06.1998	13.08.1998	LH	D-ALCC
628	48784	LH	4	D-ALCD	LH	4	11F	35	CF6-80C2	06.07.1998	17.09.1998	LH	D-ALCD
629	48785	LH	5	D-ALCE	LH	5	11F	36	CF6-80C2	03.08.1998	22.10.1998	LH	D-ALCE
630	48786	BR	6	B-16110	BR	9	11F	37	CF6-80C2	31.08.1998	14.10.1998	BR	B-16110

Fuse number	FSN	McDD config	McDD cum	Original Registration	Cust-omer	Cust cum	Model	Model cum	Engine	Assembly complete	Customer Accept	Status Config/Cust/WFU/STD/BU/L	Last/Current Registration
631	48787	BR	7	B-16111	BR	10	11F	38	CF6-80C2	30.09.1998	12.11.1998	BR	B-16111
632	48788	YM	2	PH-MCW	YM	6	11F	39	PW4462	28.10.1998	20.11.1998	YM	PH-MCW
633	48789	BAC	26	N90178	BR	11	11F	40	CF6-80C2	04.12.1998	29.07.1999	BR	B-16112
634	48790	BR	9	B-16113	BR	12	11F	41	CF6-80C2	26.01.1999	26.08.1999	BR	B-16113
635	48791	FX	20	N620FE	FX	20	11F	42	PW4462	02.03.1999	30.03.1999	FX	N620FE
636	48792	FX	21	N621FE	FX	21	11F	43	PW4462	13.04.1999	01.06.1999	FX	N621FE
637	48798	LH	6	D-ALCF	LH	6	11F	44	CF6-80C2	08.07.1999	27.08.1999	LH	D-ALCF
638	48794	FX	22	N623FE	FX	22	11F	45	PW4462	25.05.1999	29.06.1999	FX	N623FE
639	48799	LH	7	D-ALCG	LH	7	11F	46	CF6-80C2	19.08.1999	12.10.1999	LH	D-ALCG
640	48801	LH	8	D-ALCH	LH	8	11F	47	CF6-80C2	01.10.1999	24.11.1999	LH	D-ALCH
641	48800	LH	9	D-ALCI	LH	9	11F	48	CF6-80C2	12.11.1999	27.01.2000	LH	D-ALCI
642	48802	LH	10	D-ALCJ	LH	10	11F	49	CF6-80C2	12.01.2000	23.03.2000	LH	D-ALCJ
643	48803	LH	11	D-ALCK	LH	11	11F	50	CF6-80C2	24.02.2000	31.05.2000	LH	D-ALCK
644	48804	LH	12	D-ALCL	LH	12	11F	51	CF6-80C2	06.04.2000	24.08.2000	LH	D-ALCL
645	48805	BAC	27	N6069R	LH	13	11F	52	CF6-80C2	07.08.2000	22.02.2001	LH	D-ALCM
646	48806	LH	14	D-ALCN	LH	14	11F	53	CF6-80C2	02.10.2000	25.01.2001	LH	D-ALCN

Top: **China Airlines took delivery of MD-11 B-152, the third aircraft of the type in the carrier's fleet, on 30th June 1993. The aircraft was the 100th MD-11 delivered.** McDonnell Douglas

Above: **22nd February 2001. The final MD-11 delivered from the Boeing Long Beach Division takes off to enter revenue service with Lufthansa Cargo. With its departure, 30 years of tri-jet production at the facility ended.** The Boeing Company

Above right: **The Douglas Aircraft Company data plate on the first MD-11 built. MD-11F fuselage 447, serial number 48401, is in service with FedEx as N601FE.** Author's collection

Right: **The Boeing data plate of Lufthansa Cargo MD-11F D-ALCN. Fuselage 646, serial number 48806, was the last MD-11 built.** Author's collection

Chapter Five

MD-12 and MD-XX

Despite the cancellation of the former BCAL MD-11 orders, British Airways was seen as a potential customer for the MD-11X.
McDonnell Douglas

With MD-11 sales taking a downturn, MDC proposed several new variants of the aircraft: the MD-11B, the MD-11C, and the MD-11D. The different MD-11, as well as the MD-12 and MD-XX proposals are listed in the 'MD-11 Variants' table on page 95.

Although MDC seriously considered the idea of building a twin-engined derivative of the MD-11, as it had similarly postulated the DC-10 Twin for the DC-10 family, the proposal was not progressed.

The most prominent proposals were the MD-12X, the double-deck MD-12 and the MD-XX. Whereas the MD-12X and MD-12 had been planned as further members of the MDC airliner family, the MD-XX variants were to replace the MD-11.

The 1990 MD-12X proposal dated back to the original MD-12 (renamed MD-11 Super Stretch) proposal from 1987. The aircraft was conceived as a direct competitor to the 747-400. The MD-12X would feature a 35ft (10.6m) stretch of the basic MD-11, with a 20ft (6.06m) barrel with door added forward of the overwing section and a 15ft (4.54m) barrel with a new

door aft of the overwing section. With a total length of 237ft 11in (72m) the aircraft would be 4.29ft (1.3m) longer than the 747-400. The MD-12X concept featured an all-new wing with a wingspan of 212.5ft (64.39m). A four-wheel centre landing gear design would support an envisaged MTOW of 851,000 lb (386,354kg), which was almost a 30 percent increase over the MD-11. The MD-12X incorporated features such as a three-axis Fly-by-Wire flight control system, electronically controlled engines, and a two-crew flightdeck with digital avionics, six cathode ray tube instrument displays, and a fully integrated flight management system. The basically identical MD-11 and MD-12X cockpits would allow flight crew cross-qualification. As a complement to the MD-11 fleet, the MD-12X, with a predicted range of 7,900nm (14,630km), would offer the required flexibility to service long-range, high-capacity markets with improved efficiency. The engines offered for the MD-12X included the General Electric GE90-D1, Pratt & Whitney PW4484 and Rolls-Royce Trent 775. The typical three-class seating arrangement consisted of six-abreast first

class sleeperettes, seven-abreast business class, and a nine-abreast economy class that accommodated a total of 375 passengers, a 26 percent increase over the MD-11. The so-called 'Panorama Deck', originally proposed for the MD-11SS in 1987, was also studied for the MD-12X. The forward lower deck compartment would provide space for 57 passengers in a business class configuration. With the 'Panorama Deck' installed, the aircraft would carry up to 440 passengers in a three class seating arrangement. On 25th October 1991 the MDC Board of Directors gave the green light for the sales department to offer the MD-12X to the airlines. The launch of the new aircraft was expected to take place in 1992. With a first flight and start of the flight test programme scheduled for 1995, certification and deliveries to launch customers was planned for 1997.

said that MDC was too far ahead in time with the daring MD-12, the feasibility of a programme of that magnitude was nevertheless proven by Airbus with the launch of their A380 in December 2000.

When Harry C Stonecipher was elected president and chief executive officer of MDC in 1994, he proclaimed: 'If we weren't already in the commercial aircraft business, we'd get into it'.

With the battle for a 500 plus seat aircraft now being fought between Airbus Industrie and Boeing, MDC concentrated on a 300-400 seat aircraft and planned to offer two versions of a new MD-11 derivative which would ultimately replace it on the production line. The decision to develop two variants responded to discussions with potential airline customers who demanded aircraft with more passenger capacity and also wanted more range capability. Plans for the new high-capacity, long-range tri-jet were unveiled at the Farnborough International Air Show in September 1996. The MD-XX Stretch would be 32ft (9.7m) longer than the MD-11 and have a 7,020nm (13,000km) range. In a typical three-class 18 first, 70 business and 287 economy seat arrangement, the 'Stretch' would provide seating for a total of 375 passengers With all-economy seating, the aircraft would carry up to 515 passengers. With this aircraft MDC aimed at the 747-200 and 747-300 market.

The smaller, MD-11-sized, MD-11 XX LR (Long Range) version was intended to compete with the Airbus A340 and Boeing 777, offering a range of 8,320nm (15,400km). In a typical first, business and economy mix, 18, 58 and 233 passengers respectively could be accommodated.

Both aircraft would feature a new wing with a wingspan of 213ft (64.54m) and a total wing area of 5,200ft^2 (483.1m^2). A patented supercritical air foil shape would have made it the most aerodynamically efficient wing in the airline industry. A 22 percent weight saving in the tail section could have been accomplished by the installation of a new composite vertical stabiliser.

At the time discussions had been underway with all three major engine manufacturers - General Electric, Pratt & Whitney and Rolls-Royce- to use their engines on the new aircraft. It had been planned to use engines in the 65,000 lb thrust range. With the Advanced Common Flightdeck installed, the MD-XX would have offered complete operational commonality with the MD-11. A major difference from the MD-11 would have been the installation of a of a six-wheel main landing gear bogie and a four-wheel centre gear. Design studies included plans for using lower deck space for a sky lounge, sleeping compartments and airborne offices for business travellers.

The MDC concept of growth potential, as exercised before with the DC-10 and MD-11 family, also foresaw a freighter version of both MD-XX versions.

In order to be able to offer the aircraft to interested airlines and to meet the projected launch date of January 1997, an MDC board of directors approval was needed by November 1996. During the board meeting on 25th October it was decided to terminate the MD-XX programme. Contrary to his earlier statements, Stonecipher said: 'I don't see McDonnell Douglas as a major standalone player in commercial airliners. The investment required to make us into a full-fledged major player is probably in order of $15 billion over the next ten years.' At the time the decision to abandon the MD-XX plans was announced, the Boeing Company and MDC had already been in talks about a possible collaboration. On 3rd December 1996 Boeing announced that an agreement had been reached with MDC to work together on the development of future Boeing wide-body airliner programmes. Within two weeks, Phil Condit, president and chief executive officer of Boeing, and Harry Stonecipher, president and chief executive officer of MDC, jointly announced on 15th December that a definitive agreement had been signed for the two companies to merge into the world's largest aerospace company. The merger became official on 30th July 1997. Thus the MD-XX plans were to be the last to date for any new wide-body tri-jet airliner.

MD-11 Variants – Real...

MD-11	Baseline passenger model (DAC: MD-11P), derivative of DC-10-30 with CF6-80C2/ PW4460-4462 engines, winglets, glass cockpit
MD-11AH	Advanced Heavy, Swissair name for upgrade with MGTOW 630,500 lb, aerodynamic PIP modifications, and composite panels
MD-11A-1	(DAC), MD-11 fitted with A-1 modification package
MD-11C	Combi passenger/freighter model with rear fuselage left side cargo door (originally called MD-11CB by DAC)
MD-11ER	Extended Range (DAC), removable 3,000 US gallon belly tank in forward cargo compartment, MGTOW 630,500 lb (DAC: MD-11ER, MD-11ERP)
MD-11F	Freighter, or Convertible Freighter (DAC: MD-11CF), with forward cargo door

...and Imagined

MD-11ADV	Advanced Stretch, proposed (1985) 40ft stretch for 380 seats
MD-11B	Proposed (late 1992) increased gross weight
MD-11B1	MD-11B with stretch for 20 more seats
MD-11B2	MD-11B short-fuselage for 250 seats
MD-11C	Proposal (late 1992) for stretch with 125in wing root plugs
MD-11C1	MD-11C for 329 seats
MD-11C2	MD-11C for 353 seats
MD-11CC	Proposed (May 1996) 31ft stretch with new wing

MD-11D	Proposal (1993) for forward lower 'Panorama Deck', 43 business-class seats
MD-11D1	MD-11D with increased gross weight
MD-11D2	MD-11D with increased gross weight and range
MD-11ER	Extended Range, proposed (1985) combination of MD-11 features with DC-10 fuselage (dropped 1988)
MD-11LR	Long Range, proposed (December 1994) with wing tip extension and other refinements from MD-11 Stretch
MD-11M	Medium, proposed (1986) successor to MD-11XMR, centre gear removed
MD-11MRS	Medium Range Stretch, revised (1988) name for original MD-11SS
MD-11S	Stretch, proposal (1987) with 18ft stretch
MD-11S/PD	Stretch/Panorama Deck, MD-11S variant, later with new wing
MD-11SS	Super Stretch, MD-11S proposal with 35ft stretch and lower 'Panorama Deck', renamed MD-12XX
MD-11	Proposed (1994) 22ft stretch for 363 passengers Simple Stretch
MD-11	Proposed (1994) 200-240in stretch with wing tip extensions, centre fuselage tank Stretch
MD-11 Twin	Proposals (1994) for twin-jet with MD-11LR wing, short-fuselage, long-haul, and 'optimised' stretch versions
MD-11X	Proposal (September 1984) for upgraded (power plants, avionics, structures) US domestic DC-10
MD-11X-10	Proposed (September 1984) DC-10-30ER development

MD-11X-20	Proposed (September 1984) 22ft 3in stretch of DC-10-30
MD-11XMR	Medium-Range, proposed (1985) version of MD-11X-20
MD-12	Proposed (1987) 35ft stretch of MD-11 with new wing, Fly by Wire (FBW) control system, renamed MD-11SS, then MD-12X
MD-12X	Proposed (October 1990) 35ft stretch of MD-11 for 375-400 seats, new wing, FBW controls
MD-12	Four-engine, double-deck proposal (1992)
MD-12XMR	MD-12X for US transcontinental market, 450 seats (two class configuration)
MD-12XSTR	MD-12X with 15ft stretch, 450 seats (three class configurations)
MD-12XX	MD-12X with further stretch, 550 seats
MD-XX	Proposal (February 1996) for new wing with 'Panorama Deck', MD-95 cockpit
MD-XXLR	Long Range, MD-XX with 309 seats
MD-XX Stretch	MD-XX with 32ft stretch, 375-515 seats
MD-XXX	Original proposal (March 1984) for improved DC-10-30 with possible stretch, which led to the MD-11X
AM-300	Proposed (1988) designation of MD-11SS if launched as joint Airbus/MDC project
KC-10B	Proposed (1987) USAF tanker/transport version of MD-11

Bold indicates official (FAA) designations from type certificate
DAC = Douglas Aircraft Company in-house nomenclature
Source: John Wegg, Airways

A further study for the 21st century was the MD-XX 'Stretch'. The aircraft was a proposal for a 747-200 and 747-300 replacement. McDonnell Douglas

The MD-XX LR (Long Range) was intended to compete with the Airbus A340 and Boeing 777. McDonnell Douglas

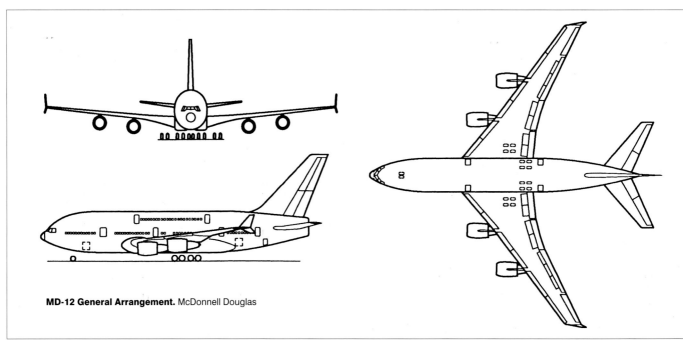

MD-12 General Arrangement. McDonnell Douglas

Chapter Six

MD-10 – A Refined Workhorse

If the launch date of 25th April 1968 for the DC-10 programme can be considered an important date, 16th September 1996 may ultimately prove to be of equal importance in the aircraft's history. On this day McDonnell Douglas and freight and small package giant Federal Express Corporation announced the MD-10 programme. The agreement included the conversion of 70 DC-10s, and an option to retrofit an additional 50 aircraft, into advanced technology freighters. The conversion project occurs in two phases. In the first phase of the FedEx MD-10 programme passenger-configured DC-10s are converted to freighters and redelivered to FedEx.

At the time MDC selected Dimension Aviation at Goodyear, Arizona, as the principal centre for converting the former United Airlines and American Airlines aircraft. Today the site is operated by Aviation Management Systems, Inc. as a maintenance repair and overhaul facility. The massive programme however required further conversion sites. Prior to the commencement of the FedEx MD-10 programme, long-time McDonnell Douglas partner Aeronavali in Italy had already converted DC-10 aircraft for operators including Gemini Air Cargo, DAS Air Cargo and United Airlines. The company was selected to be the second source location for the FedEx MD-10 conversion programme.

In 1998 the Boeing Company decided to enter the conversion scene with its newly formed Boeing Aerospace Support Center (BASC) located at former Kelly Air Force Base in San Antonio, Texas. The division was initially contracted to convert a single DC-10-10 which arrived at the BASC site in September 1998. As mentioned in the Chapter Two, Boeing Airplane Services was launched in 1999, with modification centres in Wichita, Kansas and San Antonio, Texas. As well as Aeronavali and Israel Aircraft Industries' Bedek division, Singapore-based ST Aviation Services Co (SASCO), a subsidiary of Singapore Technologies Aerospace (ST Aero), became a partner of Boeing Airplane Services' international network of modification and engineering facilities in February 2000. SASCO rolled out the first DC-10 freighter in November 2000 and will also play an important role in future DC-10 and MD-11 modifications.

The conversion programme, which began in February 1997, takes about 120 days per aircraft. It includes a heavy maintenance check, standardisation and reliability upgrades, and removal of passenger accommodations. Other main conversion activities include the main deck cargo door installation, the rigid barrier installation and structural changes to increase the maximum takeoff gross weight. McDonnell Douglas designed special tooling for fabricating and installing the cargo door to minimise the time the aircraft is out of service and to improve flexibility in production rates.

The cargo door is installed in the forward port side fuselage and is common to that used on the MD-11 freighter. The rigid cargo barrier (RCB) replaces the standard cargo net. (See Chapter 2 – Pure Freighters – for more details) A higher maximum take-off gross weight (MTOGW) for both the DC-10-10 and -30 aircraft has been achieved by structural changes made during the conversion. The Series -10 freighter's gross payload has risen from 124,000 lb (56,240kg) to 143,500 lb (65,091kg). The gross payload of a Series -30 freighter has been increased from 163,000 lb (73930kg) to 180,000 lb (81,720kg).

The second phase of the programme includes the installation of the Advanced Common Flightdeck (ACF) in the modified aircraft and other FedEx DC-10s, converting the three-crew cockpit into a two-crew 'glass cockpit'. The ACF is operationally based on Honeywell's integrated cockpit design for the two-crew MD-11, with six-across 8in x 8in (20.3cm x 20.3cm) flat panel, liquid crystal displays (LCD) showing all flight and systems information. Another major benefit of the ACF is derived from the Aircraft System Controllers originally designed for the MD-11. The system manages the functions of all major aircraft systems such as the electrical, hydraulic and fuel systems, thus eliminating the need for a flight engineer. The ACF also uses state-of-the-art high-speed, high-capacity computers built around Honeywell's innovative Versatile Integrated Avionics (VIA) design, the VIA 2000. Three of the VIA computers, coupled with a pair of new aircraft interface units linking them to the aircraft systems, replace 22 separate computers in the existing DC-10 design. With other changes in the avionics bay, an overall savings of approximately 1,000 lb (454kg) in removed equipment is achieved as a result of the ACF modification.

Other major improvements during the ACF conversion will be the fitting of an advanced weather radar system with predictive windshear detection, a Category IIIb autoflight system, landing gear reliability improvements as well as aerodynamic drag reductions.

The operational reliability of the aircraft will be further enhanced by Satellite Communications (SATCOM), Global Positioning System (GPS) navigation capabilities, Future Air Navigation System (FANS) compatibility and an On-Board Maintenance Terminal. The MD-95 100-passenger airliner, which was renamed Boeing 717 in January 1998, features a similar set of advanced cockpit displays and systems which were also to be available for planned McDonnell Douglas aircraft. (MD-11 variants see page 95)

Early artist's impression shows the MD-10 bedecked in the green, dark and light blue McDonnell Douglas last 'house colours'.
McDonnell Douglas

The new ACF technology offers significant cockpit and systems commonality between the MD-10 and MD-11 which results in remarkable savings in crew training and operating costs. In March 1998, SAir Services' company SR Technics in Zürich, Switzerland, was selected to perform flightdeck conversions as part of the Boeing MD-10 programme. The first of 57 planned conversions was completed by subsidiary SR Technics America Inc in March 2001 at the company's Palmdale, California facility. When the installation of the advanced technology flightdeck is completed, the upgraded DC-10 freighter will receive the new designation MD-10.

The ACF installation in a flight test DC-10 started in 1998. Although it had originally been planned to use three aircraft, only two modified DC-10s participated in the flight test programme. On 19th March 1999, the first MD-10 was rolled out during a ceremony held at Long Beach.

The first MD-10, N386FE, took off on its inaugural flight from Long Beach Municipal Airport at 12.55 PM local time on Saturday 10th April, 1999 and landed 4 hours and 25 minutes later at Williams Gateway Airport (formerly Williams Air Force Base) in Mesa, Arizona. This aircraft was a former United DC-10-10, N1821U (f/n 138), and dubbed 'T1'.

Boeing pilot Captain Joe Goodlove, co-pilot Captain Gary McCellan and flight-test engineer Wayne Anselmo put the MD-10 through its paces during its first flight. During the first flight all the planned flight-test parameters for the mission were completed.

A Local Area Augmentation System (LAAS) was also tested on the T1 test aircraft. The avionics system, sponsored by NASA, used a Global Positioning System (GPS) unit with experimental software and hardware to enhance landing navigation at airports without Instrument Landing System (ILS). During the test program additional 'FedEx, FAA, Boeing and LAAS Test Team' titles were added on the forward lower fuselage.

The second aircraft which joined the flight test program was designated 'T2'. The aircraft involved was a FedEx DC-10-30F, N316FE (f/r

444). The two aircraft completed a rigorous yearlong flight test programme that spanned 1,060 hours in 802 flights. Boeing and FedEx conducted the programme using a unique 'team' approach that involved FedEx maintenance mechanics, pilots, and engineering staff and their Boeing counterparts. The aircraft flew to 33 different airports and made over 1,400 landings, approaches and go-arounds. These flights were just a portion of the rigorous Federal Aviation Administration (FAA)-approved certification process. On 9th May 2000, Boeing announced that the FAA had granted the company an amended type certificate and a production certificate of airworthiness for the MD-10 freighter. The amended type certificate allows modification of DC-10 aircraft into MD-10 aircraft, while the production certificate of airworthiness is required for the aircraft to go into service. On the same day Boeing delivered the first of 89 MD-10s to FedEx at a joint Boeing-FedEx-FAA ceremony at Williams Gateway Airport. Once the last modified aircraft is delivered to FedEx, the carrier will have a stable of like-new freighters.

Boeing offers the MD-10 programme to the owners of all 404 DC-10s in service or storage, giving the programme the potential to become the largest aircraft modification effort in commercial aircraft history. The MD-10 will continue the enviable reputation of her sistership, the DC-10. On 1st February 2001, the DC-10 and MD-10 aircraft had flown 12,763,299,939 statute miles and undertaken a total of 26,769,488 revenue hours.

When the MD-10 programme was announced McDonnell Douglas publications showed artist's impressions of the aircraft bedecked in the company's last green, dark and light blue 'house' colours. Following the McDonnell Douglas-Boeing merger the aircraft was renamed Boeing MD-10. The first ACF-converted aircraft displayed a dark blue 'Boeing MD-10 freighter' title on the white fuselage with a slanted dark blue 'MD-10' title on the tail fin. 'Experimental' titles were placed above the forward and rear entry doors. It should be noted that the aircraft at the time had not been converted to the freighter role as yet and was still equipped with passenger windows.

MD-10-10F Freighter General Specifications

Capacity

Main and lower deck total	17,096ft^3	484m^3
Main deck	13,116ft^3	371m^3
Lower deck	3,980ft^3	113m^3

Dimensions

Wingspan	155ft 4in	47.35m
Length overall	182ft 3.1in	55.55m
Height overall	58ft 1in	17.70m

Wing area

Including aileron	3,550ft^2	329.8m^2
Sweepback	35°	

Landing gear

Tread (main wheels)	35ft 0in	10.67m
Wheel base (fore & aft)	72ft 5in	22.07m

Engines

	GE CF6-6D1	
Take-off thrust	40,000 lb	177.9kN

Standard delivery weights

Max take-off weight	446,000 lb	202,484kg
Des landing weight	363,500 lb	164,854kg
Max zero fuel weight	335,000 lb	151,956kg
Operator's empty weight	212,500 lb	96,415kg
Max payload	143,500 lb	65,149kg
Fuel capacity	145,810 lb	66,139kg

Performance

Level flight speed	600+ mph	965km/h
FAA take-off field length, standard weight	8,900ft	2,625m
FAA landing field length, standard weight	5,200ft	1,585m
Range, with max payload	2,000nm	3,700km

MD-10-30F Freighter General Specifications – Where differing from the MD-10-10F

Dimensions

Wingspan	165ft 4in	50.40m
Length overall	181ft 7.2in	55.35m

Wing area

Including aileron	3,647ft^2	338,8m^2

Engines

	GE CF6-50C2	
Take-off thrust	52,500 lb	233.5kN

Standard delivery weights

Max take-off weight	580,000 lb	263,320kg
Des landing weight	421,000 lb	190,965kg
Max zero fuel weight	401,000 lb	181,940kg
Operator's empty weight	238,000 lb	107,956kg
Max payload	180,000 lb	81,720kg
Fuel capacity	245,566 lb	111,388kg

Performance

FAA take-off field length, standard weight	9,650ft	2,847m
FAA landing field length, standard weight	5,960ft	1,758m
Range, with max payload	3,700nm	6,852km

The first test aircraft, dubbed T-1, was also used for the testing of the 'Local Area Augmentation System'. Harald M Helbig

The MD-10, equipped with the Advanced Common Flightdeck, took off on its inaugural flight from Long Beach to Williams Gateway Airport, Arizona, on 10th April, 1999. The Boeing Company

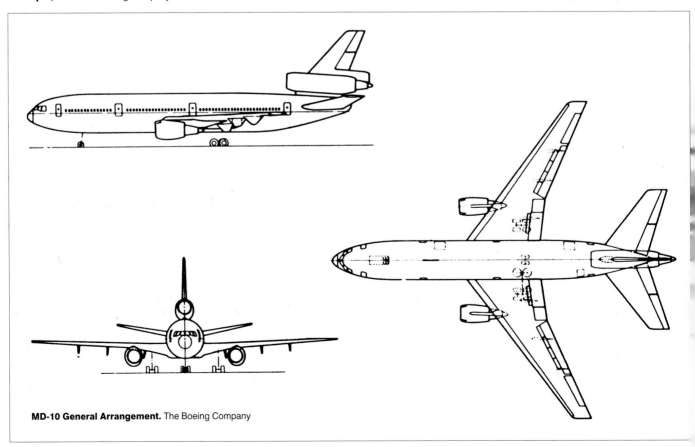

MD-10 General Arrangement. The Boeing Company

IATA/ICAO Codes of DC-10/MD-11 Operators

To aid reference, the IATA/ICAO codes are followed by the airline's name and country of origin. Where IATA codes are not applicable, three letter ICAO codes are given. This listing includes the original and current operators as shown in Chapter Six 'DC-10 Production'. Operators without a designator are included for completeness.

AA/AAL	American Airlines, USA
AM/AMX	Aeromexico, Mexico
AY/FIN	Finnair, Finland
AZ/AZA	Alitalia, Italy
A2/EXD	Cielos del Peru, Peru
BB/BBB	Balair, Switzerland
BG/BBC	Biman Bangladesh Airlines, Bangladesh
BR/BCA	British Caledonian Airways, UK
CO/COA	Continental Airlines, USA
CP/CPC	CP Air, Canada
DF/CFG	Condor, Germany
DK/VKG	Premiair, Denmark
DL/DAL	Delta Airlines, USA
EB/EWW	Emery Worldwide Airlines, USA
EG/JAA	Japan Asia Airways, Japan
ELD	Electra, Greece
FG/AFG	Ariana Afghan Airlines, Afghanistan
FM/FDX	Federal Express (until July 1996), USA
FX/FDX	Federal Express (July 1996 on), USA
GA/GIA	Garuda Indonesia, Indonesia
GH/GHA	Ghana Airways, Ghana
GK	Laker Airways, UK
GR/GCO	Gemini Air Cargo, USA
HA/HAL	Hawaiian Air, USA

IB/IBE	Iberia, Spain
IJ/LIB	Air Liberté, France
IW/AOM	AOM French Airlines, France
JD/JAS	Japan Air System, Japan
JL/JAL	Japan Airlines, Japan
JU/JAT	Jugoslovenski AT, Yugoslavia
JO/JAZ	JAL Ways, Japan
KE/KAL	Korean Air Lines, Korea
KL/KLM	KLM Royal Dutch Airlines, The Netherlands
LH/DLH	Lufthansa, Germany
MH/MAS	Malaysian Airline System, Malaysia
MP/MPH	Martinair, The Netherlands
MS/MSR	Egypt Air, Egypt
MT/JMC	JMC AIR, UK
MX/MXA	Mexicana, Mexico
NA/NAL	National Airlines, USA
NG/LDA	Lauda Air, Austria
NW/NWA	Northwest Airlines, USA
NZ/ANZ	Air New Zealand, New Zealand
OV/ONA	Overseas National Airways, USA
PK/PIA	Pakistan Int'l Airlines, Pakistan
PR/PAL	Philippine Airlines, Philippines
QC/AZR	Air Zaire, Zaire
QSC	ASA African Safari Airways, Kenya
RG/VRG	VARIG, Brazil
RK/RKA	Air Afrique, Ivory Coast
SE/DSR	DAS Air Cargo, Uganda
SK/SAS	Scandinavian Airlines System, Sweden
SKJ	Skyjet, Antigua
SJF	Skyjet France, France
SN/SAB	Sabena, Belgium
SQ/SIA	Singapore Airlines, Singapore
SR/SWR	Swissair, Switzerland
SU/AFL	Aeroflot Russian Int'l Airlines, Russia
SY/SCX	Sun Country Airlines, USA

TG/THA	Thai Airways International, Thailand
TK/THY	Turk Hava Yollari, Turkey
TLX	Cargo Lion, Luxembourg
TNI	Transair International, Brazil
TV/TIA	Trans Int'l Airlines, USA
UA/UAL	United Airlines, USA
UT/UTA	Union de Transports Aériens, France
VA/VIA	VIASA, Venezuela
VE/AVE	AVENSA, Venezuela
VZ/AIH	Airtours International, UK
WA/WAL	Western Airlines, USA
WD/WDA	Wardair, Canada
WE/CWC	Challenge Air Cargo, USA
WO/WOA	World Airways, USA
WT/NGA	Nigeria Airways, Nigeria
X9/OAE	Omni Air International, USA
YV	Air Siam, Thailand
ZA	USAF, internal MDC code
ZB/MON	Monarch Airlines, UK
ZU/AKC	ARCA Columbia, Columbia
RYN	Ryan International Airlines, USA
4Q/AEY	AeroLyon, France
–	Orbis International
–	RNAF, Royal Netherlands Air Force

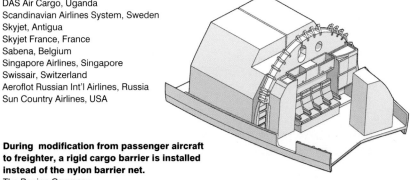

Formerly operated by United Airlines as DC-10-10 N1821U, FedEx N386FE was the first aircraft to be converted to an MD-10.
The Boeing Company

During modification from passenger aircraft to freighter, a rigid cargo barrier is installed instead of the nylon barrier net.
The Boeing Company

Chapter Seven

DC-10 Production

American Airlines DC-10-10 N102AA was the second aircraft in the airline's large DC-10 fleet. After 61,444 flying hours the aircraft was sold to FedEx in February 1997. McDonnell Douglas

Federal Express DC-10-30s will additionally be equipped with the Advanced Common Flightdeck and receive the new MD-10 designation. Federal Express Corporation

This table covers the complete McDonnell Douglas DC-10 production run and describes the present status of each aircraft at 1st February, 2001. Since the start of the MD-10 conversion programme FedEx has acquired an impressive number of used DC-10-10s from American Airlines and United Airlines. To underline the importance of DC-10 operations of the parcel and document carrier, all fuselage and serial numbers of aircraft in the fleet are printed boldfaced. The same has been done with the carrier's FX code and the aircraft variant in the status column. The majority of the DC-10-10 aircraft will first be converted to freighter with the advanced common flightdeck being installed in the second phase, as described in Chapter Six.

Aircraft which are no longer in the fleet of an airline are marked with an asterisk (*) and the name of the current owner/leasing company. An aircraft is considered withdrawn from use (WFU) when it is temporarily or permanently withdrawn from airline service. The abbreviation (STD) is used when an aircraft has been placed into short or long term shortage.

Although Boeing uses the abbreviation SF (Special Freighter) for freighter aircraft converted by BAS and its partners, all dedicated freighters are marked (F) in the table.

An aircraft that has been broken up is shown (BU) while aircraft that have been lost in an accident are marked (L).

Fuse number	FSN	McDD config	McDD cum	Original Registration	Cust-omer	Cust cum	Model/Series	Model cum	Engine	Assembly complete	Customer Accept	Status Config/Cust/WFU/STD/BU/L	Last/Current Registration
1	**46500**	AA	1	N101AA	AA	1	10	1	CF6-6D	29.07.1970	08.12.1972	**FX**	N101AA
2	46501	GK	1	G-BELO	GK	4	10	2	CF6-6D1	17.12.1970	03.06.1977	ORBIS	N220AU
3	46502	AA	2	N102AA	AA	2	10	3	CF6-6D	16.10.1970	27.06.1972	**FX**	N102AA
4	**46600**	UA	1	N1801U	UA	1	10	4	CF6-6D	18.01.1971	25.05.1972	**MD-10-10F/FX**	N364FE
5	46503	AA	3	N103AA	AA	3	10	5	CF6-6D	11.02.1971	29.07.1971	**FX**	N103AA
6	**46601**	UA	2	N1802U	UA	2	10	6	CF6-6D	08.03.1971	29.07.1971	**10F/FX**	N365FE
7	46504	AA	4	N104AA	AA	4	10	7	CF6-6D	30.03.1971	17.09.1971	BU	N104AA
8	**46602**	UA	3	N1803U	UA	3	10	8	CF6-6D	21.04.1971	03.06.1972	**10F/FX**	N366FE
9	**46505**	AA	5	N105AA	AA	5	10	9	CF6-6D	11.05.1971	09.11.1971	**FX**	N533FE
10	46603	UA	4	N1804U	UA	4	10	10	CF6-6D	28.05.1971	27.09.1971	BU	N1804U
11	46604	UA	5	N1805U	UA	5	10	11	CF6-6D	16.06.1971	29.10.1971	BU	N1805U
12	**46506**	AA	6	N106AA	AA	6	10	12	CF6-6D	30.06.1971	10.12.1971	**FX**	N534FE
13	**46507**	AA	7	N107AA	AA	7	10	13	CF6-6D	15.07.1971	15.12.1971	**FX**	N535FE
14	**46700**	NA	1	N60NA	NA	1	10	14	CF6-6D	28.07.1971	01.11.1971	**FX**	N145AA
15	**46605**	UA	6	N1806U	UA	6	10	15	CF6-6D	10.08.1971	23.12.1971	**10F/FX**	N367FE
16	**46701**	NA	2	N61NA	NA	2	10	16	CF6-6D	23.08.1971	19.11.1971	**FX**	N537FE
17	**46606**	UA	7	N1807U	UA	7	10	17	CF6-6D	03.09.1971	20.12.1971	**10F/FX**	N368FE
18	46702	NA	3	N62NA	NA	3	10	18	CF6-6D	16.09.1971	21.12.1971	X9/BU	N147AA
19	**46703**	NA	4	N63NA	NA	4	10	19	CF6-6D	28.09.1971	12.01.1972	**FX**	N539FE
20	**46508**	AA	8	N108AA	AA	8	10	20	CF6-6D	08.10.1971	31.01.1972	**FX**	N540FE
21	46509	AA	9	N109AA	AA	9	10	21	CF6-6D	19.10.1971	21.01.1972	BU	N109AA
22	46510	AA	10	N110AA	AA	10	10	22	CF6-6D	29.10.1971	28.02.1972	L	N110AA
23	46511	AA	11	N111AA	AA	11	10	23	CF6-6D	10.01.1972	15.03.1972	BU	N111AA
24	**46512**	AA	12	N112AA	AA	12	10	24	CF6-6D	14.01.1972	30.03.1972	**FX**	N541FE
25	**46607**	UA	8	N1808U	UA	8	10	25	CF6-6D	20.01.1972	27.02.1972	**FX**	N369FE
26	**46608**	UA	9	N1809U	UA	9	10	26	CF6-6D	02.02.1972	29.02.1972	**10F/FX**	N370FE
27	**46609**	UA	10	N1810U	UA	10	10	27	CF6-6D	09.02.1972	20.04.1972	**10F/FX**	N371FE
28	46750	NW	1	N141US	NW	1	40	1	JT9D-20	25.01.1972	13.06.1973	NW	N141US
29	46704	TK	1	TC-JAV	TK	1	10	28	CF6-6D	15.02.1972	10.12.1972	L	TC-JAV
30	46513	AA	13	N113AA	AA	13	10	29	CF6-6D	21.02.1972	20.04.1972	BU	N113AA
31	46514	AA	14	N114AA	AA	14	10	30	CF6-6D	28.02.1972	17.05.1972	BU	N114AA
32	**46610**	UA	11	N1811U	UA	11	10	31	CF6-6D	03.03.1972	24.04.1972	**10F/FX**	N372FE
33	**46705**	TK	2	TC-JAU	TK	2	10	32	CF6-6D	09.03.1972	02.12.1972	**10F/FX**	N68058
34	46900	CO	1	N68041	CO	1	10	33	CF6-6D	15.03.1972	14.04.1972	10F/EB	N68041
35	**46611**	UA	12	N1812U	UA	12	10	34	CF6-6D	20.03.1972	27.04.1972	**10F/FX**	N373FE
36	46751	NW	2	N142US	NW	2	40	2	JT9D-20	24.03.1972	16.02.1973	TZ/L	N184AT
37	**46515**	AA	15	N115AA	AA	15	10	35	CF6-6D	03.04.1972	26.05.1972	**FX**	N542FE
38	46706	NA	5	N64NA	NA	5	10	36	CF6-6D	08.04.1972	10.05.1972	X9	N360AX
39	**46612**	UA	13	N1813U	UA	13	10	37	CF6-6D	18.04.1972	27.05.1972	**FX**	N374FE
40	46901	CO	2	N68042	CO	2	10	38	CF6-6D	22.04.1972	22.05.1972	10F/EB	N68042
41	46902	CO	3	N68043	CO	3	10	39	CF6-6D	29.04.1972	19.05.1972	10F/EB	N68043
42	**46613**	UA	14	N1814U	UA	14	10	40	CF6-6D	06.05.1972	23.06.1972	**10F/FX**	N375FE
43	46903	CO	4	N68044	CO	4	10	41	CF6-6D	15.05.1972	09.06.1972	10F/EB	N68044
44	46904	CO	5	N68045	CO	5	10	42	CF6-6D	20.05.1972	23.06.1972	L	N68045
45	**46614**	UA	15	N1815U	UA	15	10	43	CF6-6D	07.06.1972	07.07.1972	**FX**	N1815U
46	46550	KL	1	PH-DTA	KL	1	30	1	CF6-50A	27.05.1972	15.03.1974	The Memphis Group	N12089
47	46905	GK	2	G-AZZC	GK	1	10	44	CF6-6D1	14.06.1972	26.10.1972	SY/BU	N573SC
48	**46516**	AA	16	N116AA	AA	16	10	45	CF6-6D	21.06.1972	14.07.1972	**FX**	N116AA
49	**46517**	AA	17	N117AA	AA	17	10	46	CF6-6D	28.06.1972	21.07.1972	**FX**	N545FE
50	**46906**	GK	3	G-AZZD	GK	2	10	47	CF6-6D1	06.07.1972	16.11.1972	**FX**	N546FE
51	**46518**	AA	18	N118AA	AA	18	10	48	CF6-6D	11.07.1972	29.07.1972	**FX**	N547FE
52	**46519**	AA	19	N119AA	AA	19	10	49	CF6-6D	18.07.1972	11.08.1972	**FX**	N119AA
53	46752	NW	3	N143US	NW	3	40	3	JT9D-20	24.07.1972	10.11.1972	NW	N133JC
54	**46520**	AA	20	N120AA	AA	20	10	50	CF6-6D	28.07.1972	24.08.1972	**FX**	N549FE
55	**46521**	AA	21	N121AA	AA	21	10	51	CF6-6D	03.08.1972	01.09.1972	MD-10-10F/**FX**	N550FE
56	46522	AA	22	N122AA	AA	22	10	52	CF6-6D	10.08.1972	18.09.1972	HA	N122AA
57	46575	SR	1	HB-IHA	SR	1	30	2	CF6-50A	16.08.1972	30.11.1972	EU	PP-SFB
58	**46523**	AA	23	N123AA	AA	23	10	53	CF6-6D	22.08.1972	20.10.1972	**FX**	N123AA
59	47965	DL	1	N601DA	DL	1	10	54	CF6-6D	28.08.1972	10.10.1972	**10F/FX**	N377FE
60	46551	KL	2	PH-DTB	KL	2	30	3	CF6-50A	01.09.1972	03.12.1972	NW	N229NW
61	46707	NA	6	N65NA	NA	6	10	55	CF6-6D	08.09.1972	13.10.1972	HA	N152AA
62	46708	NA	7	N66NA	NA	7	10	56	CF6-6D	15.09.1972	19.10.1972	HA	N153AA
63	46850	UT	1	F-BTDB	UT	1	30	4	CF6-50A	21.09.1972	18.02.1973	CO	N13088
64	47966	DL	2	N602DA	DL	2	10	57	CF6-6D	26.09.1972	10.11.1972	**FX**	N1834U
65	46524	AA	24	N124AA	AA	24	10	58	CF6-6D	30.09.1972	17.11.1972	USAF	N910SF
66	46753	NW	4	N144US	NW	4	40	4	JT9D-20	05.10.1972	12.12.1972	NW	N144JC
67	47967	DL	3	N603DA	DL	3	10	59	CF6-6D	07.10.1972	28.11.1972	UA/WFU/STD	N1835U
68	**46709**	NA	8	N67NA	NA	8	10	60	CF6-6D	14.10.1972	30.11.1972	**FX**	N154AA
69	47846	NZ	1	ZK-NZL	NZ	1	30	5	CF6-50A	26.10.1972	11.01.1973	AA/L	N136AA
70	46710	NA	9	N68NA	NA	9	10	61	CF6-6D	31.10.1972	12.12.1972	HA	N160AA
71	46552	KL	3	PH-DTC	KL	3	30	6	CF6-50A	03.11.1972	06.02.1973	NW	N230NW
72	46525	AA	25	N125AA	AA	25	10	62	CF6-6D	09.11.1972	19.12.1972	HA	N125AA
73	46576	SR	2	HB-IHB	SR	2	30	7	CF6-50A	14.11.1972	05.02.1973	CO/WFU/STD	N19072
74	47968	DL	4	N604DA	DL	4	10	63	CF6-6D	20.11.1972	05.01.1973	UA/WFU/STD	N1836U
75	47861	AZ	1	I-DYNA	AZ	1	30	8	CF6-50A	27.11.1972	06.02.1973	CO	N39081
76	**46615**	UA	16	N1816U	UA	16	10	64	CF6-6D	01.12.1972	30.01.1973	**FX**	N381FE
77	46890	RK	1	TU-TAL	RK	1	30	9	CF6-50A	06.12.1972	28.02.1973	IW/L	F-GTDI
78	**46907**	TK	3	TC-JAY	TK	3	10	65	CF6-6D	11.12.1972	27.02.1973	**10F/FX**	N68059
79	46754	NW	5	N145US	NW	5	40	5	JT9D-20	15.12.1972	31.01.1973	NW	N145US
80	47969	DL	5	N605DA	DL	5	10	66	CF6-6D	03.01.1973	16.02.1973	UA/WFU/STD	N1837U
81	46825	OV	1	N1031F	OV	1	30CF	1	CF6-50A	09.01.1973	21.04.1973	L	N1031F
82	46553	KL	4	PH-DTD	KL	4	30	10	CF6-50A	13.01.1973	28.02.1973	CO/WFU/STD	N14090
83	46727	GK	4	G-BBSZ	GK	3	10	67	CF6-6D1	18.01.1973	20.05.1974	10F/ZU/STD	N104WA
84	46554	KL	5	PH-DTE	KL	5	30	11	CF6-50A	24.01.1973	09.03.1973	GH	9G-PHN
85	46851	UT	2	F-BTDC	UT	2	30	12	CF6-50A	30.01.1973	19.03.1973	IW	F-GTDH
86	**46616**	UA	17	N1817U	UA	17	10	68	CF6-6D	03.02.1973	22.03.1973	**10F/FX**	N383FE
87	46925	IB	1	EC-CBN	IB	1	30	13	CF6-50A	08.02.1973	20.03.1973	L	EC-CBN
88	47862	AZ	2	I-DYNE	AZ	2	30	14	CF6-50A	14.02.1973	21.03.1973	CO	N12064
89	**46617**	UA	18	N1818U	UA	18	10	69	CF6-6D	20.02.1973	06.04.1973	**10F/FX**	N384FE
90	47886	QC	1	9Q-CLI	QC	1	30	15	CF6-50A	24.02.1973	08.06.1973	QC/WFU/STD	9Q-CLI
91	46555	KL	6	PH-DTF	KL	6	30	16	CF6-50A	01.03.1973	13.04.1973	AA/WFU/STD	N143AA
92	47800	CO	6	N68046	CO	6	10	70	CF6-6D	07.03.1973	12.04.1973	The Memphis Group/BU	N68046

Fuse number	FSN	McDD config	McDD cum	Original Registration	Cust-omer	Cust cum	Model/ Series	Model cum	Engine	Assembly complete	Customer Accept	Status Config/Cust/WFU/STD/BU/L	Last/Current Registration
93	46852	UT	3	N54629	UT	3	30	17	CF6-50A	13.03.1973	01.05.1973	L	N54629
94	47863	AZ	3	I-DYNI	AZ	3	30	18	CF6-50A	17.03.1973	20.04.1973	CO	N14062
95	46908	WA	1	N901WA	WA	1	10	71	CF6-6D	22.03.1973	19.04.1973	FX	N166AA
96	46800	TV	1	N101TV	TV	1	30CF	2	CF6-50A	27.03.1973	19.04.1973	30F/FX	N301FE
97	46755	NW	6	N146US	NW	6	40	6	JT9D-20	31.03.1973	09.05.1973	NW	N146US
98	47801	CO	7	N68047	CO	7	10	72	CF6-6D	05.04.1973	10.05.1973	10F/EB	N68047
99	46926	IB	2	EC-CBO	IB	2	30	19	CF6-50A	10.04.1973	19.05.1973	CO	N37078
100	46927	IB	3	EC-CBP	IB	3	30	20	CF6-50A	14.04.1973	29.05.1973	CO	N14079
101	47802	CO	8	N68048	CO	8	10	73	CF6-6D	24.04.1973	23.05.1973	FX	N68048
102	46756	NW	7	N147US	NW	7	40	7	JT9D-20	28.04.1973	02.06.1973	NW	N147US
103	46801	TV	2	N102TV	TV	2	30CF	3	CF6-50A	03.05.1973	04.06.1973	30F/FX	N302FE
104	46928	WA	2	N902WA	WA	2	10	74	CF6-6D	09.05.1973	12.06.1973	Aero Controls Inc./BU	N902WA
105	46711	NA	1	N80NA	NA	10	30	21	CF6-50A	15.05.1973	11.06.1973	AA/BU	N139AA
106	46712	NA	2	N81NA	NA	11	30	22	CF6-50A	19.05.1973	18.06.1973	HA	N140AA
107	46929	WA	3	N903WA	WA	3	10	75	CF6-6D	24.05.1973	21.06.1973	L	N903WA
108	46757	NW	8	N148US	NW	8	40	8	JT9D-20	31.05.1973	06.07.1973	NW	N148US
109	46826	OV	2	N1032F	OV	2	30CF	4	CF6-50A	06.06.1973	29.06.1973	L	N1032F
110	46802	TV	3	N103TV	TV	3	30CF	5	CF6-50A	11.06.1973	02.07.1973	30F/FX	N303FE
111	46758	NW	9	N149US	NW	9	40	9	JT9D-20	15.06.1973	25.07.1973	NW	N149US
112	46930	WA	4	N904WA	WA	4	10	76	CF6-6D	21.06.1973	20.07.1973	FX	N167AA
113	46759	NW	10	N150US	NW	10	40	10	JT9D-20	27.06.1973	31.07.1973	NW	N150US
114	46577	SR	3	HB-IHC	SR	3	30	23	CF6-50A	02.07.1973	10.09.1973	NW	N220NW
115	47906	SN	1	OO-SLA	SN	1	30CF	6	CF6-50A	09.07.1973	18.09.1973	30F/SE	5X-JOE
116	47847	NZ	2	ZK-NZM	NZ	2	30	24	CF6-50A	13.07.1973	14.09.1973	AA/WFU/STD	N137AA
117	47921	LH	1	D-ADAO	LH	1	30	25	CF6-50A	20.07.1973	12.11.1973	30F/GR	N601GC
118	46618	UA	19	N1819U	UA	19	10	77	CF6-6D	27.07.1973	12.04.1974	L	N1819U
119	46619	UA	20	N1820U	UA	20	10	78	CF6-6D	03.08.1973	22.02.1974	10F/FX	N385FE
120	46760	NW	11	N151US	NW	11	40	11	JT9D-20	10.08.1973	30.10.1973	NW	N151US
121	47864	AZ	4	I-DYNO	AZ	4	30	26	CF6-50A	17.08.1973	13.11.1973	CO	N14063
122	47922	LH	2	D-ADBO	LH	2	30	27	CF6-50A	24.08.1973	15.01.1974	30F/GR	N603GC
123	47923	LH	3	D-ADCO	LH	3	30	28	CF6-50A	31.08.1973	11.02.1974	30F/GR	N602GC
124	46761	NW	12	N152US	NW	12	40	12	JT9D-20	10.09.1973	07.11.1973	NW	N152US
125	47887	YV	1	HS-VGE	YV	1	30	29	CF6-50C	17.09.1973	25.11.1974	KE/L	HL7328
126	46762	NW	13	N153US	NW	13	40	13	JT9D-20	21.09.1973	14.11.1973	NW	N153US
127	46891	MP	1	PH-MBG	MP	1	30CF	7	CF6-50A	25.09.1973	13.11.1973	A2	OB-1749
128	46763	NW	14	N154US	NW	14	40	14	JT9D-20	08.10.1973	28.11.1973	NW	N154US
129	47924	LH	4	D-ADDO	LH	4	30	30	CF6-50A	15.10.1973	15.02.1974	30F/GR	N604GC
130	46764	NW	15	N155US	NW	15	40	15	JT9D-20	23.10.1973	12.12.1973	NW	N155US
131	46578	SR	4	HB-IHD	SR	4	30	31	CF6-50A	30.10.1973	06.12.1973	NW	N228NW
132	46579	SR	5	HB-IHE	SR	5	30	32	CF6-50A	06.11.1973	06.02.1974	NW	N221NW
133	46944	RG	1	PP-VMA	RG	1	30	33	CF6-50C	13.11.1973	29.05.1974	Pacific Air Corp*	N940PG
134	46853	UT	4	N54639	UT	4	30	34	CF6-50A	20.11.1973	18.01.1974	IW	F-BTDE
135	47865	AZ	5	I-DYNU	AZ	5	30	35	CF6-50A	29.11.1973	22.01.1974	IJ	F-GPVD
136	47848	NZ	3	ZK-NZN	NZ	3	30	36	CF6-50A	06.12.1973	18.01.1974	AA/WFU/STD	N144AA
137	46931	PK	1	AP-AXC	PK	1	30	37	CF6-50C	12.12.1973	01.03.1974	30F/GR	N832LA
138	46620	UA	21	N1821U	UA	21	10	79	CF6-6D	20.12.1973	13.02.1974	MD-10-10F/FX	N386FE
139	47803	CO	9	N68049	CO	9	10CF	1	CF6-6D	07.01.1974	04.02.1974	FX	N68049
140	46621	UA	22	N1822U	UA	22	10	80	CF6-6D	14.01.1974	25.04.1974	10F/FX	N387FE
141	46940	PK	2	AP-AXD	PK	2	30	38	CF6-50C	21.01.1974	02.04.1974	CO/WFU/STD	N76073
142	47804	CO	10	N68050	CO	10	10CF	2	CF6-6D	28.01.1974	04.03.1974	FX	N68050
143	46765	NW	16	N156US	NW	16	40	16	JT9D-20	01.02.1974	08.03.1974	NW	N156US
144	46622	UA	23	N1823U	UA	23	10	81	CF6-6D	11.02.1974	02.05.1974	FX	N388FE
145	47805	CO	11	N68051	CO	11	10CF	3	CF6-6D	18.02.1974	08.04.1974	FX	N68051
146	46556	VA	1	PH-DTG	KL	7	30	39	CF6-50A	25.02.1974	03.04.1974	IB/WFU/STD	EC-GTB
147	46936	AM	1	XA-DUG	AM	1	30	40	CF6-50C	04.03.1974	17.04.1974	30F/EB	N831LA
148	47806	CO	12	N68052	CO	12	10CF	4	CF6-6D	11.03.1974	11.04.1974	FX	N68052
149	47866	AZ	6	I-DYNB	AZ	6	30	41	CF6-50A	18.03.1974	19.04.1974	CO	N13067
150	47980	IB	4	EC-CEZ	IB	4	30	42	CF6-50A	25.03.1974	19.05.1974	IB/WFU/STD	EC-CEZ
151	46766	NW	17	N157US	NW	17	40	17	JT9D-20	01.04.1974	17.05.1974	NW	N157US
152	46937	AM	2	XA-DUH	AM	2	30	43	CF6-50C	08.04.1974	16.05.1974	30F/EB	N833LA
153	46938	WA	5	N905WA	WA	5	10	82	CF6-6D	15.04.1974	14.05.1974	FX	N168AA
154	46623	UA	24	N1824U	UA	24	10	83	CF6-6D	22.04.1974	19.06.1974	10F/FX	N389FE
155	46624	UA	25	N1825U	UA	25	10	84	CF6-6D	29.04.1974	26.06.1974	10F/FX	N390FE
156	46945	RG	2	PP-VMB	RG	2	30	44	CF6-50C	06.05.1974	18.06.1974	VE	YV-50C
157	47907	SN	2	OO-SLB	SN	2	30CF	8	CF6-50A	13.05.1974	10.06.1974	NMB Air Operations Corp.	N10MB
158	46932	QC	2	9Q-CLT	QC	2	30	45	CF6-50A	20.05.1974	26.06.1974	30F/GR	N609GC
159	46933	PR	1	PH-DTI	KL	8	30	46	CF6-50C	28.05.1974	27.06.1974	GH	9G-ANC
160	46934	KE	1	HL7315	KE	1	30	47	CF6-50C	04.06.1974	20.06.1974	NW	N236NW
161	46767	NW	18	N158US	NW	18	40	18	JT9D-20	11.06.1974	19.07.1974	NW	N158US
162	46942	NA	10	N69NA	NA	12	10	85	CF6-6D	18.06.1974	25.06.1975	X9	N450AX
163	46943	NA	11	N70NA	NA	13	10	86	CF6-6D	25.06.1974	23.06.1975	FX	N162AA
164	46768	NW	19	N159US	NW	19	40	19	JT9D-20	02.07.1974	09.08.1974	NW	N159US
165	46713	NA	3	N82NA	NA	14	30	48	CF6-50A	10.07.1974	20.06.1975	HA	N141AA
166	47925	LH	5	D-ADFO	LH	5	30	49	CF6-50A	17.07.1974	14.11.1974	30F/GR	N605GC
167	46714	NA	4	N83NA	NA	15	30	50	CF6-50A	24.07.1974	16.06.1975	Ages Aircraft/BU	N142AA
168	46769	NW	20	N160US	NW	20	40	20	JT9D-20	31.07.1974	10.09.1974	NW	N160US
169	46625	UA	26	N1826U	UA	26	10	87	CF6-6D	07.08.1974	27.02.1975	10F/FX	N391FE
170	47926	LH	6	D-ADGO	LH	6	30	51	CF6-50A	14.08.1974	03.01.1975	CO	N59083
171	46868	SK	1	LN-RKA	SK	1	30	52	CF6-50A	21.08.1974	01.10.1974	NW	N211NW
172	46935	PK	3	AP-AXE	PK	3	30	53	CF6-50C	28.08.1974	19.10.1974	L	AP-AXE
173	47807	CO	13	N68053	CO	13	10CF	5	CF6-6D	05.09.1974	18.02.1975	FX	N68053
174	46869	SK	2	SE-DFD	SK	2	30	54	CF6-50A	12.09.1974	04.11.1974	IW	F-GTLZ
175	46770	NW	21	N161US	NW	21	40	21	JT9D-20	19.09.1974	05.11.1974	NW	N161US
176	46941	RG	3	PP-VMQ	RG	3	30	55	CF6-50C	26.09.1974	07.11.1974	American Air Carriers/BU	PP-VMQ
177	47808	CO	14	N68054	CO	14	10CF	6	CF6-6D	03.10.1974	10.03.1975	FX	N68054
178	47867	AZ	7	I-DYNC	AZ	7	30	56	CF6-50A	10.10.1974	18.02.1975	CO/WFU/STD	N41068
179	46949	BR	1	G-BEBL	BR	1	30	57	CF6-50C	17.10.1974	31.03.1977	30F/RG	N16949
180	46771	NW	22	N162US	NW	22	40	22	JT9D-20	25.10.1974	06.12.1974	NW	N162US
181	47956	AY	1	OH-LHA	AY	1	30	58	CF6-50C	01.11.1974	27.01.1975	IJ	F-GPVA
182	46910	NZ	4	ZK-NZP	NZ	4	30	59	CF6-50A	08.11.1974	13.12.1974	L	ZK-NZP
183	46580	SR	6	HB-IHF	SR	6	30	60	CF6-50A	15.11.1974	11.01.1975	NW	N223NW
184	46581	SR	7	HB-IHG	SR	7	30	61	CF6-50A	22.11.1974	14.02.1975	NW	N224NW

Fuse number	FSN	McDD config	McDD cum	Original Registration	Cust-omer	Cust cum	Model/Series	Model cum	Engine	Assembly complete	Customer Accept	Status Config/Cust/WFU/STD/BU/L	Last/Current Registration
185	46952	PR	2	PH-DTL	KL	9	30	62	CF6-50A	03.12.1974	26.02.1975	QSC	5Y-MBA
186	47981	IB	5	EC-CLB	IB	5	30	63	CF6-50A	10.12.1974	24.01.1975	CO	N12080
187	46582	SR	8	HB-IHH	SR	8	30	64	CF6-50A	17.12.1974	21.02.1975	NW	N225NW
188	46912	KE	2	HL7316	KE	2	30	65	CF6-50C	24.12.1974	07.02.1975	NW	N234NW
189	46911	NZ	5	ZK-NZQ	NZ	5	30	66	CF6-50C	08.01.1975	20.02.1975	CO	N14074
190	47927	LH	7	D-ADHO	LH	7	30	67	CF6-50A	15.01.1975	28.02.1975	CO	N49082
191	47809	CO	15	N68055	CO	15	10CF	7	CF6-6D	22.01.1975	17.03.1975	FX/L	N68055
192	47928	LH	8	D-ADJO	LH	8	30	68	CF6-50A	29.01.1975	10.03.1975	30F/WO	N17087
193	46854	UT	5	N54649	UT	5	30	69	CF6-50A	05.02.1975	19.03.1975	IW	F-GTDF
194	47810	CO	16	N68056	CO	16	10CF	8	CF6-6D	12.02.1975	24.03.1975	FX	N68056
195	46914	PR	3	PH-DTK	KL	10	30	70	CF6-50C	19.02.1975	27.03.1975	GE Caapital Corp.*	N163AA
196	47929	LH	9	D-ADKO	LH	9	30	71	CF6-50A	26.02.1975	31.03.1975	30F/GR	N606GC
197	46557	VA	2	PH-DTH	KL	11	30	72	CF6-50A	05.03.1975	15.04.1975	Avteam/BU	N431AV
198	46626	UA	27	N1827U	UA	27	10	88	CF6-6D	12.03.1975	25.04.1975	10F/FX	N392FE
199	46915	KE	3	HL7317	KE	3	30	73	CF6-50C	19.03.1975	25.04.1975	NW	N235NW
200	47868	AZ	8	I-DYND	AZ	8	30	74	CF6-50A	26.03.1975	05.05.1975	Finova Capital*/WFU/STD	N305FV
201	47957	AY	2	OH-LHB	AY	2	30	75	CF6-50C	03.04.1975	06.05.1975	CO	N17085
202	46916	RG	4	PP-VMD	RG	4	30	76	CF6-50C	17.04.1975	12.06.1975	Spire Pacific*/WFU/STD	N46916
203	46939	WA	6	N906WA	WA	6	10	89	CF6-6D	29.04.1975	03.06.1975	FX	N357FE
204	46892	RK	2	TU-TAM	RK	2	30	77	CF6-50A	09.05.1975	19.06.1975	IW	F-GNEM
205	46627	UA	28	N1828U	UA	28	10	90	CF6-6D	16.05.1975	23.06.1975	FX	N1828U
206	46913	JL	1	JA8534	JL	1	40-I	23	JT9D-59A	16.06.1975	23.11.1976	EG	JA8534
207	46628	UA	29	N1829U	UA	29	10	91	CF6-6D	20.06.1975	24.07.1975	UA/WFU/STD	N1829U
208	46629	UA	30	N1830U	UA	30	10	92	CF6-6D	30.06.1975	04.08.1975	10F/FX	N395FE
209	46630	UA	31	N1831U	UA	31	10	93	CF6-6D	11.07.1975	20.08.1975	FX	N1831U
210	46631	UA	32	N1832U	UA	32	10	94	CF6-6D	18.07.1975	23.09.1975	10F/FX	N397FE
211	46917	LH	10	D-ADLO	LH	10	30	78	CF6-50C	28.07.1975	01.12.1975	ILFC*	N13086
212	46920	JL	2	JA8530	JL	2	40-D	24	JT9D-59A	06.08.1975	09.04.1976	40F/WE	N140WE
213	47849	NZ	6	ZK-NZR	NZ	6	30	79	CF6-50C	22.08.1975	02.10.1975	IW	F-GNDC
214	46921	BR	2	G-BEBM	BR	2	30	80	CF6-50C	10.09.1975	23.02.1977	30F/GR	N608GC
215	47908	SN	3	OO-SLC	SN	3	30CF	9	CF6-50C	26.09.1975	27.10.1975	FX	N322FE
216	46923	JL	3	JA8531	JL	3	40-D	25	JT9D-59A	14.10.1975	12.04.1976	EG	JA8531
217	46870	SK	3	OY-KDA	SK	3	30	81	CF6-50A	18.11.1975	18.12.1975	IW	F-GHOI
218	46924	MP	2	PH-MBN	MP	2	30CF	10	CF6-50C	29.10.1975	26.11.1975	L	PH-MBN
219	46871	SK	4	LN-RKB	SK	4	30	82	CF6-50C	08.12.1975	23.01.1976	30F/FX	N311FE
220	46660	JL	4	JA8532	JL	4	40-D	26	JT9D-59A	31.12.1975	16.04.1976	40-I/EG	JA8532
221	46922	IB	6	EC-CSJ	IB	6	30	83	CF6-50C	19.01.1976	23.02.1976	WO	N14075
222	46946	WA	7	N907WA	WA	7	10	95	CF6-6D	04.02.1976	22.06.1976	The Memphis Group/BU	N946LL
223	46918	GA	1	PK-GIA	GA	1	30	84	CF6-50C	20.02.1976	22.03.1976	GA	PK-GIA
224	46661	JL	5	JA8533	JL	5	40-D	27	JT9D-59A	09.03.1976	25.05.1976	40F/WE	N141WE
225	46953	IB	7	EC-CSK	IB	7	30	85	CF6-50C	24.03.1976	14.05.1976	IB/WFU/STD	EC-GNG
226	46919	GA	2	PK-GIB	GA	2	30	86	CF6-50C	13.04.1976	29.05.1976	GA	PK-GIB
227	46954	NZ	7	ZK-NZS	NZ	7	30	87	CF6-50C	29.04.1976	07.06.1976	IW	F-GTLY
228	46955	MH	1	9M-MAS	MH	1	30	88	CF6-50C	17.05.1976	02.08.1976	30F/SE/L	N800WR

nch customer United Airlines operated an extensive fleet of DC-10-10s. N1801U was delivered in 1972 and was the airline's first DC-10. After 25 years of passenger service the aircraft was sold to FedEx in 1997 and entered service as a MD-10 freighter in 2001. McDonnell Douglas

Fuse number	FSN	McDD config	McDD cum	Original Registration	Cust-omer	Cust cum	Model/ Series	Model cum	Engine	Assembly complete	Customer Accept	Status Config/Cust/WFU/STD/BU/L	Last/Current Registration
229	47889	PK	4	AP-AYM	PK	4	30	89	CF6-50C	03.06.1976	25.08.1976	Finova Capital*/WFU/STD	N306FV
230	46662	JL	6	JA8535	JL	6	40-I	28	JT9D-59A	21.06.1976	13.08.1976	JL	JA8535
231	46957	WT	1	5N-ANN	WT	1	30	90	CF6-50C	27.07.1976	14.10.1976	WT	5N-ANN
232	46958	PR	4	RP-C2003	PR	1	30	91	CF6-50C	31.08.1976	22.10.1976	CO/WFU/STD	EI-DLA
233	46872	SK	5	SE-DFE	SK	5	30	92	CF6-50C	06.10.1976	02.12.1976	4Q	F-GLYS
234	46959	TG	1	HS-TGD	TG	1	30	93	CF6-50C	20.12.1976	03.03.1977	GH	9G-ANB
235	46956	MP	3	PH-MBP	MP	3	30CF	11	CF6-50C	11.11.1976	23.12.1976	KDC-10/RNLAF	T-235
236	46961	TG	2	HS-TGE	TG	2	30	94	CF6-50C	01.02.1977	05.05.1977	NW	N232NW
237	46960	OV	3	N1033F	OV	3	30CF	12	CF6-50C1	08.03.1977	09.05.1977	KE/L	HL7339
238	46962	OV	4	N1034F	OV	4	30CF	13	CF6-50C1	13.04.1977	06.06.1977	BX/L	EC-DEG
239	46964	GA	3	PK-GIC	GA	3	30	95	CF6-50C	16.05.1977	03.10.1977	GA	PK-GIC
240	46640	MH	2	9M-MAT	MH	2	30	96	CF6-50C	27.05.1977	21.09.1977	NW	N233NW
241	46969	SR	9	HB-IHI	SR	9	30	97	CF6-50C	28.06.1977	21.10.1977	NW	N227NW
242	46950	NZ	8	ZK-NZT	NZ	8	30	98	CF6-50C	22.07.1977	10.11.1977	AA/WFU/STD	N164AA
243	46968	WT	2	5N-ANR	WT	2	30	99	CF6-50C	12.08.1977	18.10.1977	L	5N-ANR
244	46963	UT	6	F-BTDD	UT	6	30	100	CF6-50C	02.09.1977	02.11.1977	4Q	F-BTDD
245	46965	LH	11	D-ADMO	LH	11	30	101	CF6-50C	26.09.1977 *	09.12.1977	30F/GR	N600GC
246	46951	GA	4	PK-GID	GA	4	30	102	CF6-50C	17.10.1977	13.01.1978	GA	PK-GID
247	46947	AA	26	N126AA	AA	26	10	96	CF6-6D	07.11.1977	10.02.1978	HA	N126AA
248	46975	WO	1	N103WA	WO	1	30CF	14	CF6-50C1	23.11.1977	07.03.1978	UA	N1856U
249	46948	AA	27	N127AA	AA	27	10	97	CF6-6D	09.12.1977	20.03.1978	WFU/STD	N127AA
250	46984	AA	28	N128AA	AA	28	10	98	CF6-6D	23.12.1977	01.05.1978	HA	N128AA
251	46977	WA	8	N908WA	WA	8	10	99	CF6-6D	16.01.1978	13.03.1978	RYN	N572RY
252	46983	WA	9	N909WA	WA	9	10	100	CF6-6D	30.01.1978	18.05.1978	VZ	G-TDTW
253	46986	WO	2	N104WA	WO	2	30CF	15	CF6-50C1	02.05.1978	15.06.1978	UA	N1857U
254	46976	WD	1	C-GXRB	WD	1	30	103	CF6-50C1	23.05.1978	14.12.1978	30F/SE	N400JR
255	46987	WO	3	N105WA	WO	3	30CF	16	CF6-50C1	13.06.1978	04.08.1978	UA	N1858U
256	46978	WD	2	C-GXRC	WD	2	30	104	CF6-50C1	27.06.1978	03.11.1978	30F/GR	N607GC
257	**46992**	OV	5	N1035F	OV	5	30CF	17	CF6-50C1	12.07.1978	08.09.1978	**30F/FX**	N304FE
258	46971	VA	3	YV-135C	VA	1	30	105	CF6-50C	26.07.1978	21.09.1978	BU	YV-135C
259	46981	JU	1	YU-AMA	JU	1	30	106	CF6-50C1	09.08.1978	08.12.1978	CO	N37077
260	46990	SQ	1	9V-SDA	SQ	1	30	107	CF6-50C1	23.08.1978	23.10.1978	VZ	G-BYDA
261	46991	SQ	2	9V-SDC	SQ	2	30	108	CF6-50C1	07.09.1978	31.01.1979	HA	N35084
262	46966	JL	7	JA8536	JL	7	40-D	29	JT9D-59A	21.09.1978	20.11.1978	40F/WE	N142WE
263	46993	SQ	3	9V-SDB	SQ	3	30	109	CF6-50C1	03.10.1978	29.11.1978	BG	S2-ACO
264	46985	MP	4	PH-MBT	MP	4	30CF	18	CF6-50C	13.10.1978	20.12.1978	KDC-10/RNLAF	T-264
265	46967	JL	8	JA8537	JL	8	40-D	30	JT9D-59A	26.10.1978	18.01.1979	40-I/EG	JA8537
266	46590	BR	3	G-BFGI	BR	3	30	110	CF6-50C	06.11.1978	22.01.1979	SE	N68065
267	46998	BB	1	HB-IHK	BB	1	30	111	CF6-50C	15.11.1978	31.01.1979	30F/WO	N526MD
268	46540	CP	1	C-GCPC	CP	1	30	112	CF6-50C1	29.11.1978	27.03.1979	Sapphire Aviation Leasing *	N304SP
269	**46970**	GK	5	G-GFAL	GK	5	10	101	CF6-6D	07.12.1978	27.02.1979	**10F/FX**	N10060
270	46996	AA	29	N129AA	AA	29	10	102	CF6-6D	16.12.1978	27.02.1979	HA	N129AA
271	**46989**	AA	30	N130AA	AA	30	10	103	CF6-6D	03.01.1979	15.03.1979	**FX**	N130AA
272	**46973**	GK	6	G-GSKY	GK	6	10	104	CF6-6D1	12.01.1979	21.03.1979	**10F/FX**	N40061
273	46994	AA	31	N131AA	AA	31	10	105	CF6-6D	22.01.1979	03.04.1979	WFU/STD	N131AA
274	46974	JL	9	JA8538	JL	9	40-I	31	JT9D-59A	30.01.1979	04.04.1979	JL	JA8538
275	46995	SQ	4	9V-SDD	SQ	4	30	113	CF6-50C1	08.02.1979	30.03.1979	BG	S2-ACP
276	46972	VA	4	YV-136C	VA	2	30	114	CF6-50C	16.02.1979	20.04.1979	IB/BU	EC-GTC
277	**46835**	WO	4	N106WA	WO	4	30CF	19	CF6-50C2	24.02.1979	27.04.1979	**FX**	N317FE
278	46988	JU	2	YU-AMB	JU	2	30	115	CF6-50C1	05.03.1979	14.05.1979	JU	YU-AMB
279	47982	IB	8	EC-DEA	IB	8	30	116	CF6-50C	12.03.1979	14.05.1979	IB/WFU/STD	EC-DEA
280	46836	WO	5	N107WA	WO	5	30CF	20	CF6-50C2	20.03.1979	21.05.1979	WO	N107WA
281	46541	CP	2	C-GCPD	CP	2	30	117	CF6-50C1	28.03.1979	19.07.1979	30F/WO	N541SA
282	**46837**	WO	6	N108WA	WO	6	30CF	21	CF6-50C2	06.04.1979	29.05.1979	**FX**	N318FE
283	46645	WA	10	N912WA	WA	10	10	106	CF6-6D	16.04.1979	19.07.1979	RYN	N571RY
284	46685	GA	5	PK-GIE	GA	5	30	118	CF6-50C	24.04.1979	27.07.1979	L	PK-GIE
285	46646	WA	11	N913WA	WA	11	10	107	CF6-6D	02.05.1979	26.07.1979	VZ	G-DPSP
286	46686	GA	6	PK-GIF	GA	6	30	119	CF6-50C	10.05.1979	22.08.1979	GA	PK-GIF
287	46591	BR	4	G-BGAT	BR	4	30	120	CF6-50C	18.05.1979	08.08.1979	CO	N13066
288	46997	RK	3	TU-TAN	RK	3	30	121	CF6-50C	29.05.1979	10.08.1979	IW	F-GTDG
289	46999	SQ	5	9V-SDE	SQ	5	30	122	CF6-50C2	06.06.1979	29.08.1979	30F/SU	M524MD
290	46982	VA	5	YV-137C	VA	3	30	123	CF6-50C	14.06.1979	05.10.1979	IB/WFU/STD	EC-GTD
291	47888	FG	1	YA-LAS	FG	1	30	124	CF6-50C2	22.06.1979	21.09.1979	Stansborough Investment *	N47888
292	46583	SR	10	HB-IHL	SR	10	30	125	CF6-50C	02.07.1979	03.03.1980	NW	N226NW
293	46584	SR	11	HB-IHM	SR	11	30	126	CF6-50C	11.07.1979	01.02.1980	CO	N15069
294	47827	AA	32	N132AA	AA	32	10	108	CF6-6D	19.07.1979	13.11.1979	HA	N132AA
295	46542	CP	3	C-GCPE	CP	3	30	127	CF6-50C2	27.07.1979	02.11.1979	BG	S2-ADN
296	46632	UA	33	N1838U	UA	33	10	109	CF6-6D	06.08.1979	30.11.1979	The Aircraft Group*	N1838U
297	46633	UA	34	N1839U	UA	34	10	110	CF6-6D	14.08.1979	15.02.1980	WFU/STD	N1839U
298	**46634**	UA	35	N1841U	UA	35	10	111	CF6-6D	22.08.1979	31.01.1980	**FX**	N1841U
299	46595	DF	1	D-ADPO	LH	12	30	128	CF6-50C2	30.08.1979	21.11.1979	X9	N540AX
300	47817	SQ	6	PP-VMR	SQ	6	30	129	CF6-50C2	10.09.1979	30.11.1979	BG	S2-ACQ
301	46596	DF	2	D-ADQO	LH	13	30	130	CF6-50C2	18.09.1979	15.12.1979	X9	N630AX
302	**47811**	GK	1	G-BGXE	GK	7	30	131	CF6-50C2	26.09.1979	15.12.1979	**30F/FX**	N323FE
303	47812	GK	2	G-BGXF	GK	8	30	132	CF6-50C2	04.10.1979	05.01.1980	30F/UA	N1853U
304	47822	JL	10	JA8539	JL	10	40-I	32	JT9D-59A	12.10.1979	07.01.1980	JO	JA8539
305	47818	SQ	7	PP-VMS	SQ	7	30	133	CF6-50C2	23.10.1979	25.01.1980	MT	G-LYON
306	47823	JL	11	JA8540	JL	11	40-D	33	JT9D-59A	31.10.1979	24.12.1979	Ten Forty Corporation*	N804AZ
307	46635	UA	36	N1842U	UA	36	10	112	CF6-6D	08.11.1979	28.02.1980	WFU/STD	N1842U
308	47824	JL	12	JA8541	JL	12	40-I	34	JT9D-59A	16.11.1979	20.03.1980	JO	JA8541
309	46636	UA	37	N1843U	UA	37	10	113	CF6-6D	28.11.1979	14.03.1980	WFU/STD	N1843U
310	47825	JL	13	JA8542	JL	13	40-I	35	JT9D-59A	06.12.1979	17.04.1980	JL	JA8542
311	48200	ZA	1	79-0433	ZA	1	30CF	22	CF6-50C2	14.12.1979	01.10.1981	KC-10A/USAF	79-0433
312	47813	GK	3	G-BGXG	GK	9	30	134	CF6-50C2	24.12.1979	24.03.1980	30F/UA	N1854U
313	47826	JL	14	JA8543	JL	14	40-I	36	JT9D-59A	09.01.1980	22.05.1980	JL	JA8543
314	47819	WO	7	N109WA	WO	7	30CF	23	CF6-50C2	17.01.1980	09.04.1980	30F/UA	N1859U
315	47814	GK	4	G-BGXH	GK	10	30	135	CF6-50C2	25.01.1980	30.04.1980	IW	F-GLMX
316	47816	BR	5	G-BHDH	BR	5	30	136	CF6-50C	04.02.1980	30.04.1980	30F/EB	N47816
317	**47820**	WO	8	N112WA	WO	8	30CF	24	CF6-50C2	12.02.1980	14.05.1980	**FX**	N319FE
318	47832	WA	12	N914WA	WA	12	10	114	CF6-6D	20.02.1980	12.05.1980	VZ	G-TAOS
319	47828	AA	33	N133AA	AA	33	10	115	CF6-6D	28.02.1980	15.05.1980	HA	N133AA
320	47821	WO	9	N113WA	WO	9	30CF	25	CF6-50C2	07.03.1980	27.05.1980	L	N113WA

Fuse number	FSN	McDD config	McDD cum	Original Registration	Cust-omer	Cust cum	Model/Series	Model cum	Engine	Assembly complete	Customer Accept	Status Config/Cust/WFU/STD/BU/L	Last/Current Registration
321	47829	AA	34	N134AA	AA	34	10	116	CF6-6D	17.03.1980	23.05.1980	**FX**	N134AA
322	47833	WA	13	N915WA	WA	13	10	117	CF6-6D	25.03.1980	05.06.1980	Aircraft Investment Inc.*	N833AA
323	47830	AA	35	N135AA	AA	35	10	118	CF6-6D	03.04.1980	09.06.1980	HA	N135AA
324	47834	IB	9	EC-DHZ	IB	9	30	137	CF6-50C	11.04.1980	23.06.1980	IB/WFU/STD	EC-DHZ
325	47815	GK	5	G-BGXI	GK	11	30	138	CF6-50C2	21.04.1980	24.06.1980	IW	F-GKMY
326	47835	SN	4	OO-SLD	SN	4	30CF	26	CF6-50C2	29.04.1980	09.07.1980	**FX**	N320FE
327	47831	BR	6	G-BHDI	BR	6	30	139	CF6-50C	07.05.1980	21.07.1980	30F/TLX	LX-TLD
328	47837	NA	5	N84NA	NA	16	30	140	CF6-50C	15.05.1980	06.08.1980	UA/WFU/STD	N1855U
329	47841	RG	5	PP-VMT	RG	5	30	141	CF6-50C2	23.05.1980	31.07.1980	30F/RG	PP-VMT
330	47836	SN	5	OO-SLE	SN	5	30CF	27	CF6-50C2	03.06.1980	14.08.1980	**FX**	N321FE
331	47850	CO	1	N68060	CO	17	30	142	CF6-50C2	11.06.1980	28.08.1980	HA	N68060
332	47842	RG	6	PP-VMU	RG	6	30	143	CF6-50C2	19.06.1980	05.09.1980	30F/RG	PP-VMU
333	48201	ZA	2	79-0434	ZA	2	30CF	28	CF6-50C2	27.06.1980	17.03.1981	KC-10A/USAF	79-0434
334	47851	CO	2	N12061	CO	18	30	144	CF6-50C2	08.07.1980	25.09.1980	HA	N12061
335	47843	RG	7	PP-VMV	RG	7	30	145	CF6-50C2	16.07.1980	09.10.1980	30F/SE	N335SJ
336	47844	RG	8	PP-VMW	RG	8	30	146	CF6-50C2	24.07.1980	10.11.1980	NW	N237NW
337	47840	BR	7	G-BHDJ	BR	7	30	147	CF6-50C	01.08.1980	16.10.1980	30F/GR	N612GC
338	47838	PR	5	RP-C2114	PR	2	30	148	CF6-50C2	11.08.1980	25.11.1980	MT	G-GOKT
339	47870	NG	1	N305FE	FM	1	30CF	29	CF6-50C2	19.08.1980	07.09.1984	**30F/FX**	N305FE
340	47852	JL	15	JA8544	JL	15	40-I	37	JT9D-59A	27.08.1980	09.12.1980	JO	JA8544
341	46543	CP	4	C-GCPF	CP	4	30	149	CF6-50C2	05.09.1980	26.11.1980	BG	S2-ACS
342	48252	DF	3	D-ADSO	LH	14	30	150	CF6-50C2	17.09.1980	22.01.1981	X9	N720AX
343	47853	JL	16	JA8545	JL	16	40-I	38	JT9D-59A	29.09.1980	19.12.1980	JL	JA8545
344	48260	UA	38	N1844U	UA	38	10	119	CF6-6D	09.10.1980	09.04.1981	**FX**	N361FE
345	48265	AY	3	N345HC	AY	3	30	151	CF6-50C2	22.10.1980	11.08.1981	IJ	F-GPVC
346	48258	MX	1	N1003L	MX	1	15	1	CF6-50C2F	03.11.1980	15.06.1981	ELC	SX-CPH
347	48261	UA	39	N1845U	UA	39	10	120	CF6-6D	13.11.1980	24.04.1981	**FX**	N362FE
348	48266	MS	1	N3016Z	QZ	1	30	152	CF6-50C2	25.11.1980	20.07.1984	ZB	G-DMCA
349	47855	JL	17	JA8546	JL	17	40-D	39	JT9D-59A	09.12.1980	25.03.1981	Ten Forty Corporation *	N805AZ
350	48283	MH	3	9M-MAV	MH	3	30	153	CF6-50C2	19.12.1980	20.02.1981	WFU/STD	9M-MAV
351	48262	UA	40	N1846U	UA	40	10	121	CF6-6D	20.01.1981	08.05.1981	10F/ FX	N399FE
352	48285	CP	5	C-GCPG	CP	5	30	154	CF6-50C2	08.01.1981	27.02.1981	Centre Solutions/WFU/STD	N285CR
353	48263	UA	41	N1847U	UA	41	10	122	CF6-6D	30.01.1981	22.05.1981	**FX**	N363FE
354	48277	BR	8	G-DCIO	BR	8	30	155	CF6-50C2	11.02.1981	15.04.1981	BA	G-DCIO
355	48282	RG	9	PP-VMY	RG	9	30	156	CF6-50C2	27.02.1981	30.04.1981	NW	N241NW
356	47845	RG	10	PP-VMX	RG	10	30	157	CF6-50C2	17.03.1981	03.06.1981	NW	N242NW
357	48259	MX	2	N10045	MX	2	15	2	CF6-50C2F	03.04.1981	29.06.1981	SY/BU	N154SY
358	48275	AM	1	N10038	AM	3	15	3	CF6-50C2F	21.04.1981	30.06.1981	SKJ	V2-SKY
359	48202	ZA	3	79-1710	ZA	3	30CF	30	CF6-50C2	07.05.1981	30.07.1981	KC-10A/USAF	79-1710
360	48203	ZA	4	79-1711	ZA	4	30CF	31	CF6-50C2	26.05.1981	28.08.1981	KC-10A/USAF	79-1711
361	48204	ZA	5	79-1712	ZA	5	30CF	32	CF6-50C2	11.06.1981	22.09.1981	KC-10A/USAF	79-1712
362	48276	AM	2	N1003N	AM	4	15	4	CF6-50C2F	29.06.1981	12.11.1981	SY	N153SY
363	48205	ZA	6	79-1713	ZA	6	30CF	33	CF6-50C2	16.07.1981	23.10.1981	KC-10A/USAF	79-1713
364	48288	CP	6	C-GCPH	CP	6	30	158	CF6-50C2	03.08.1981	02.11.1981	Centre Solutions/WFU/STD	N482CR

Many airlines are attracted by the DC-10's capability as a freighter aircraft. This former Martinair Holland DC-10-30CF entered service as a freighter with Cielos del Peru in late 2000. Exavia

Fuse number	FSN	McDD config	McDD cum	Original Registration	Cust-omer	Cust cum	Model/Series	Model cum	Engine	Assembly complete	Customer Accept	Status Config/Cust/WFU/STD/BU/L	Last/Current Registration
365	48289	MX	3	N1003W	MX	3	15	5	CF6-50C2F	19.08.1981	03.12.1981	The Memphis Group/BU	N152SY
366	47856	JL	18	JA8547	JL	18	40-I	40	JT9D-59A	04.09.1981	08.12.1981	JO	JA8547
367	47857	JL	19	JA8548	JL	19	40-D	41	JT9D-59A	23.09.1981	25.01.1982	JL	JA8548
368	48292	SR	12	HB-IHN	SR	12	30	159	CF6-50C2	09.10.1981	27.02.1982	CO	N87070
369	48286	GH	1	9G-ANA	GH	1	30	160	CF6-50C2	02.11.1981	25.02.1983	GH	9G-ANA
370	48296	CP	7	C-GCPI	CP	7	30	161	CF6-50C2	23.11.1981	19.02.1982	Centre Solutions/WFU/STD	N296CR
371	48293	SR	13	HB-IHO	SR	13	30	162	CF6-50C2	16.12.1981	01.04.1982	CO/WFU/STD	N83071
372	48294	MX	4	XA-MEW	MX	4	15	6	CF6-50C2F	18.01.1982	13.01.1983	ELC	SX-CVP
373	48206	ZA	7	79-1946	ZA	7	30CF	34	CF6-50C2	10.02.1982	25.05.1982	KC-10A/USAF	79-1946
374	48295	MX	5	XA-MEX	MX	5	15	7	CF6-50C2F	05.03.1982	13.01.1983	SY	N151SY
375	48207	ZA	8	79-1947	ZA	8	30CF	35	CF6-50C2	30.03.1982	21.06.1982	KC-10A/USAF	79-1947
376	48208	ZA	9	79-1948	ZA	9	30CF	36	CF6-50C2	23.04.1982	23.07.1982	KC-10A/USAF	79-1948
377	48209	ZA	10	79-1949	ZA	10	30CF	37	CF6-50C2	18.05.1982	09.08.1982	KC-10A/USAF	79-1949
378	48210	ZA	11	79-1950	ZA	11	30CF	38	CF6-50C2	11.06.1982	08.09.1982	KC-10A/USAF	79-1950
379	**48264**	UA	42	N1848U	UA	42	10CF	9	CF6-6D	06.08.1982	20.09.1982	**FX**	N68057
380	48211	ZA	12	79-1951	ZA	12	30CF	39	CF6-50C2	31.08.1982	18.11.1982	KC-10A/USAF	79-1951
381	48301	JL	20	JA8549	JL	20	40-D	42	JT9D-59A	19.10.1982 *	15.03.1983	JL	JA8549
382	48212	ZA	13	82-0190	ZA	13	30CF	40	CF6-50C2	20.12.1982	06.04.1983	KC-10A/USAF/L	82-0190
383	48213	ZA	14	82-0191	ZA	14	30CF	41	CF6-50C2	08.02.1983	19.04.1983	KC-10A/USAF	82-0191
384	48214	ZA	15	82-0192	ZA	15	30CF	42	CF6-50C2	22.03.1983	20.05.1983	KC-10A/USAF	82-0192
385	48215	ZA	16	82-0193	ZA	16	30CF	43	CF6-50C2	04.05.1983	28.07.1983	KC-10A/USAF	82-0193
386	48216	ZA	17	83-0075	ZA	17	30CF	44	CF6-50C2	16.06.1983	23.08.1983	KC-10A/USAF	83-0075
387	48217	ZA	18	83-0076	ZA	18	30CF	45	CF6-50C2	29.07.1983	16.09.1983	KC-10A/USAF	83-0076
388	48218	ZA	19	83-0077	ZA	19	30CF	46	CF6-50C2	12.09.1983	02.11.1983	KC-10A/USAF	83-0077
389	48219	ZA	20	83-0078	ZA	20	30CF	47	CF6-50C2	25.10.1983	13.12.1983	KC-10A/USAF	83-0078
390	48220	ZA	21	83-0079	ZA	21	30CF	48	CF6-50C2	08.12.1983	27.02.1984	KC-10A/USAF	83-0079
391	48221	ZA	22	83-0080	ZA	22	30CF	49	CF6-50C2	17.02.1984	28.03.1984	KC-10A/USAF	83-0080
392	48222	ZA	23	83-0081	ZA	23	30CF	50	CF6-50C2	27.04.1984	07.06.1984	KC-10A/USAF	83-0081
393	48223	ZA	24	83-0082	ZA	24	30CF	51	CF6-50C2	12.06.1984	19.07.1984	KC-10A/USAF	83-0082
394	48224	ZA	25	84-0185	ZA	25	30CF	52	CF6-50C2	26.07.1984	04.09.1984	KC-10A/USAF	84-0185
395	48225	ZA	26	84-0186	ZA	26	30CF	53	CF6-50C2	30.08.1984	15.10.1984	KC-10A/USAF	84-0186
396	48226	ZA	27	84-0187	ZA	27	30CF	54	CF6-50C2	05.10.1984	27.11.1984	KC-10A/USAF	84-0187
397	48227	ZA	28	84-0188	ZA	28	30CF	55	CF6-50C2	12.11.1984	19.12.1984	KC-10A/USAF	84-0188
398	48228	ZA	29	84-0189	ZA	29	30CF	56	CF6-50C2	19.12.1984	05.02.1985	KC-10A/USAF	84-0189
399	48229	ZA	30	84-0190	ZA	30	30CF	57	CF6-50C2	01.02.1985	16.03.1985	KC-10A/USAF	84-0190
400	48230	ZA	31	84-0191	ZA	31	30CF	58	CF6-50C2	08.03.1985	18.04.1985	KC-10A/USAF	84-0191
401	48231	ZA	32	84-0192	ZA	32	30CF	59	CF6-50C2	12.04.1985	04.06.1985	KC-10A/USAF	84-0192
402	48232	ZA	33	85-0027	ZA	33	30CF	60	CF6-50C2	10.05.1985	21.08.1985	KC-10A/USAF	85-0027
403	48233	ZA	34	85-0028	ZA	34	30CF	61	CF6-50C2	10.06.1985	01.08.1985	KC-10A/USAF	85-0028
404	48234	ZA	35	85-0029	ZA	35	30CF	62	CF6-50C2	09.07.1985	04.09.1985	KC-10A/USAF	85-0029
405	48235	ZA	36	85-0030	ZA	36	30CF	63	CF6-50C2	06.08.1985	19.09.1985	KC-10A/USAF	85-0030
406	48236	ZA	37	85-0031	ZA	37	30CF	64	CF6-50C2	04.09.1985	10.10.1985	KC-10A/USAF	85-0031
407	48237	ZA	38	85-0032	ZA	38	30CF	65	CF6-50C2	25.09.1985	04.11.1985	KC-10A/USAF	85-0032
408	48238	ZA	39	85-0033	ZA	39	30CF	66	CF6-50C2	16.10.1985	03.12.1985	KC-10A/USAF	85-0033
409	**48287**	FM	1	N306FE	FM	2	30F	1	CF6-50C2	07.11.1985	24.01.1986	**FX**	N306FE
410	48239	ZA	40	85-0034	ZA	40	30CF	67	CF6-50C2	02.12.1985	04.02.1986	KC-10A/USAF	85-0034
411	48240	ZA	41	86-0027	ZA	41	30CF	68	CF6-50C2	30.12.1985	27.02.1986	KC-10A/USAF	86-0027
412	**48291**	FM	2	N307FE	FM	3	30F	2	CF6-50C2	21.01.1986	07.03.1986	**FX**	N307FE
413	48241	ZA	42	86-0028	ZA	42	30CF	69	CF6-50C2	11.02.1986	29.03.1986	KC-10A/USAF	86-0028
414	48242	ZA	43	86-0029	ZA	43	30CF	70	CF6-50C2	04.03.1986	25.04.1986	KC-10A/USAF	86-0029
415	48243	ZA	44	86-0030	ZA	44	30CF	71	CF6-50C2	25.03.1986	09.05.1986	KC-10A/USAF	86-0030
416	**48297**	FM	3	N308FE	FM	4	30F	3	CF6-50C2	16.04.1986	28.05.1986	**FX**	N308FE
417	48244	ZA	45	86-0031	ZA	45	30CF	72	CF6-50C2	07.05.1986	23.06.1986	KC-10A/USAF	86-0031
418	48245	ZA	46	86-0032	ZA	46	30CF	73	CF6-50C2	29.05.1986	18.07.1986	KC-10A/USAF	86-0032
419	**48298**	FM	4	N309FE	FM	5	30F	4	CF6-50C2	19.06.1986	31.07.1986	**FX**	N309FE
420	48246	ZA	47	86-0033	ZA	47	30CF	74	CF6-50C2	11.07.1986	27.08.1986	KC-10A/USAF	86-0033
421	48247	ZA	48	86-0034	ZA	48	30CF	75	CF6-50C2	01.08.1986	30.09.1986	KC-10A/USAF	86-0034
422	**48299**	FM	5	N310FE	FM	6	30F	5	CF6-50C2	22.08.1986	30.09.1986	**FX**	N310FE
423	48248	ZA	49	86-0035	ZA	49	30CF	76	CF6-50C2	15.09.1986	31.10.1986	KC-10A/USAF	86-0035
424	48249	ZA	50	86-0036	ZA	50	30CF	77	CF6-50C2	06.10.1986	30.11.1986	KC-10A/USAF	86-0036
425	48250	ZA	51	86-0037	ZA	51	30CF	78	CF6-50C2	28.10.1986	24.12.1986	KC-10A/USAF	86-0037
426	48251	ZA	52	86-0038	ZA	52	30CF	79	CF6-50C2	18.11.1986	31.01.1987	KC-10A/USAF	86-0038
427	48303	ZA	53	87-0117	ZA	53	30CF	80	CF6-50C2	05.01.1987	28.02.1987	KC-10A/USAF	87-0117
428	48304	ZA	54	87-0118	ZA	54	30CF	81	CF6-50C2	09.02.1987	17.04.1987	KC-10A/USAF	87-0118
429	48305	ZA	55	87-0119	ZA	55	30CF	82	CF6-50C2	16.03.1987	26.05.1987	KC-10A/USAF	87-0119
430	48306	ZA	56	87-0120	ZA	56	30CF	83	CF6-50C2	21.04.1987	30.06.1987	KC-10A/USAF	87-0120
431	48307	ZA	57	87-0121	ZA	57	30CF	84	CF6-50C2	27.05.1987	21.08.1987	KC-10A/USAF	87-0121
432	48308	ZA	58	87-0122	ZA	58	30CF	85	CF6-50C2	01.07.1987	17.11.1987	KC-10A/USAF	87-0122
433	**48300**	FM	6	N312FE	FM	7	30F	6	CF6-50C2	06.08.1987	30.09.1987	**MD-10-30F/FX**	N312FE
434	48267	TG	3	HS-TMA	TG	3	30	163	CF6-50C2	11.09.1987	01.12.1987	NW	N238NW
435	48290	TG	4	HS-TMB	TG	4	30	164	CF6-50C2	16.10.1987	22.12.1987	NW	N239NW
436	48315	JD	1	JA8550	JD	1	30	165	CF6-50C2	20.11.1987	30.03.1988	NW	N243NW
437	48316	JD	2	JA8551	JD	2	30	166	CF6-50C2	05.01.1988	29.07.1988	NW	N244NW
438	48319	TG	5	HS-TMC	TG	5	30	167	CF6-50C2	02.02.1988	26.05.1988	NW	N240NW
439	48309	ZA	59	87-0123	ZA	59	30CF	86	CF6-50C2	01.03.1988	24.08.1988	KC-10A/USAF	87-0123
440	**48311**	FM	7	N313FE	FM	8	3OF	7	CF6-50C2	29.03.1988	28.05.1988	**FX**	N313FE
441	48310	ZA	60	87-0124	ZA	60	30CF	87	CF6-50C2	25.05.1988	30.09.1988	KC-10A/USAF	87-0124
442	**48312**	FM	8	N314FE	FM	9	30F	8	CF6-50C2	23.06.1988	26.08.1988	**FX**	N314FE
443	**48313**	FM	9	N315FE	FM	10	30F	9	CF6-50C2	22.07.1988	29.09.1988	**FX**	N315FE
444	**48314**	FM	10	N316FE	FM	11	30F	10	CF6-50C2	19.08.1988	28.10.1988	**MD-10-30F/FX**	N316FE
445	48317	BG	1	S2-ACR	BG	1	30	168	CF6-50C2	19.09.1988	30.12.1988	BG	S2-ACR
446	48318	WT	3	N3042W	WT	3	30	169	CF6-50C2	17.10.1988	27.07.1989	Star & Sun Leasing*	N117WA

ValuJet was the launch customer for the MD-95. Following the merger with AirTran, the new airline took delivery of the first aircraft, by then known as the Boeing 717, in September 1999.
The Boeing Company

Chapter Eight

Epilogue

Following the merger of McDonnell Douglas and Boeing into the world's largest aerospace company on 1st August 1997, on that day the name of the Douglas Aircraft company was changed to Douglas Products Division. The operations of the new Boeing Company began on Monday 4th August 1997.

It still was publicly unknown then what far reaching effects the merger would have on the Long Beach employees and the fine products built by them. As mentioned in the introduction, Boeing announced the phase-out of the MD-80 and MD-90 in November 1997. TWA took delivery of its final MD-83 from Boeing on 28th December 1999. The aircraft, N984TW, was also the last of the MD-80 series to be built at the Long Beach production facility and was appropriately named 'Spirit of Long Beach'. Saudi Arabian Airlines was the last customer for the MD-90 with an order for 29 aircraft of the type. Production of the MD-90 ceased in Spring 2000.

The announcement of the phase-out of the MD-11 on 3rd June 1998, came as another blow to the Long Beach site. Thousands of jobs had already been lost and following Boeing's decision thousands more employees would have to go. Neither was this decision easily accepted by some operators. At least three freight carriers -FedEx, Lufthansa Cargo and Gemini Air Cargo- had shown an interest in acquiring further new examples of the rugged workhorse.

Celebrating the arrival of the first two MD-11 freighters Lufthansa Cargo held a press conference on 1st July 1998. Speaking during the ceremony at Frankfurt/Main Airport Wilhelm Althen, former chairman of Lufthansa Cargo, criticised Boeing's decision to stop production of the MD-11: 'As a customer I cannot understand why this decision was taken' and added 'Boeing now is a monopoly player in the heavy freighter business, an unacceptable situation from a customer's point of view. It would be healthy for another manufacturer to develop an alternative freighter aircraft to break this monopoly.'

However, two aircraft will carry on MDC's legendary reputation of designing and building profitable and reliable products. In October 1995, MDC launched the 100-passenger MD-95, powered by latest technology BMW Rolls-Royce BR715 engines. The aircraft was renamed Boeing 717-200 in January 1998. The first deliveries to launch customer AirTran, formerly ValuJet, took place in September 1999. Boeing aims to go ahead with the development of a regional jet version of the 717, dubbed the 717-100X . Parallel studies for a stretched 125-seat 300X version are also conducted.

The C-17A Globemaster III is another workhorse from the MDC days. A total of 120 have been ordered by the US Air Force. The military airlifter is capable of carrying up to 169,000 lb (76,395kg) of cargo, yet can land on austere fields as short as 3,000ft (1,000m). The C-17A shares the same flightdeck configuration and shape as the MD-11. The first aircraft was delivered to the 437th Airlift Wing and associate 315th AFRES Airlift Wing, Air Mobility Command, Charleston Air Force Base, South Carolina, who jointly operate the aircraft. C-17As are also stationed with the 97th Airlift Wing at Altus Air Force Base, Oklahoma, and the 62nd Airlift Wing and associate 446th AFRES Airlift Wing at McChord Air Force Base, Washington. At the time of writing 68 examples of 'The best moving van in the world' had been delivered to the USAF. In May 2000, the UK Ministry of Defence announced its intention to lease four C-17As for the Royal Air Force beginning 2001. In 1996, MDC presented a model of the MD-17, the civil cargo version of the C-17A. Although the project rested for several years, Boeing revived plans for this version, dubbed BC-17X, in 2000. With a possible launch in July 2001, Boeing expects to complete the first civil aircraft in 2004.

In August 1998, Boeing announced a series of consolidations and realignments to improve the efficiencies of it operations. These changes included the opening a next-generation 737 assembly line in Long Beach, supplementing the capacity in Renton, Washington. However, this important change was never realised and was followed by the decision to only build the Boeing 717 in Long Beach. In conjunction with the planned production of the 737, the commercial airplane operation in Long Beach was renamed the Long Beach Division. With this transformation the Douglas name disappeared forever. However, employees, visitors and passers-by will be constantly reminded of a glorious past as the famous 'Fly DC JETS' neon sign will remain as a landmark on Building 80,

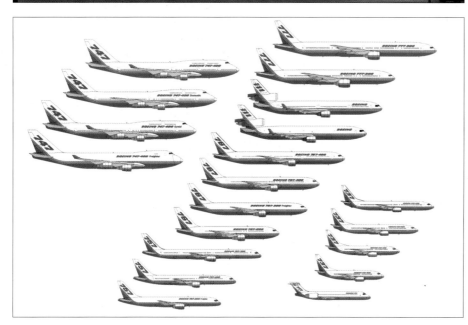

the building where the Boeing 717 is now assembled.

Even if the combination of the surnames of fellow Scotsmen James Smith McDonnell and Donald Wills Douglas may never again adorn a new civil or military aircraft, they will not be forgotten as important aviation pioneers and manufacturers of some of the most famous and finest products in aviation history.

On 22nd November 2000, sixty years had passed to the day Donald W Douglas turned a spade of earth to start construction of an assembly facility next to Daugherty Field, which today is Long Beach Airport. Only thirteen months after that memorable day the first aircraft rolled out of the hangar destined for service in the Second World War. The first aircraft built was a C-47 Skytrain, the military version of the famous DC-3. Long Beach quickly developed into one of America's Arsenals of Democracy, the manufacturing sites developed to support US and Allied armed forces in Europe and the Pacific. Since then, over 15,000 Douglas and McDonnell Douglas commercial and military aircraft have been built at the Long Beach facilities.

The MD-11 unfortunately was the last member of a famous wide-body jetliner family built by the Long Beach manufacturer. The rigidity and reliability of the world's most recognised and prestigious wide-body tri-jet ensure that the MD-11, together with other legendary McDonnell Douglas products, will grace the skies for many years to come.

Top: **C-17A Globemaster III 60106 of the 437th AW at Charleston AFB, South Carolina, is one of the new workhorses operated by the USAF.** McDonnell Douglas

Centre: **The historical landmark 'Fly DC Jets' sits on top of the MD-80 and MD-90 assembly building. Today Building 80 is 'Home of the Boeing 717'.** McDonnell Douglas

Left: **The MD-11, bedecked in the Boeing white, red and blue house colours, was shown in Boeing advertisements and publications until mid-1998.** The Boeing Company

Above: **A commemorative bumper sticker issued by Boeing in 2001 to celebrate 30 years of tri-jets.** The Boeing Company

Opposite page: **A 'get together' of three Delta Air Lines MD-11s.** McDonnell Douglas

Index

The MD-11 aircraft will continue to serve her owners for many years to come. McDonnell Douglas